THE PERSIAN CARPET

The Vision of a Whole People

For My Friend Mat

Good Luck For 2008

THE PERSIAN CARPET

The Vision of a Whole People

James Turner & Iraj Nouraie

TABAR

Published in Canada by TABAR
www.tabar.ca

ISBN 978-0-9784187-0-0

Library and Archives Canada Cataloguing in Publication

Turner, James, 1944-
The Persian carpet : the vision of a whole people / James Turner, Iraj Nouraie.

Includes bibliographical references and index.
ISBN 978-0-9784187-0-0 (bound)

1. Rugs, Persian. 2. Rugs, Persian--Social aspects. I. Nouraie, Iraj, 1940- II. Title.

NK2809.P4T87 2007 746.7′55 C2007-904875-7

Design by RMS Design
Photography by Paul McCarthy
Set in Palatino LT Std: Light, Light Italic, Medium and Medium Italic
Printed and bound in Canada by Transcontinental Printing
Printed on acid-free paper

Foreword by Dr. Fazlollah Reza

For centuries, the Persian carpet has been one of the principal methods of expression for Iranians at all cultural levels. Individuals, families, local communities, regions and the nation have joined in a shared creative endeavor. At the peak of activity in recent decades, it is estimated that as many as two million people in Iran have been involved in all aspects of carpet production. Together with classical Persian poetry, the carpet has served famously as an ambassador of Iranian culture to the world.

Despite this long history and the obvious social importance of this cultural enterprise, there have been relatively few attempts to go beyond mainly technical understandings or aesthetic appreciations of formal qualities. James Turner and Iraj Nouraie have chosen a different path. Combining technical, aesthetic and cultural knowledge, they relate modern Persian carpets to their social and intellectual contexts and to some of the oldest themes of Iranian culture. Since carpets have engaged many areas of Iranian life, the story they tell is necessarily a complicated one. We remember that the words text and textile have a common origin and at times almost a common meaning.

The Persian Carpet: The Vision of a Whole People examines the origins of carpet designs in the ideas and imagery of Greek metaphysical philosophy, Islamic mysticism, Shi'a Islam and Iranian folk traditions. In a convincing way, the authors have reconnected these sources to present-day concerns. They are willing to confront the controversial question of the symbolic meanings of carpet designs. They have articulated what most Iranians and many others have long known wordlessly. This art form has been and continues to be a profound expression of Iranian spiritual culture.

Many centuries ago, Farrukhi Seistani wrote that he had woven his thoughts together in his poetry like a carpet, but one that time would not diminish and neither water nor fire would be able to destroy. The complex patterns of Persian carpets may be seen as solutions to difficult geometrical and intellectual puzzles, and they reveal the sophistication of the world view of the designers and weavers who created them. Drawing on many sources, their anonymous creators developed a visual language of personal and social expression that has resisted the damages of time.

A familiar image in Iranian culture is the *jam-e Jam*, the all-seeing bowl of Jamshid Shah and the other mythical kings who ruled with its help in prehistory. In the *Shahnameh (The Book of Kings)*, the national epic poem of Iran, Jamshid is credited with bringing the arts of technology to mankind including the arts of weaving. Long before modern communications, the great king was able to see everything in his kingdom by looking into the magical bowl. In a similar image from Islamic mysticism, the dervish on the spiritual journey strives to make his heart a perfectly polished mirror that will reflect the cosmic or divine pattern without any distortion.

The ideals of complete visibility and total understanding expressed by these unforgettable images have strong resonances in Iranian thought. The traditional designs of Persian carpets are also expressions of these transcendent ideals. With some imagination, they may serve roles very similar to Jamshid's bowl or the flawlessly polished heart of the spiritual seeker. Iranians learn over a lifetime that these carpets have a remarkable power. Viewed in the right way, they reflect or reveal what we are as individuals and as members of a diverse human community sharing a common heritage. Even more, they present a constant invitation to participate in and renew the ordinary life of our community.

To write more personally, I recognized in this book some of the concerns that have motivated me during a long career. When I spoke a few years ago at the millennial conference in Tehran celebrating the writing of the *Shahnameh* by Ferdowsi, it was quite moving to see in the many contributors the same desire to achieve a comprehensive understanding that inspired one Iranian writer a thousand years before. I was reminded that the major difficulty in arriving at a scientific, literary, religious or spiritual understanding has always been to think simply. This humbling task is indispensable in order to see the timeless patterns and coherent values that lie behind the confusing multiplicities and the many contradictions of experience.

In this search for genuine understanding, Persian carpets may play a role that has rarely been fully admitted. We learn here in explicit terms what we have probably known intuitively. Viewing a well-designed carpet over a long period of time may be experienced as a constantly repeated mental and spiritual exercise. Emerging from a serious contemplation of the complexity of the design, a unified pattern or wholeness may eventually be revealed.

From all we know of art and science, there is one truth we must accept with some regret. It is very unlikely there have ever been any flying carpets. However, an Iranian proverb expresses the imaginative truth that lies behind this old image. If you step onto a carpet, it will take you where you desire to go. That is the surprising approach of this book, and it does take us where we fervently want to go. At the very least, it indicates to the willing reader how the journey should begin.

Like the designs of Persian carpets, the pattern that emerges here combines religious, aesthetic, intellectual and practical motivations in a compelling unity. It is finally a comprehensive pattern or vision striving to unite the human and the divine that is revealed through the Persian carpet. This is the vast design that may be called the vision of a whole people.

Fazlollah Reza

Ottawa, Canada
September 2007

Preface

This book studies some of the historical and social contexts of a widely appreciated but poorly understood art form. Since the publication of the classic survey *The Persian Carpet* by A.C.Edwards more than a half-century ago, subsequent works have classified and compared the great variety of designs. These range from the bold linear geometries of tribal textiles to the strong patterns of village weavings and the intricate curvilinear designs of town carpets. Difficult questions of identification and dating have been resolved, and the commercial expansion of the Iranian carpet industry in the modern period beginning in the 1870s has been well documented.

It may now be time for a different emphasis. We explore the cultural significance of the Persian carpet as a means of personal and social expression, and we examine the sources of carpet design in relation to the main themes of Iranian culture. Our primary goal is not to identify Persian carpets, but instead to identify with them. We seek to make possible a genuine participation in one of the world's great cultural traditions. A central question is the continuing ability of this art form to serve as a carrier of social meaning.

Both the mundane and the profound elude attempts at satisfactory reductions to words. The Persian carpet is problematic at both extremes since it unites the most ordinary human concerns and the deepest spiritual motivations. Even the indispensable term "the Persian carpet" is not without its difficulties and ambiguities. It describes a wide range of textiles produced by different peoples who are not entirely confined within the present boundaries of Iran. Additional difficulties derive from the nature of Iranian culture where encoded communication has been a well-accepted cultural norm.

A familiar proverb hints at these complexities: "Those who know don't speak; those who speak don't know." Concealment of personal beliefs and the desire to create physical and psychological refuges are centuries-old Iranian values that are very understandable in historical terms. "Stretch your feet to the length of your blanket." "If you plan to steal the minaret, first dig a well." "Do not let your fruit tree grow over the garden wall." These and many other popular sayings express strong social preferences for ambiguity, protecting appearances, and considering consequences.

This deeply-ingrained cultural attitude encourages acceptance of personal limits and favors indirect forms of communication. It discourages new interpretations or open examinations of controversial subjects. To close our discussion before it begins, we could follow a time-honored Iranian custom by finding a cryptic quotation from *The Golestan (The Rose Garden)* of Sa'adi, a compendium of popular wisdom from the thirteenth century. "From a little we judge of much; a handful is a sample of an ass-load." "It is a rule of reason that the archer should have patience, for when the arrow has left the bow it will not return."

Sociologists have described Iranian life as a high-context, implicit culture in which the participants have thoroughly assimilated its many customs and rules since early childhood. In any traditional culture whose members follow mostly unspoken rules of which they are only partially aware, the observations of outsiders are often the most penetrating. For the same reasons, their perceptions may be the most confused and uncomprehending.

A Year Amongst the Persians by the English traveler Edward G. Browne is the account of his year of discovery in Iran in 1887 and 1888. One of his observations about Iranians has been frequently quoted: "The most striking feature of the Persians as a nation is their passion for metaphysical speculation. This passion, so far from being confined to the learned classes, permeates all ranks, and manifests itself in the shopkeeper and the muleteer, as well as in the scholar and the man of letters." In a culture whose members carefully guard appearances, it should not be surprising to find a balancing belief in hidden motivations and meanings. Metaphysics is the branch of philosophy that attempts to go beyond appearances and surface meanings to a deeper understanding of the nature of reality.

A few years later, the English writer Gertrude Bell was living in Tehran. With an Iranian collaborator Sheikh Hassan, she translated the mystical poetry of the fourteenth-century poet Hafez. She describes their working methods in *Safarnameh: Persian Pictures* which was first published anonymously in 1894. Beginning with a word-for-word translation, Bell and Hassan would try to discover the concealed meanings: "The Sheikh would then proceed to annotate them in halting French, pointing out that a pun was contained in every rhyme, that half the words bore at the smallest computation two or three different meanings, and that therefore the lines might be done in several English versions, each with an entirely different significance, and with an equally truthful rendering of the Persian."

Before this daunting complexity, Bell retreated to the simplest interpretations: "Women were women and wine red wine for me, the cup-bearer was the person whose advent was most eagerly to be greeted; roses and nightingales, soft winds and blooming gardens, were all part of a beautiful imaginative world, and fit setting for a poet's dreams." However, she came to regret the limitations of her literal approach and the lost opportunity for a deeper understanding. She wrote, "If I had listened to the wisdom of Sheikh Hassan, I should have realized that we were in the midst of sublime abstractions, and that the most rigid morality and the strictest abstinence were inculcated by these glowing lines."

Do these observations have any relevance to Persian carpets in the contemporary world? Some personal experiences suggest these cultural values have a continuing significance. A Kurdish villager from the region near Bijar in northwest Iran had made the journey to Tehran to sell some carpets in the bazaar. When the visitor who purchased his carpets was preparing a list, the Kurdish man said he began his own lists with the number 110. He explained that 110 stood for *ya Ali* (Oh, Ali!) in *abjad*, the ancient number symbolism that assigns a numerical value to each letter. To bring good fortune to his enterprise, the villager invoked the revered memory of Ali who was the first convert to Islam. The national religion of Iran is Shi'a Islam which is properly referred to as *shi'a Ali*, the followers of Imam Ali and his successors.

Another time, the traveler met a young Qashqai woman at her home in Firuzabad, a town in the mountainous region south of Shiraz in Fars province. Some months before, she had agreed to make a *gabbeh* carpet for a Shiraz merchant. These loosely-knotted, thick-piled carpets with simplified designs were then in great demand. Instead of the *gabbeh* ordered with a completely black open field, the weaver had added her own intricate patterns in vibrant colors to the somber design. She said without any apologies, "I am a young woman and happily married. I need to have color and life in my carpets. You should ask a widow to make those sad things!"

In Lahore, Pakistan, he was in the modest business premises of an Afghani carpet dealer who was a recent refugee from years of turmoil in Afghanistan. The walls of the small room were covered with quotations from Jalaluddin Rumi, the thirteenth-century poet whose extensive metaphysical works have been called the Persian *Quran*. The visitor asked, "Why do you have that writing on the walls?" He was told only, "That is Rumi." Pretending not to know, the traveler asked a second question, "Who is Rumi?" Surprised and disappointed, the carpet dealer was for a moment at a loss for words. He then answered with another question, "How can you be in the carpet business and not know Rumi?"

The small Tabriz carpet illustrated (c.1970) is unusual in several ways. There is almost no border, a rare occurrence in Persian carpets. It has the niche design of a prayer carpet although the proportions are slightly too square for that purpose and the black background color is not commonly seen in prayer carpets. The central design is elusive; birds celebrating the joy of spring, a stylized vase of flowers, the royal crown, or the cap worn by a wandering dervish. The carpet may simply have a beautiful design, the original creation of a designer's aesthetic imagination and a weaver's skill.

There may be another way to see this puzzling design. Turn the page and view it upside down. There should emerge the unmistakable frontal view of the head of a cow, an animal revered both in Islam and the Zoroastrian religion. *The Cow* is the title of the first *sura* (chapter) of the *Quran*, and that religious allusion may be the primary intended reference in the Tabriz carpet. But, as Gertrude Bell found in translating Hafez, there are always different possibilities and equally truthful renderings.

In the *Shahnameh (The Book of Kings)*, the epic poem written by Ferdowsi in the eleventh century, we may read that the noble Feridoun had a cow-headed mace made for him by the rebel blacksmith Kaveh. The mace's design recalled the cow that had nourished Feridoun in infancy. He uses the mace to break the skull of the evil foreign tyrant Zahhak who had misruled Iran for centuries. Ever since, the image of a cow's head has been understood by Iranians as a symbol of their desire for liberation from tyranny.

0.1 Tabriz *Concealed Design* *(c.1970, 2.02 x 1.52)*
Some designs do not reveal all of their intended meanings immediately.

The hidden cow's head design found in the Tabriz textile does not occur very often in contemporary weavings, although it is seen in some older carpets from Kerman and Ravar. Concealed ram's heads are more frequently seen, especially in Isfahan carpets. They are often intended to symbolize the renewal of life at the time of *Nouruz*, the Iranian New Year celebrated at the spring equinox. These concealed designs suggest we may expect to find some other surprising reversals of meaning when we encounter Persian carpets.

A living culture is an extended conversation in which accepted meanings are negotiated. Familiar images and symbols make possible the ordinary communications that maintain and renew any community. The active participants in a culture are those who respond to their opportunities for socially meaningful expression. In conventional and creative ways, they participate in the everyday rituals and conversations that define their communities. Our aim is to experience the Persian carpet as a traditional and evolving form that has contributed to the shared conversations of Iran and the entire human community.

For those experiencing Persian carpets for the first time, the many names such as Tabriz, Bijar and Qashqai used to identify carpets may be initially bewildering. The elaborate classifications by time and place of origin, by local variations of designs, and by materials and techniques of knotting convey a great deal of information. However, they do not address some questions we find more fundamental. Our primary concerns are the social contexts and meaning content of Persian carpets, and we view them in ways that are significant in Iranian culture. This leads to a critical analysis of approaches strongly influenced by commercial concerns or the concepts of European aesthetics.

We focus on the modern period conveniently dated from the revival of carpet making in the 1870s initially in response to foreign interest. The illustrations are not intended to be representative of the total phenomenon although a wide selection is included ranging from tribal textiles to village and town carpets. Some are major works by accomplished twentieth-century designers. Others are more modest when judged by conventional standards, but often with immodest symbolic interpretations and cultural significance.

This book is the result of an extended conversation in which many have participated. Before our arrow leaves the bow and we offer our sample for judgment, we would like to express our appreciation to the contributors to that conversation. May it continue with many new participants responding in their own ways to the communication of meaning in Persian carpets. We are grateful to Dr. Fazlollah Reza for his continued interest and encouragement as the work progressed. Like the great variety of carpet designs, the many dimensions of his careers in science, literature, education and diplomacy have provided a demonstration of the permanent values and unity of Iranian culture.

I cannot now think symbols less than the greatest of all powers whether they are used consciously by the masters of magic, or half unconsciously by their successors, the poet, the musician, and the artist. … Whatever the passions of men have gathered about becomes a symbol in the great memory, and in the hands of him who has the secret it is a worker of wonders, a caller-up of angels or of devils.

W.B.Yeats in the essay “Magic” (1901)

No thought or image was unnatural to me; I could understand the secrets of ancient paintings, the mysteries of forms and norms, because at this moment I was participating in the revolution of the earth and the planets, in the growth of the plants and in the activities of the animal world. The past and the future, far and near, shared my sentient life and were at one with me.

Sadeq Hedayat in *Buf-e Kur (The Blind Owl*, 1936)

1 Yeki Bud, Yeki Nabud

Where do we begin? Early in 1935, Reza Shah Pahlavi decreed that the country he ruled would no longer be known to the world as Persia. From March 21 of that year, his realm would be known for all official purposes as the Kingdom of Iran. This well-publicized gesture acted in several symbolic and practical directions. Taking effect at the joyful time when Iranians celebrate the coming of a new year, the royal decree signaled to the outside world a new beginning for a great nation that was rediscovering its true identity.

The proclamation contributed to a strongly promoted government policy encouraging a renewal of the connections of contemporary Iranian culture with the historical cultures of pre-Islamic and ancient Iran. *Airya* was the divinely guided kingdom known from the *Avesta*, the holy book of the Zoroastrians, and *Ariana* was the powerful empire of Darius the Great and the other Achaemenian kings. In the social and political contexts of 1935, the decree was intended to make some other connections to ideas of the aryan race that were then current. The modern word aryan was itself derived from *arya* meaning noble or honorable in Sanskrit and old Persian.

By his imperial command, Reza Shah attempted to correct a very old error. The international name Persia with its many legendary and historical associations was originally derived from the Greek word *Persis*. Outside Iran, the more familiar name immediately brought to mind the many centuries of conflict of successive Iranian dynasties with the invading armies of Greece, Rome and Byzantium.

The decree symbolized to the whole world a nation that was modernizing rapidly at the same time it was remembering its ancient origins. Reza Shah's order also gave a small but visible demonstration of his ability to extend his power and influence even beyond the recognized borders of Iran. To enforce his command internationally, he ordered that all letters addressed to Persia after that date were to be refused entry to the country. They were to be returned unopened to their senders.

From modest beginnings in the northern province of Mazanderan, Reza Khan had risen quickly through the ranks of the Cossack Brigade in the unsettled period of the 1910s. Participating in a successful coup d'état in 1921 against the fragile Qajar monarchy, it soon became known that his command of the military gave him effective control of the new government. By late 1923, his decisive influence became apparent to all when he was formally appointed to head the national government as prime minister.

In 1924, Reza Khan and his government moved to consolidate further his predominant position. Careful plans were made to depose the powerless monarch Ahmad Shah Qajar a short time before March 21 and to simultaneously proclaim the establishment of the Republic of Iran. The government leader Reza Khan would be persuaded to serve as the first president of the new republic. However, the opportunity for this major constitutional reform was narrowly missed due to some contemporaneous events in a neighboring country.

A few weeks before the planned date, the reform-minded government in Turkey abolished the centuries-old Ottoman Caliphate and introduced programs that would greatly diminish the official role of Islam in their national life. Religious schools were closed throughout Turkey and influential Islamic organizations were ordered to disband. These far-reaching changes led almost immediately to widespread public protests in Iran. There were loud demonstrations in the major cities against the possibility of similar actions by the Iranian government.

When these protests continued and gathered strength, Reza Khan attempted various measures to calm the increasingly volatile and unpredictable situation. Unaccustomed to vocal opposition, the nervous prime minister traveled hastily to the holy city of Qom to consult with some of the most prominent religious leaders of the country. On April 1, he issued a proclamation to all Iranians declaring solemnly that the republican form of government was not consistent with Islamic law.

Self-crowned as king in 1926, Reza Shah Pahlavi constantly tested and expanded his powers by a carefully calculated stream of decrees. The commercial code adopted in 1925 had already deprived the religious establishment of most of its traditional role in the administration of justice. This was followed in 1926 by a modern criminal code. Also in 1925, a solar calendar with the months identified by their pre-Islamic names replaced the Islamic calendar for official purposes. In 1927, compulsory national military service was introduced. According to one significant provision of the new law, all students of theology would be required to pass an examination before an official board in order to be exempted from military duty.

During the next year, a critical transforming event occurred in Qom, the religious city where there had been a steadily growing discontent with the effects of these many decrees. The unplanned incident was quickly seized upon by Reza Shah and immediately turned to his advantage. He seemed even to welcome the local disturbances in Qom. They provided an opportunity to demonstrate the great changes he had made in a few years to the traditional balance of powers in the country. The events were later recalled by Henry Filmer, an American traveler in Iran, in his travel journal *The Pageant of Persia* (1936).

Unlike his uncertain response to the dangerous situation four years earlier, the new king acted much more resolutely in this crisis. More confident of his governing abilities and his almost unchallenged authority, he did not take the time to consult with the religious leaders of the city.

> Early in 1928 the Queen, his consort, mother of the Crown Prince, visited Kum, a shrine particularly sacred to Moslem women as the burial place of Fatima, in order to participate in the Persian New Year services at the mosque. Having inadvertently exposed her face during the service, she was severely admonished by the officiating mullah, who proceeded to denounce the tendencies of modern Persian women to depart from the traditional customs of the Islamic faith. As a result, the fanatical crowd was aroused to make a demonstration against the Queen.
>
> Upon being acquainted with the occurrence the Shah immediately ordered two armoured cars and a body of troops to Kum, and he himself

> followed them there the next day. Arriving at the mosque he entered its portals without removing his boots, in accordance with customary Islamic procedure, and having found the offending mullah he proceeded to administer to him corporal punishment. He further humiliated the clergy of Kum by giving orders for the arrest of three criminals who had taken sanctuary within the precincts of the mosque, in spite of the age-old claim of immunity from justice of refugees who found asylum there.

In this encounter, Reza Shah and his soldiers broke boldly and decisively with some of the longest accepted rules and customs of the Iranian community. The king's tall military boots became a part of Iranian folklore, a distinctive visual symbol of the forcible methods he used to achieve his reforms.

In the same year as the dramatic events in Qom, orders were given that the famous mosques of Isfahan would be required to admit foreign visitors. In the following years, this policy was gradually extended to include many other religiously important buildings throughout the country. By 1935, all but the most sacred shrines and mosques in Iran were open to foreigners with police protection provided when necessary.

One perceptive observer of the consequences of these changes was the English writer Onera Amelia Merritt-Hawkes who traveled extensively in Iran in 1934. She was there to advise the Iranian government on health issues, especially as they affected women. In Isfahan, she visited the beautiful buildings of the *Medrasseh Chahar Bagh* located on the *Chahar Bagh*, the great public square of the city. Until March 1933, this famous *medrasseh* had been one of the most important religious schools in the country.

Each year for several centuries past, about a hundred students at age fourteen had entered the school to begin studies lasting ten years to become mullahs. With some obvious skepticism, Merritt-Hawkes repeats the official explanation for the recent change. She writes, "They have now been sent away to a number of small schools in order, it is said, that it may become a national historic monument."

In her travels, she frequently saw the winged figure of Ahura Mazda, the guardian symbol of the Zoroastrian religion and the kings of ancient Iran. She describes its new uses in modern Iran: "This figure is now seen everywhere in Persia, on buildings, on rings, on brass and silver work. It has become a symbol of the new nationalism, of a return to all that is purely Persian, to pre-Islamic, pre-Arabic days. To the idealists, it means light and salvation for Persia, but to others it is mere jingoism."

During her long journey recounted in fond detail in her travel memoir *Persia: Romance and Reality* (1935), Merritt-Hawkes was a keen observer of the many recent innovations but she also showed a great interest in learning about traditional Iranian folklore and popular beliefs. To her regret, this was an interest she found was not often shared by the educated people she was meeting in the towns and cities. With little success, she attempted to impress upon them the importance of recording the old stories and the folk wisdom they contained before they were completely forgotten.

She mentions one typically discouraging encounter in Isfahan. There a thoroughly modern Iranian woman told her, "If you in Europe like to tell your children fairy stories, I am very sorry for you; it shows you are not as educated as Persians. I do not believe that even in the little villages any Persian has such ideas. We must get rid of these things." Attempting to find a common ground, the visitor cautiously replied, "Of course, but do get records of them first."

The progressive woman from Isfahan was not in a mood to tolerate such backwardness. She answered, "Why? That would be to write us down as fools." Disappointed by their complete failure to communicate, Onera Merritt-Hawkes sadly concluded that only the ruins of Persepolis seemed to inspire pride among Iranians. And that was not primarily for their beauty, she added, but as the remaining visible evidence of the past greatness of their nation.

Robert Byron was an English writer who traveled extensively in Iran and Soviet Turkestan in 1933 and 1934. He recorded his experiences and impressions in *The Road to Oxiana* (1937) which is now considered to be a classic of modern travel literature. Byron spent a short time in Tus, a very old city near Meshed in Khorasan province. There he visited the burial site of the famous poet Ferdowsi (d.1020). He was the writer of the *Shahnameh (The Book of Kings)* which has been recognized for a millennium as the national epic poem of Iran.

Contrary to his expectations, Byron was favorably impressed by the preparations then being made in Tus for the celebration of the thousandth anniversary of Ferdowsi's birth. They included extensive additions and renovations to the great poet's tomb which had been previously neglected.

> [The cenotaph], which is almost built, proved a pleasant surprise. A square cone, to be covered with white stone, stands on a broad flight of steps. In front of it lies a long pool, framed by lines of trees and announced by a pair of classical pavilions. … the design is admirable. The Western part of it, the cenotaph, is as simple as can be: the Persian part, the garden, is beautiful as always; and the two are blended by good proportions.

On his return journey some months later, the curious traveler revisited the construction site to view the progress made since his first visit. Byron was severely disappointed to find that drastic changes were then being made to the new monument.

> A crowd of workmen were busy demolishing it. Iron railings hid the pool. Municipal flower-beds lay ready for cannas and begonias. And at the end, instead of the unostentatious pyramid I admired in November, rose half-built copies of the bull's head columns at Persepolis.

After returning to Tehran, the traveler learned the probable reason for the unfortunate changes. He heard rumors that Reza Shah had been shown photographs of the originally planned memorial as it was being built. Without hesitating, the decisive ruler of Iran declared that the monument was too plain.

This new visual language was intended to impose a modern national identity on a diverse and traditional country. The Pahlavi crown used for the first time at the 1926 coronation became a prominent public symbol of this social renewal. In obvious or subtle ways, the distinctive crown became a frequently seen design element in Persian carpets during the Pahlavi period. European clothing was made compulsory for men by a decree in 1929 banning the customary tribal and regional clothing. This was followed by the "international hat" which became obligatory for men in 1935. To enforce these decrees, merchants in the bazaars were forbidden to sell the traditional clothing.

In these years of relentless changes, the police were given orders to forcibly remove the plain wool cloaks worn by the dervishes, and they were ordered to cut the long hair and beards that were primary signs of an ancient way of life. The dervishes were the itinerant holy men with few possessions who had chosen to be followers of Sufism, selflessly dedicating the remainder of their lives to the mystical traditions of Islam.

For more than ten centuries, the Sufi mystics had wandered about Iran and the neighboring countries seeking to abandon themselves and this world. Some dervishes proclaimed their freedom from all confining obligations by their unkempt appearance and careless behavior. Defying conventional social rules, their only remaining goal in life was to achieve a spiritual union with God. The national government of Reza Shah decreed that their undisciplined and outmoded way of life would have no place in modern Iran.

During this period, straight roads called Pahlavi avenues were ordered built in many towns and villages. Local governors were commanded to demolish any buildings standing in the way of this progressive measure. Usually crossing at right angles in a central Pahlavi square, the new roads cut through the knotted complexity of long-established communities in a way worthy of Alexander of Macedon. In some remote areas, the dislocations necessary to create these public squares and unnaturally straight roads were the first signs of the national program of modernization.

Many familiar place-names, especially names with Turkish or Arabic associations, were changed to reflect the different priorities of the new order. Sultanabad, an important carpet-making city in western Iran, was renamed Arak. In the same region, Senneh became Sanandaj. The oasis town Tun in Khorasan province became Ferdows ("Paradise") as a result of one of these royal decrees, but most visitors would have agreed that it did not immediately become a paradise after the sudden change of name.

Also in northeast Iran, the old city Turshiz was renamed Kashmar. This name recalled the legendary cypress tree believed to have been planted by Zardosht (Zoroaster) in the village Kashmar, a legend retold by Ferdowsi in the *Shahnameh*. It commemorated the joy of Zardosht and his followers caused by the acceptance of Zoroastrian beliefs and practices by the ruler of the country. The ancient tree had thrived for more than a thousand years until it was cut down in the seventh century. This sorrowful event occurred a few years after the Arab conquest when the new rulers needed the strong wood of the sacred tree of the Zoroastrians to build a great palace for the Caliph in Baghdad.

When the enormous tree was felled, it was said that the whole earth trembled. So many birds flew away from the shelter of its branches that they darkened the sky. Thirteen centuries later, the most famous cypress tree of Iran was restored to memory by Reza Shah's command.

In the 1930s, the town renamed Kashmar became known for some new carpet designs called *zir haq* ("under the ground"). These crowded designs served a contemporary social purpose by expressing an idea that was being officially encouraged by the central government. The complex patterns of these carpets displayed the long concealed treasures and neglected resources that were being brought to light everywhere in that industrious time. This unprecedented achievement was credited officially to the common enterprise of the Iranian people and the farsightedness of their chosen leader.

The *zir haq* carpet illustrated (c.1935) shows very prominently the winged figure of Ahura Mazda and the familiar *chehel minar*, the "forty pillars" of the ruins of Persepolis. Together with the Pahlavi crown and the portrait of Reza Shah, these historical images were imposed and promoted at every opportunity. They were intended to be seen by all as the key symbols of the vigorous government program of national renewal that was then in progress.

The storks and the other birds featured prominently in the busy design of the Kashmar carpet require some cultural interpretation. Until as recently as the 1930s, visitors to the ruins of Persepolis reported seeing storks nesting on the famous pillars. In Iran, the storks were commonly referred to as pilgrims. They were treated with reverence because, according to popular beliefs, they built their nests on minarets and they made the pilgrimage to Mecca each year. Returning in spring from the holy city, the constantly repeated call of the storks was heard as *lak, lak, lak*. This was interpreted to mean "to Thee, to Thee, to Thee" in Arabic. This repeated phrase is a *zikr Allah*, a remembrance or *zikr* from the holy birds of the divine source of all.

1.1 Kashmar *Zir Haq* *(c.1935, 3.97 x 2.94)*

Kashmar was identified in the 1930s with the ***zir haq*** *or under the ground designs expressing the synthesis of modern reforms with a rediscovered heritage.*

The loud crowing of the roosters was another important reminder to the faithful of the religious obligations of Islam. Early each morning, their insistent crowing called the believers to the dawn prayer. Another more contemporary meaning may also have been intended. The proud roosters seem to be calling on a somnolent Iran to awake to its destiny. In the *zir haq* carpet designs, symbols from ancient Iran were combined in this way with familiar symbols from Islam and traditional folk beliefs, suggesting the new synthesis of tradition and modernity that was being forcibly created.

The year 1935 saw the founding of *Sherket Farsh Iran,* the Iran Carpet Company. Making a virtue out of the necessities of the time, the new company was formed initially by nationalizing and merging some of the foreign and Iranian firms that were experiencing serious economic difficulties. Working closely in the following years with faculty and students at the recently established Tehran College of Art, the company organized the systematic study of traditional carpet designs and it directed the development of many innovative patterns.

This centralizing policy had several intended effects. It gradually decreased the strong regional identifications of designs, and it coordinated local artistic activity with the current programs and social objectives of the national government. Reflecting this unifying approach, a company publication in the 1970s classified the design types of Persian carpets under nineteen uninformative headings such as spiral patterns, intertwined fish patterns, tribal patterns, and composites.

One of these nineteen design classifications was called "patterns of historic monuments and Islamic buildings,°" an indication of the social and political program that lay behind many of the company's activities. Following the reforming spirit of the time, this objective classification served an obvious purpose of the central government in its policy of diminishing the prominent role of religion in public life. In a not very subtle way, the combined classification implied that the sacred mosques and shrines of Shi'a Islam were considered officially to be comparable to secular historical buildings.

By the early 1970s, the Iran Carpet Company was at the height of its influence. According to its own estimates in that period, it produced in its workshops and factories or by contracts with home weavers only about one percent of all Persian carpets. However, the company's influence was much more widespread than this small percentage of total production would seem to indicate. In a trade catalogue illustrating some of the company's current designs, the company president described in the foreword his considerable difficulties in fulfilling the ambitious mandate he had been given. He wrote that his company was mandated by the government to exercise some degree of supervision over the production of all carpets throughout the country.

1.2 Qashqai *Royal Crown* *(c.1930, 2.00 x 1.35)*

The new royal crown was frequently seen in carpet patterns during the Pahlavi period (1926–1979), usually in more concealed ways than this realistic depiction.

Asking for cooperation from his Iranian readers and appealing for their sympathetic understanding of the great magnitude of this task, the company president wrote, "One can only imagine how difficult it would be to go from one village or loom to another to supervise and study the conditions of the more than one million people weaving carpets." Despite the many practical difficulties, he did acknowledge somewhat reluctantly his company's overall responsibility. He wrote, "It is the duty of the Company to make every effort to find ways and means on the country level and then assume guidance and leadership for carpet producers in the private sector all over the country."

Perhaps we should begin our wandering at a much earlier time, a thousand years ago when Ferdowsi was composing the *Shahnameh*. Combining myth, legend and history, the epic narrative required three decades to complete. It extends in time from the creation of the world to the defeat of the Sassanian dynasty (224-641) by the Arab invaders. Roughly equal in length to all of Shakespeare's plays, the many stories and images from this immense work have remained a constant wellspring of the imagination for Iranians.

The *Shahnameh* divides naturally into two separate works; the mythology of the prehistoric period and the semi-legendary, semi-historical stories of the Sassanian kings. The figure dividing the two epochs of mythology and history is Iskander, the world-conqueror Alexander. In times of personal difficulties or disruptive social changes, these ancient stories have always been told again by Iranians. Like the stories of Homer in Greek culture, they have been used repeatedly in Iran to rediscover old values and in a search for new insights.

We should not be surprised to learn that Ferdowsi's epic poem was given a new emphasis by the national government during the Pahlavi period when it acquired an important political significance. Schoolchildren were often required to memorize some of the lengthy passages from the *Shahnameh*, especially those passages that were interpreted as glorifying the histories of the kings of ancient Iran.

During the politically unsettled years from 1896 to the 1920s, pictorial carpets typically illustrating episodes from Ferdowsi and scenes from the *Quran* were produced in large numbers. Many were made in the old city Kashan which was an important center for political activity in this period. A Kashan carpet from this time illustrates the tragic story of Khosrow, Farhad and Shirin told in the *Shahnameh*. The famous story was retold more elaborately by the twelfth-century writer Nizami (d.1209).

Khosrow Parviz was one of the last Sassanian kings, ruling Iran from 590 to 628. He seemed destined to marry the beautiful Armenian princess Shirin. However, due to a series of misunderstandings and failures of recognition, this event was repeatedly postponed. The legendary Farhad was a renowned stonemason and builder who also passionately loved Shirin.

To remove his rival, Khosrow gave him the impossibly difficult task of building a road and tunnel through a mountainous area. In return, the king agreed he would give up Shirin if Farhad succeeded. When he learned to his surprise that the tunnel was nearing completion,

1.3 Kashan *Safavid Design* *(c.1970, 4.82 x 3.20)*

Many familiar elements of this contemporary design are adapted from the classic carpet patterns of the Safavid era (1501-1722).

1.4 Kashan
Khosrow, Farhad and Shirin
(c.1915, 2.10 x 1.32)

The ***Shahnameh*** *records how Khosrow Shah and the master builder Farhad competed for Shirin's love in the final period of Sassanian rule (224-641).*

Khosrow Parviz sent the false news that Shirin had died. Overwhelmed by grief and despair, Farhad threw himself off the mountain. There are some further misadventures that end with the murder of Khosrow and the untimely death of Shirin.

Like many other episodes in the *Shahnameh*, the legendary story has a subtle political and historical significance. It describes in disguised symbolic terms the repeated failures of the Zoroastrian and Christian kingdoms to recognize their common interests and achieve unity only a few years before the cataclysm of the Arab invasion. There is also a slightly discordant contemporary reference in this carpet design. Looking out of place among the legendary rulers of Iran shown in the border of the Kashan carpet, there is an awkwardly

1.5 Kashan
Bahram and Fitnah
c.1930, 2.16 x 1.37)

The impulsive slave girl Fitnah is condemned to death for refusing to praise her king. Years later, she demonstrates to Bahram what may be achieved by constant effort.

drawn portrait of the last Qajar king, the young Ahmad Shah who was soon to be removed from his throne by Reza Khan.

The second Kashan pictorial carpet was made some decades later (c.1930). It shows two scenes from the story of an earlier Sassanian king Bahram Gur (ruled 420-38) and his favorite slave girl Fitnah as told by Nizami in his poetry. In the *Shahnameh*, Ferdowsi tells a less detailed but closely related story of Bahram and the slave girl Azadeh. In Nizami's poetic version, Fitnah incurs the uncontrolled wrath of the proud king when she refuses to praise him.

She declares she is unimpressed by one of his remarkable feats of archery, saying that his achievement was only a result of practice. Sentenced to die, Fitnah is saved from execution and hidden by a high official of the royal court who understands his true loyalty to the king. They wait patiently for an opportunity to correct the situation. Years later, concealed by a disguise, Fitnah performs an almost impossible feat of strength for Bahram. She astonishes the visiting monarch by carrying a fully-grown ox up sixty steps in the officer's castle.

Courageously removing her disguise to reveal herself to the king, Fitnah explains she had not praised him for fear of attracting the evil eye. She boldly tells him she had acquired her unusual ability by constant practice, the same method he had employed to acquire his skills in archery. Each day during her years of exile, she had carried the ox up the steps of the castle beginning when it was a small calf. Surprised and delighted to find her alive, Bahram immediately repents of his former impulsive behavior and he marries Fitnah. By her constancy in adversity over a long period of time, Fitnah was transformed from a willful young woman into a spiritual guide capable of leading Bahram to an understanding of the true nature of kingship.

In a complex way, the well-known story brings together many timeless and universal themes. The unforgettable narrative focuses in turn on pride and anger, failure of communication, sincerity, loyalty, patience, endurance, courage, concealment, recognition, judgment, and guidance. In the twelfth century, Nizami wrote that his poetry was intended to teach man the nature of his own design. Beyond its many separate themes, this story evokes an ancient ideal that continues to resonate in Iranian public life. The perfect ruler should combine in his person the dual roles of religious leader and king.

One of the most remembered narratives in the *Shahnameh* is the tragic story of the three brothers Iraj, Salm and Tur. They were the sons of the mythological king Feridoun whose five hundred year rule had been a period of harmony and prosperity after the long tyranny of Zahhak. This interval of enlightened rule ends abruptly when a complacent Feridoun decides to divide his kingdom among his three sons. Salm is given the western part (*Rum*, Asia Minor) and Tur acquires the northern part (*Turan*, Central Asia).

Feridoun's youngest son Iraj had always been his favorite. He is chosen to inherit the kingdom of Iran and the golden throne of his father. Motivated by jealousy and opportunism, Salm and Tur later form an alliance to kill Iraj and claim his territory. This tragic event marks the beginning of a centuries-long struggle for dominance between Iran and Turan, the kingdoms known as *Airya* and *Turya* in the *Avesta*.

From a careful analysis of small changes in the author's style of writing, scholars have concluded that Ferdowsi began his thirty years labor composing the *Shahnameh* with his telling of the story of the forbidden love of Bijan and Manijeh. Familiar to all Iranians, the romantic story describes one of the most memorable incidents in the long period of conflict between Iran and Turan.

Remarkably, Ferdowsi precedes his retelling of the old story with a dramatic account of a personal experience. He begins with a description of himself sleeping in his garden on a dark night. Waking suddenly and seized by an overwhelming terror of the total darkness, the young man that he then was calls out anxiously for light. His companion sees his great distress and she hurriedly brings lighted candles.

To overcome his remaining fears, she tries to distract Ferdowsi by telling him an old story. She chooses to relate the story of Bijan's cruel imprisonment chained in a well where he has been left to perish. He was confined there by Manijeh's father who was the ruler of Turan. Bijan is kept alive by the faithful Manijeh until he can be rescued from his hopeless situation by Rustam, the legendary hero of the ancient conflicts between Iran and Turan.

With the light of a few candles and by entering into the created world of the story told by his companion, Ferdowsi regained his composure. He was able to escape imaginatively from uncontrollable fears and from the unnamed evils he perceived to be surrounding him in every direction. We may believe that the old story of the constant lovers and the vivid memory of his rescue from his deepest fears on that dark night exerted a profound influence on Ferdowsi. It is possible they became the inspiration and model for his life's work.

The story of Bijan's miraculous escape from the well finds echoes in another story told in the *Quran* and the Bible. We should recall the fortunate rescue of Joseph from the well where his envious brothers had left him to die. For centuries, these two stories and their related images have created profound resonances in the Iranian imagination. Like the designs of the *zir haq* carpets of the 1930s, the rescues of Bijan and Joseph from their dark confinements under the ground recall the most central Zoroastrian beliefs. In the ancient religion of Iran, the world was a place of eternal conflict between Ahriman and Ahura Mazda representing the forces of darkness and the forces of light.

1.6 Kashan
Rescue of Joseph
(c.1915, 2.03 x 1.32)

Weak from hunger and blinded by the light, Joseph is helpless at the moment of his rescue from the dark well by the merchants of a passing caravan.

There is another significant spiritual interpretation that may be given to these familiar narratives. In Islamic mysticism, the earthbound condition of man is often compared to the situation of Joseph in the dark well waiting impatiently to be rescued. The spiritual seekers on the mystical journey are all like Joseph. They are waiting for the rope or the ladder that will allow them to escape from their confinement in the darkness of the material world.

The Kashan carpet illustrated (c.1915) expresses this well-known spiritual meaning of the rescue of Joseph and it is combined with a more concealed but unmistakable contemporary reference. The choice to weave this pictorial design was almost certainly related to the strong desire at the time the carpet was made for extensive social changes and a complete national renewal.

There are many other possible beginnings. The collection of six short stories *Yeki Bud, Yeki Nabud (It was, It was not)* by Mohammed Ali Jamalzadeh published in 1921 is considered by many to be the first major work of modern Iranian prose literature. The title chosen by Jamalzadeh is a very significant one for all Iranians since *yeki bud, yeki nabud* is the traditional beginning phrase of Iranian stories for children. It plays the same role as the conventional phrase "Once upon a time" that begins children's stories in English.

"It was, it was not" seems to be more expressive in the way it suggests there will be an oscillation between seen and unseen or between reality and imagination in the story that follows. Immediately, these few familiar words act on the suggestible minds of Iranian children to create a receptive uncertainty. They produce an eager willingness to enter the imaginative logic of a story. In 1921, Jamalzadeh sought very consciously to create a similar awareness in his adult readers.

Consistent with his goals of a greater transparency in Iranian life and a mutual comprehensibility, Jamalzadeh is careful to explain his motivations very clearly in the preface to his book.

> My purpose is to create stories in a literary style which, from the point of view of language, may contain words and expressions in current use by the common people and the man in the street, and, from the point of view of description of the life of the different classes, may be a mirror to describe society.

Jamalzadeh writes further that the highly developed European literary forms of the short story and the novel were best suited to faithfully reflect the customs and thoughts of ordinary Iranians at all levels of society. Living in permanent exile in Europe, the author was very aware of the great contributions made by these more contemporary forms to self-awareness and social solidarity.

In the best-known story of the collection, *Farsi Shekar Ast* ("Persian is Sweet"), Jamalzadeh communicates these motivations to his readers by means of some strong metaphors. The simple story takes place in a small jail in an Iranian border town. The three prisoners in the jail are a cross-section of Iranian society, a common laborer, a mullah, and an intellectual newly returned from Europe. They find they are unable to communicate with each other since their vocabularies, concepts and experiences are all so different.

The story *Bile Dig, Bile Chokondar* ("As the Beetroot, So the Pot") proved to be the most controversial. It presents a confused and scandalous account by a European bath attendant of his several years in Iran. He had been invited to accompany an official delegation to Iran to serve as a masseur for one of the leaders. There, due to some misunderstandings and failures of communication, the bath attendant became an important and surprisingly successful government official in a very short time. In this prominent position, the confused European visitor gained a unique if highly distorted perspective on Iranian life.

The unusual title of Jamalzadeh's disturbing story refers to a well-known tale from the province of Azerbaijan. It tells of two peasants from nearby villages who happened to meet. One villager boasted, "In my village, we grow beets as big as houses." Not to be outdone, the other proudly replied, "In my village, we make cooking pots as big as mosques." Puzzled, the first man asked, "Why do you do that?" The second villager answered very innocently, "We need them to cook your beets!"

In his stories and essays, Jamalzadeh argues eloquently for the necessity of a shared language in which all could communicate, a common language capable of accurately reflecting present-day society. The two villagers from Azerbaijan in the old story, the prisoners in the border jail, and the perplexed European visitor to Iran experienced almost the same difficulties but in very different circumstances. We might add the real-life example of Onera Merritt-Hawkes attempting in vain to communicate with a modern Iranian woman in Isfahan. None of them were successful in negotiating the appropriate common levels of description and discourse, metaphorical or pragmatic, which would make possible a true sharing of ideas and experiences.

This preoccupation with language and communication has been a central concern of Iranian culture at least since the time of Ferdowsi. In the *Shahnameh*, written more than three centuries after the Arab conquest, Ferdowsi very consciously attempted to renew the resources of the Persian language. On a smaller scale, this was also the primary aim of Jamalzadeh almost ten centuries later. In their writings, they both sought to explore and expand the potential of the vernacular language of their times as a vital means of personal and cultural expression.

In *Iranian Nationality and the Persian Language* (1992), Meskoob Shahrokh examines the central role of language in the construction of a national identity in modern times. He makes a comparison with other peoples where various social and cultural factors as well as the arts have a national importance that is well understood and generally accepted. With the exception of architecture, Shahrokh observes, the national culture of Iranians lacked almost all of these other unifying factors. He concludes, "Thus our task was more difficult: our nationality had no abode except language."

Surprisingly, Shahrokh makes no reference to the unique possibilities of the Persian carpet and the evident achievements of Iranian textile and visual arts in playing a significant historical and contemporary role in the expression of a national character. Another scholarly study of Iranian national identity, *Iran as Imagined Nation* (1993) by Mostafa Vaziri, examines similar questions but it has a different emphasis. It focuses with considerable skepticism on the possible continuity of language and art from the time of the Achaemenian empire to the present and their roles in creating a comprehensive national heritage. This supposed continuity had been almost an article of faith during the Pahlavi period (1926-1979).

The dominant motivation of Jamalzadeh was to renew the possibilities of individual and national expression in the Persian language. This aim has been shared by many less well-known prose writers and poets in modern times. The American traveler and author Robert Payne toured Iran in 1949, and he described his experiences in *Journey to Persia* (1951). During his brief stay in Iran, he took a strong interest in current literary developments. In Shiraz, he met a young poet who told him in response to his questions, "It's all changing now. The wine and the roses — it won't be long before the Persian poets speak of tractors. Yet the odd thing is that we keep on going back to Hafiz. … we shall probably be the last to write social poetry."

Asked again by Payne about recent trends in modern poetry, the Shirazi poet answered his visitor's insistent questions in a reluctant and evasive way. Apparently unwilling to be drawn into a detailed discussion with his visitor, he continued to reply in a more general manner. He answered, "There is too much. Everyone in Persia is a poet – it is one of our national failings. At the end of a dinner everyone writes a poem. They are truly magnificent poems, but they are always about eating dinners."

In 1934, Merritt-Hawkes spent her last evening in Isfahan attending a meeting of a poetry club, one of several in the city and hundreds in the country. The members took turns reading their new poems quietly or dramatically, some almost singing their verses in the traditional way. She noted an important difference among the readers. Some preferred to express their own ideas in their compositions while others put more emphasis on technique and faithfulness to the classical models.

Finally, the turn came for the poet sitting next to her to read his poetry. Her host for the evening did not follow the others in reciting his recent work, but instead he chose to make a long speech pleading for the modernization of the themes and techniques of contemporary Iranian poetry. With some emotion, he said, "All we are doing is to make bad copies of the great poets, Ferdowsi, Nizami, Sa'adi, but it would be better if we followed the example of the Europeans, altered the form and introduced modern ideas, so that poetry might be a photograph of life today."

Stronger criticisms are contained in the writings of Sadeq Hedayat, the most prominent Iranian literary figure of the 1930s and 1940s. As advocated by the anonymous Isfahan poet, Hedayat introduced many European models and ideas to Iranian literature. Best known for his short stories and novels, he also wrote travel journals, plays, folklore studies, translations and critical essays. To a great extent, his work did provide a photograph of contemporary Iranian life in an eventful period.

In "The Stray Dog," the title story from the short story collection *Sag-e Velgard* (1942), Hedayat deals metaphorically with the theme of the problematic reception of foreign ideas in a traditional culture. The story tells of the difficult life of a dog that has been lost or abandoned by its European owners in an Iranian town. The bewildered dog is unable to understand the rejection it finds from all directions.

In 1932, Hedayat and three other writers formed the *Rab'a* ("The Four" in pseudo-Arabic) to discuss and encourage new writing. Until it disbanded in 1936 under government pressure, this literary group provided an informal setting for the socially committed writers of Tehran to exchange ideas about current trends in literature. The members of the *Rab'a* had strong negative opinions on the continued dominance of the classical models of Persian literature. They criticized the conventional products of the literary establishment of their day as "grave digging" and "the science of fossils." These epithets were mocking references to the *zir haq* ("under the ground") idea that was being officially promoted.

In *Tup-e Morvari* (*The Pearl Cannon*), a bitterly critical late work completed in 1947, Hedayat satirized again some of the cultural pretensions of the current Pahlavi period which he compared unfavorably to the previous Qajar era.

> Without experts in patriotic propaganda, the people showed a greater attachment to their land. Without throwing a christening party and changing the country's name, it looks as if the name and reputation of this country among the foreigners was much greater. ... There was not such heat in the air about public education, but there were more learned people and many more good books were published.

Hedayat was never impressed by the noisy propaganda accompanying the many symbolic gestures of the national government. This included the royal decree in 1935 that changed the international name of the country from Persia to Iran.

A letter to Hassan Shahid-Nourai who was his closest friend during his last years addresses similar themes. It further indicates Hedayat's disillusion with the Iranian literary scene of the time and with the traditional visual imagery of Iranian art and literature. One of their writer friends had recently died, and he was being mourned in death far more than he had ever been celebrated in life.

> On the whole the poor fellow had an unhappy life, and spent it all wandering about in hardship. But what can you do? This is typical of many people's lives in the country of roses and nightingales.

In a letter to Jamalzadeh also written at this time, Hedayat pointed to the difficulty of genuine human communication as the central problem: "In our life, environment and everything else, there's a terrifying rift such that we can no longer understand each other's language."

Almost the same scene described by Merritt-Hawkes at the meeting of the poetry club in Isfahan occurs in fictional form in the novel *Identity Card* (1966) by F.M.Esfandiary. The central character is Daryush Aryana, an unexceptional young man with a very significant name. He has returned to Iran from America for no particular reason he can articulate beyond a curiosity to see again the country he had left with his family in childhood.

Soon after his arrival in Iran, Aryana learns that a document he had lost many years before may be very important. Without a *shenaznameh*, the national identity card issued to every Iranian citizen at birth, he will not be allowed to leave the country. To his dismay, Aryana does not find the land he had imagined from childhood stories. Instead of an heroic nation inspired by the epic tales in the *Shahnameh*, he discovers the nervously uncertain country of the *shenaznameh*. What began as a journey to rediscover his Iranian identity becomes a Kafkaesque struggle to obtain an identity card from an impenetrable bureaucracy.

Early in the novel, Daryush Aryana is invited to a social evening at a wealthy north Tehran home. Several poets with a local reputation are in attendance. After a brief show of reluctance, they agree to recite some of their very conventional, uninspired poetry. As a distinguished foreign visitor to Iran, Aryana is asked politely for his opinion of their works. Without hesitating to consider his words, he hears himself saying to the others that poetry is dead. He tells them very definitely, "The age of poetry has passed, it is gone, it is finished, finished."

There is a strong negative reaction from the other guests to these unexpected words, an understandable response that the host immediately attempts to smooth over. Apologizing for the unfortunate misunderstanding, he deflects the criticism onto himself. Searching for the right words, he says, "I am the guilty one, because I should have explained to you beforehand that Mr. Aryana has been abroad many years, many many years, and therefore speaks in a different spirit, how shall I say, he has a different vocabulary – yes, that's it, he has a different vocabulary."

One of the guests also tries to restore the situation by saying helpfully, "I am sure what he meant was that some poems – not the ones that were recited here – but others, are now, perhaps, a little, well, how shall we say, a little outmoded and I am sure we all agree with that."

Aryana does not seize this opportunity but instead adds considerably to his difficulties. Unwilling to compromise, he answers, "There is no room for such silly romanticism. … The poets of today are the dedicated, inspired realists, scientists who labor day and night to help man probe deeper into himself and his environment. … A sensitive, rational man, alive to all the miseries, all the injustices, all the suffering in the world, has no patience, no inclination to sit back and passively weave stupid, idle rhymings about mountains that weep and beautiful tears of love-crazed idiots."

Replying to a guest who asserts defensively that the poems symbolize problems of the mind and society, Aryana continues to make his situation worse. In his different vocabulary and his more direct manner, he says, "I don't see the symbolism. … It is in fashion here to write meaningless things, then make all sorts of claims that they have deep hidden meanings and symbolize things."

Isolated and rejected now by the others, Daryush Aryana soon leaves the gathering. Instead of returning to his room in central Tehran, he begins to walk aimlessly. Without much thought, he turns in another direction. Following some impulse, he heads further north along the Darband road leading to the mountains. As he walks, the anger inside him grows and he thinks of even stronger words he should have used. When he reaches the village of Darband, his dark mood changes suddenly.

He regrets he had not come sooner to spend whole days and nights at the stream passing through the quiet village. Aryana feels he should have come there before everything else in order to make friends with the trees and to meet his old friend the mountain. He is not yet willing to admit the influence of the mediocre poetry he condemned so completely a few hours before. Despite this, he is strongly affected by the simple scene before him. He now understands he has concealed within him some deep memories of these trees and mountains that must date from his early childhood.

Aryana quietly ponders the calming effects of this more sympathetic environment. This brings to his mind some other regrets about what he had found in his brief time in contemporary Iran: "He was sorry that his modern countrymen did not frequent Darband, and were, as a rule, loath to lie down on the rugs in the old cafes or teahouses, as they called them, but preferred to show themselves in ostentatious restaurants, sitting stiffly on inhospitable chairs under aggressive neon lights."

In a surprising reversal, Aryana surrenders himself to the natural symbolism of the peaceful scene and the almost forgotten memories from childhood that it has reawakened in him. They combine to change his perceptions almost completely, reconciling him for the moment to the difficulties of his present situation. He whispers repeatedly to himself, "God, how I needed to come back to my country." After his disastrous social evening, Daryush Aryana realizes he is not any closer to finding his identity card. However, he understands for the first time that he is beginning to rediscover his true Iranian identity.

Some memorable advice that may serve here was given to Edward G. Browne during his first journey in Iran in 1887, as described in his travel journal *A Year Amongst the Persians*. In a village near Persepolis, the community leader or *kadkhoda* (literally, "hand of God") explained very sensitively what he thought the inexperienced English visitor should look for in Iran.

> "Perhaps you, too, will by the grace of God, be brought to believe in the religion of our Prophet. You have come to see our country from afar; do not, like the majority of the Firangis [foreigners], occupy yourself with nothing but dumb stones, vessels of brass, tiles and fabrics; contemplate the world of form, and seek for Truth rather than for curiosities. Why should you not even pay a visit to the most holy tombs of our Imams at Kerbela and Nejef? There you might see the miracles whereby they prove to all that they still live and rule. … It would be a pity that you should take back nothing with you but a collection of those curiosities and antiquities with which your people seem for the most part to be so strangely infatuated."

The village leader had expressed in the simplest terms what the classically educated visitor certainly understood as the essence of Platonic philosophy and metaphysics. In our encounters with the external world, we must always strive to go beyond the transitory world of appearances and the deceptive accidents of material form to perceive an eternal reality.

A second chance encounter made an equally strong impression on the young traveler. During his stay in Shiraz, Browne was invited one evening to a social gathering in a private home. In the background, a blind musician was playing the sitar and singing in a sweet melodious voice. When the host addressed his distinguished foreign guest as *hakim sahib* ("esteemed doctor"), the blind man overheard him. He exclaimed, "*Hakim*! … Is our guest a physician? Can he not perhaps cure my blindness and enable me to once more behold the light?"

As gently as possible, the host explained to the unfortunate musician that the honored visitor was a metaphysician (*hakim-i-ilahi*, "philosopher") and not a physician. With some evident emotion, Browne observed the very human response: "It went to my heart to see the momentary expression of anxious hope which had crossed the face of the blind minstrel pass, through a quiver of disappointment, into the look of patient sadness which his countenance habitually wore."

We know the young English visitor had already learned what would prove to be the essential lesson for him to follow during his year of exploration. From the *kadkhoda* in the village near Persepolis, he had learned there was another type of blindness that affected some visitors to Iran. This was the human blindness to more profound meanings, a common affliction that only a metaphysician could cure.

Some months before these encounters, Edward Browne was waiting impatiently in Tehran for winter to end. There he explained his earnest intentions to an Iranian friend Ferhad Mirza. Browne said that he planned to travel to Shiraz as soon as the roads became passable again at the beginning of spring. He thought Shiraz would be the best place to pursue his studies of Persian language and culture since that city was well known as the *daru'l-ilm,* the abode of knowledge (literally, "the door or gate of knowledge").

His more knowledgeable Tehrani companion reacted very skeptically when he learned of Browne's naïve plan. With unusual directness, Ferhad Mirza told his English friend he had come to Iran much too late to achieve his goal. He said, "That is quite a mistake: five hundred years ago Shiraz was the *daru'l-ilm,* but now that has passed, and it can only be called the *daru'l-fisk,* the abode of vice."

In every age, the realists such as Ferhad Mirza and Daryush Aryana will believe that the age of poetry has passed. Needless to say, Browne persisted in his original plan and the fervent hopes of the young idealist were not to be disappointed. His excited account of the last stages of the slow approach to Shiraz through the difficult mountain passes has become a classic description of its kind in travel literature.

1.7 Isfahan *Gate of **Tang-i Allahu Akbar*** *(c.1970, 1.75 x 1.23)*

In past centuries, travelers to Shiraz first saw theTang Gate and the nearby tombs of Hafez and Sa'adi. A bounding chain and birds rising to the light are cultural signs of a refuge and a spiritual journey.

> Suddenly we turned a corner, and in that moment – a moment of which the recollection will never fade from my mind – there burst upon my delighted gaze a view the like of which I never saw. We were now at that point, known to all students of Hafiz called *Tang-i Allahu Akbar,* because whoever first beholds Shiraz hence is constrained by the exceeding beauty of the sight to cry out in admiration *"Allahu Akbar"* – "God is most great!" At our very feet … lay the home of Persian culture, the mother of Persian genius, the sanctuary of poetry and philosophy, Shiraz.

After a weary journey of several weeks from Isfahan, Browne found to his great relief he had not come five centuries too late. When he passed through the narrow opening in the hills leading to Shiraz, the reality that lay before him was not a disappointment. It far surpassed the idealized vision he had conceived as a young student in England reading two popular works, James Morier's *Hajji Baba of Isfahan* and Edward Fitzgerald's translation of the *Rubaiyat of Omar Khayyam.*

About twenty-five years later, there is another beginning described by the American writer H.G.Dwight in *Persian Miniatures* (1917). This is the lively account of his travels and lengthy stay in Iran in 1913 and 1914. As the house guest for several months of an English friend A.C.Edwards, Dwight observed the introduction in the Hamadan region of carpet-making on a large scale according to foreign ideas. Edwards was the local manager for a British company, Oriental Carpet Manufacturers Ltd., founded only a few years before in London in 1906.

The new company had recently built a very large carpet factory in Hamadan with room for several hundred looms. A visible sign of the company's progressive ways was the lofty windmill erected for the carpet enterprise. As tall as a minaret, the windmill had been imported with great effort all the way from Chicago, very probably ordered from the catalogue of the Sears and Roebuck Company. As soon as the many separate pieces were assembled and the windmill erected, villagers began to travel from miles around to see the impressive mechanical marvel for themselves.

Some of them spent hours watching the ingenious windmill tirelessly drawing up great quantities of water from deep in the ground for the factory's many dyeing vats. How exactly, the villagers must have wondered to themselves, did the constantly turning windmill achieve its miracle? How did it use the unseen wind to release the precious water that for centuries had lain concealed far under the ground?

Before the company could recruit the large number of weavers needed to work on the new looms, there were some necessary and delicate negotiations with the most prominent religious authority of the city. After consulting widely among his followers in the community, he finally announced his decision to the anxious company representatives. The religious leader tolerantly agreed that the women of Hamadan would be permitted to work in the new factory if one necessary precondition was satisfied. A suitable elderly religious person would have to be appointed to serve as their chaperon in order to ensure that decorum and good manners prevailed.

An experienced master weaver had been recruited from distant Tabriz, the major center of carpet activity in the country. The company's choice met with general approval in Hamadan. Everyone could see that the master weaver wore a green turban, the recognized sign of a *seyyed*. In Shi'a Islam, this well-understood visual sign meant the wearer was a direct descendant of the Prophet Mohammed and his beloved daughter Fatima. The descent of a respected *seyyed* was through the male line from Ali who was the husband of Fatima and the first Imam of Shi'a Islam. The green turban of the Tabrizi master weaver gave some additional feelings of reassurance to the religious leader. Equally important, this sign of respectability increased substantially the confidence of the worried fathers and husbands of the new weavers.

With varying degrees of success, the pioneering carpet enterprise in Hamadan attempted to introduce rigorous controls to all stages of carpet making, preparing and dyeing its own wool in the factory and following its own designs. Finding reliable workers in sufficient numbers proved to be more difficult than expected. According to Dwight, the enormous factory had space for seven hundred looms, but there were rarely enough weavers to work at half that number.

Dwight sympathized with the inability of the weavers to understand fully the demanding requirements of capitalism. He wrote approvingly of their obstinate refusal to be governed by these pressing needs: "A religious anniversary falls due, a visitor comes to call, they are invited to a picnic, or a husband pinches their cheek, and they stay at home – while their carpet hangs idle on the loom and dealers in Firengistan [Europe] telegraph angrily about delays in filling contracts."

A small incident observed by Dwight illustrates some of the many changes produced by the introduction of factory methods. One day, a young weaver giggled as the Feranghi manager A.C.Edwards walked by her carpet loom on an inspection tour. When he seemed curious about the source of her amusement, the young girl pointed cheerfully to a yellow bird she had thought to add to the design. Acting completely on her own initiative, she had secretly woven the small bird into the floral border of the large carpet with a formal design that she was working on.

The Iranian employee responsible for supervising the weaving knew what his duty to his employer required. The *ustad* made it clear to everyone present that he did not share the weaver's innocent amusement, and he asked her to remove the trespassing bird immediately. His order would have required extensive reweaving with the loss of considerable time. On this occasion, the strict employee was overruled by the more understanding English manager. Despite the company's usual preference for rigorous control of all aspects of their carpet designs, Edwards decided impulsively to make an exception to the rules. Seeing the young weaver's happiness, he would tolerantly permit an unexpected yellow bird to stay where it was.

The keenly interested American observer who happened to be present that day to record this revealing encounter did not intervene with any suggestions of his own. However, it is immediately apparent from his sympathetic description that he strongly supported the humane decision of his English friend. Dwight was encouraged to witness an unusual victory for the irregularities he believed had been one of the principal charms of Persian carpets only a few decades before. That was in the still fondly remembered time preceding the renewal of international interest in the 1870s and the resulting introduction of the impersonal factory system throughout the country by Iranian and foreign companies.

The Qashqai rug illustrated is an example of the type made by students at the Qashqai Tribal School in Shiraz established in the 1960s. Experienced weavers were employed by the school to pass on their knowledge of carpet designs to a new generation. They taught their students the dyeing and weaving techniques that had been developed over many generations by the nomadic Qashqai people of southwest Iran. The girls and young women in the school's programs were instructed to be faithful to the old designs and methods, but they were also encouraged to find ways to put something of their own experiences and preferences into their carpets.

1.8 Qashqai
Ab Baba
(c.1970, 1.53 x 1.10)

*The words **ab** and **baba** meaning water and father are formed from the first letters of the **alephba**. Young children are eager to learn the thirty-three letters and the many words of a common language.*

This may explain why the weaver of this small rug, like the young girl in Hamadan in 1914, has included an unexpected element in the otherwise traditional design. Very inconspicuously, she has added the two meaningful words *ab* and *baba* ("water" and "father") to her carpet pattern. Both words are formed from the letters *aleph* and *ba* which are the first two letters of the *alephba* or alphabet. For that elementary reason, they are almost always the first words that Iranian children learn to write in their earliest days at school.

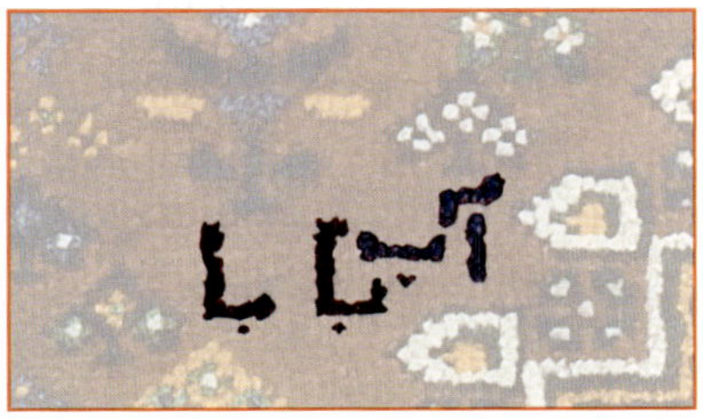

In different ways, the words *ab* and *baba* describe primary sources of life and they suggest essential requirements for all beginnings. It may be significant for our purposes to remember that the words father and pattern have a common linguistic origin. We may imagine an inexperienced young woman who was opening herself to old methods and new possibilities. In the familiar way of all beginning students, she was eager to understand her origins and anxious to join a larger world.

Acquiring the cultural and technical knowledge necessary to weave carpets and developing the requisite manual dexterity were important parts of this personal opening to new and old experiences. A young woman was learning to read and write the national language at the same time she was learning the intricate patterns of Qashqai weaving. Like many others before her, she was learning the visual language of her community and the woven symbolic record of their historical experiences. What had been a bewildering multiplicity of social influences and personal motivations became a comprehensible unity in a small carpet.

It is in these small observations and encounters that we are more likely to find the cultural meanings we seek than in the coercive decrees of Reza Shah. We prefer to believe with the poet William Butler Yeats that there are always two living countries, the one visible and the other invisible. Unlike the well-defined borders of modern Iran, the boundaries of Persia are no longer represented very well by the narrow curved lines drawn on any map. Their changeable contours are more likely to be found and explored in the world of the imagination. We will boldly challenge the king's decree and continue to use the word Persia in this spirit, reluctantly accepting the risk that our letters may not reach their intended destinations.

The phrase *yeki bud, yeki nabud* that begins children's stories in Iran is an invitation to what Yeats called a radical innocence. *It was, it was not* summons us to a child's world from which myth and magic have not vanished. *Yeki bud, yeki nabud* is a subversive invitation to a double world of reality and imagination where there is a constant oscillation between seen and unseen.

In this child's world, every moment of time is a new beginning. To understand the most profound meanings of the designs of Persian carpets, it may be necessary to find ways to recapture some of the uncalculating innocence and receptive uncertainty we knew in childhood. Before reentering this imagined world of memories and dreams, we should be warned of the possible difficulties. In the invisible country we intend to visit, there may be very few straight roads to make our journey go more easily.

But now we must make greater haste. The brave travelers who have not changed their minds have assembled at the leaving place. After a sleepless night, they are all gathered a short distance outside the city's crumbling mud walls. It is just before dawn, and they are shivering nervously in the unfamiliar cold and darkness of early morning. A crescent moon and numberless stars illuminate the scene. A few oil lamps produce a feeble light that flickers unsteadily in the penetrating wind.

The battered tin lamps cast long ghostly shadows whose constantly moving shapes fade away and then disappear completely in the surrounding void. The friends and relatives who have accompanied the travelers to the leaving place are now saying their final sad farewells. They will be returning very soon to the inviting warmth of their homes in the city. These companions will carry back with them the abandoned baggage that now seems unnecessary. Some of it proved to be impossible to load or impractical to carry great distances.

Struggling under the weight of their new burdens, the noisy camels have risen to their feet with difficulty. Even in the early morning, they are demonstrating their restless impatience by pulling repeatedly against their iron chains. The older camels have some awareness of the hardships and potential accidents that may confront the small caravan, but they are more than ready to escape from long days of monotonous confinement in the hungry city. Unlike the hesitant human travelers, the proud camels are showing no signs of reluctance to begin the long journey.

The many bad omens reported by some anxious travelers have been explained by the elderly dervish, and the recommended spells and talismans have been purchased. After glancing several times at the sky and more than once at the busy caravan leader, the holy wanderer begins to reassure the travelers that no further delay is necessary. The grey-bearded dervish announces to anyone who will listen that the important stars and planets have moved to their most auspicious positions. He assures them there will never be a better time to begin.

In any event, the heavenly bodies have become impossible to see as the bright sun is about to rise. In a few minutes more, the golden eye of heaven will appear above the low range of hills which have now become visible beneath the yellow-red glow that forms a narrow band curving along the eastern horizon. Before darkness returns, the travelers must reach a safe resting place at a *caravanserai* located somewhere in the refuge of those distant hills.

The *charvadar*, the caravan leader, has finally lost all patience with the ceaseless complaints of the merchants and pilgrims he has agreed to guide to distant places. Looking toward the east, he sees there is enough light to begin. His main concern is whether the heavily loaded camels will find their way around the obstacles of the uneven path ahead of them. At last, their rusting chains have been removed and the old lamps have been extinguished. In a rough commanding voice that silences everyone and compels obedience, the *charvadar* calls out, "Start the journey!"

آسیا با

2 The Persian Carpet

About Rug Books is the deceptively inviting title of one chapter of *Persian Miniatures*, the insightful travel journal by the American writer Harrison Griswald Dwight. Contrary to expectations, the chapter does not provide a comprehensive survey of the currently available sources of carpet knowledge combined with a measured analysis of their contents. It outlines instead a memorable warning directed to all future readers of books about oriental carpets and even to prospective writers of such books.

Dwight begins his informative but very critical account innocently enough. He disarms his readers by first conjuring up a pleasant domestic scene.

> Whenever we are hard up for amusement – as may happen even in royal Ecbatana, since Alexander went away – we turn over our rug books. Of these we have quite a collection. For the Sah'b is himself a man of rugs; and when a new book about them appears, as is sure to happen once a twelve-month, the good people at home send him out a copy.

We have already encountered the enterprising Sah'b (*saheb*, "master") who is described here as a man of rugs. A.C.Edwards was the young English manager of the new carpet factory in Hamadan with whom Dwight stayed as a house guest for some months in the ominous year 1914.

Ecbatana was the original name of the city of Hamadan more than two millennia before when it was the summer capital of the Achaemenian kings. In its ancient days of imperial glory, the royal city was renowned for its great power and overwhelming beauty. Ecbatana was the name in use at the momentous time when the invader Alexander of Macedon was briefly in residence there. In 1914, there were few visible traces remaining in the remote provincial city of Hamadan from that legendary period.

It is quickly made clear that the genial amusement so generously provided to Dwight and Edwards by their sizeable collection of rug books had a sharp edge which could cut very deeply. Their amusement was not always of the kind the mainly uninformed authors of these tomes had intended for their mostly credulous readers.

> We find it impossible to take these volumes very seriously, not even the fattest and most expensive of them, whose authors' names are pronounced in whispers by all ladies in America. They remind us too much of Babu English, and of what Persians say about our own side of the world.

In the context of the time, this was an entirely justified warning. By any reasonable standards, the available volumes were usually filled with inventive misinformation. This increased substantially the difficulties in arriving at a genuine appreciation of Persian carpets and a thorough understanding of their undoubted complexities.

Dwight does mention the existence of some honorable exceptions to these strong statements including the works of several eminent European authorities. In particular, the author exempts the contemporary American writer John Kimberly Mumford from most of his criticisms. He writes in exoneration of his faults that Mumford's limitations were primarily those of opportunity rather than those of good faith.

In the previous decade, Mumford's well-known work *Oriental Rugs* (1901) had helped to establish a new standard for systematic carpet studies. Dwight gives this book well-deserved credit for bringing some needed order to what had been little more than a picturesque chaos before its publication. If Mumford must pay the penalty of the pioneer in carpet studies, Dwight graciously concedes that so too does he deserve the glory.

A favorite book Dwight and Edwards appreciated primarily for its amusement value was a more recent addition to their library. *The Practical Book of Oriental Rugs* by Dr.G.G.Lewis became an immediate best-seller when it was published in 1911 and it remained in print in the United States for the next forty years. The unassuming title may have been intended as an implied criticism of the relative difficulty of an earlier book. Lewis's main competitor initially was Mumford's much more substantial volume which had appeared only ten years before.

Dwight is clearly not impressed by the newer author's severely limited knowledge, however practical the resulting book may have been for its unsuspecting readers. To communicate his unequivocal opinion of Lewis's efforts, he asks his own readers a sharply pointed rhetorical question.

> How can we keep straight faces when he talks about Greek Mohammedans, or reveals to us that a talismanic triangle is often tattooed on a Turk's body, or says that green is a favorite colour of Persian rug makers, or announces that a dog is considered in the Near East a sacred animal, …?

After several pages in a similar vein directed against Lewis and some other easy targets, Dwight then tries a different approach to the problem. He attempts to be helpful to future writers of rug books or preferably to discourage them from embarking on the considerable difficulties of the task.

He begins by analyzing the faulty methods he conjectures had been employed by the popular Dr. Lewis and similar authors.

> Their method, one gathers from their books, is to sit down with Mr. Mumford in one hand and a school geography in the other, dictating until they feel the need for illumination on some obscure point – when they seek enlightenment from an Armenian rug pedlar or from the buyer of a department store who has been three times to Smyrna, Constantinople, Tiflis and Tabriz.

Benefiting from his recent experiences and observations in Iran, Dwight knew that much better methods were both possible and urgently needed.

The American writer generously acknowledges his extensive consultations with a more reliable authority than himself. He credits his amiable host in Hamadan as the source of the detailed information about carpets that he provides. In his preface, Dwight had briefly changed his usually skeptical and even mocking tone to one of cautious hope. He does this just long enough to make a significant prediction. Very confidently, he predicts that his English friend could write a more competent rug book than had yet been written if he ever chose to do so.

Arthur Cecil Edwards delayed for almost four decades but he did eventually choose to write that rug book. When it was published in 1953, it fully justified Dwight's early prediction. *The Persian Carpet: A Survey of the Carpet-Weaving Industry of Persia* became immediately the authoritative work on the subject, and it remains to this day an indispensable reference. The author's extensive personal knowledge and direct experiences are apparent on every page. By the time of publication, Edwards had been involved in the Persian carpet business in London for almost fifty years of which thirteen were spent living in Iran.

Referring to himself after his retirement in 1947 from active professional concerns, he describes his intention to complete the project that had been so long delayed but never forgotten. Edwards writes, "He then resolved to occupy his leisure with a task which had long been in his mind: to produce a survey of the admirable carpet industry of Persia." His very ambitious goal was to produce an accurate and reasonably complete record of the Iranian weaving industry as it existed at that time.

More diplomatic than Dwight in his comments on other books and their authors, Edwards notes simply that there were so few previous works on Persian carpets which could with honesty be recommended. Without giving details, he also notes that errors had been repeated in successive works with "melancholy persistence." Certainly, his own research and writing methods were completely different from those of many earlier authors as described so critically by his outspoken American friend. His methods were entirely centered on his own observations and on knowledge he confirmed as much as possible from his experiences.

The Persian Carpet is given significant narrative unity as the chronological record of a very long journey. In April 1948, Edwards landed with his wife at Khorramshahr at the head of the Persian Gulf where they collected their sturdy Hillman station wagon. They then set out together on a journey of discovery which was to last nearly a year and cover 8,500 miles. This proved to be a physically and mentally challenging journey throughout Iran that Edwards described sincerely as a pilgrimage.

The greatest contribution of *The Persian Carpet* is to be found in its balanced combination of detailed local observations together with a long-term perspective on the past development and future potential of the Persian carpet. During his years in the carpet business in Iran, the author writes, he had already visited every weaving center of importance at frequent intervals. The benefits of this first-hand professional experience are very evident in his book, but Edwards occasionally feels the need to apologize to his general readers for including some boring technical details of carpet weaving. In many places, the book does read like a practical manual intended primarily for professional carpet buyers in Iran.

> The Arab weavers of the Khamseh are of special interest to the merchant, because their output is by far the largest of any of the tribes of Fars. ….
> On the whole the dyes used [by the Bakhtiari] in the Chahar Mahal are good, but the dyeing is careless. Too often grey yarns are used instead of white which produces muddy colours. ….

> Rug weaving is not with the Qashqai as it is with the Khamseh a purely commercial proposition. Their women take pride in the rugs which they produce. ....

These brief comments are typical of the detailed observations and comparisons describing local conditions in every weaving center that he visited on his final journey. Located in different areas of southwest Iran, the Khamseh, Bakhtiari and Qashqai are three important tribal groups that have been major sources of carpets and other textiles for many generations.

The countless observations small and large made by Edwards are not recorded at random or without an overall unifying design. Instead, they are made with the constant purpose of recommending commercial and artistic improvements. His underlying goal was to help reverse the serious decline of the Iranian carpet industry during the previous twenty years of economic depression, foreign military occupations and political unrest. A primary motivation for his detailed survey was to present these much-needed recommendations to the appropriate ministry of the national government.

Edwards was one of many outsiders in the modern period to take an active interest in the commercial and artistic development of the Iranian carpet industry. In 1883, S.G.W.Benjamin became the first American government official to be posted to Iran where he opened a diplomatic legation in Tehran. Living in the Iranian capital for the next three years and traveling extensively throughout the country, he became a keen and sympathetic observer of all aspects of contemporary life. In his lengthy memoir of his experiences *Persia and the Persians* (1887), Benjamin assessed the current situation of all forms of Iranian art. He described them as being in a difficult transitional state with an uncertain future.

With some evidently strong regrets, the American diplomat observed firsthand that carpet production throughout Iran was coming increasingly under European influence and control. He writes about one noticeable symptom of this major change: "Until a European firm in Persia employed some of the carpet makers to reproduce ancient patterns, it was impossible to find two rugs or carpets in Persia identical in design." Benjamin is making an important point here, but he seems to have forgotten temporarily that many Persian carpets were made in identical pairs and some in larger matching sets.

The pioneering European firm referred to by Benjamin is not difficult to identify. In the previous decade, Messrs. Ziegler and Co. of Manchester, England had been the first foreign enterprise to introduce modified carpet designs intended to satisfy the current preferences of the growing English market. At the same time, the Ziegler Company achieved more consistent results by introducing new methods to a traditional occupation.

Benjamin comments on some of the consequences of these recent reforms. He writes, "By making advances to the workmen in Sultanabad they keep them steadily employed; but one condition is that they shall not give rein to their individual taste, but like machines they shall continually reproduce the designs which are found to meet the prevailing fashions in Europe." In this passage and many others, Benjamin communicates his preference for continuing with long-established methods and his strong disapproval of the unconsidered consequences that inevitably accompanied the new ways.

2.1 Arak *Sultanabad Carpet* *(c.1880, 5.80 x 4.12)*

Sultanabad weavers made many large carpets during the Qajar era (1785–1925). This still sizeable carpet has been reduced substantially to fit a smaller room.

The Ziegler Company began its trading connection with Iran in the 1860s, initially by exporting British cotton textiles and importing raw silk in exchange from Gilan province. The company soon developed a secondary business importing old Persian carpets collected mainly in Tabriz. When international interest increased substantially in the 1870s and the available supplies of old carpets in Iran diminished rapidly, an innovative solution to the problem was found. The company began ordering new carpets that were to be made following its own designs in the sizes and colors required for British customers.

In order to maintain standards and to guarantee a steady supply, the Ziegler Company gradually took over control of all aspects of this carpet production. The office and factory in Sultanabad (now Arak) referred to by Benjamin were opened in 1883. The English company was following closely the example provided by some enterprising Tabriz merchants a short time before. In the previous decade, they had begun making carpets in Sultanabad intended mainly to satisfy the growing demands of the new European market.

Observing this increasing foreign influence on carpet making, Benjamin regretted the resulting loss of spontaneity and individuality. There was another important quality endangered by the new methods, an intangible quality that may be illustrated by one of his personal experiences.

> One day an artist of Tehran came to do a little task of gilding for me. He was a tall, portly, handsome man, with a raven-colored beard. His black eyes were thoughtful and pleasant with a far-away look, as if he were living in a world of dreams. He said he was a pupil of Aga, or A'Najeff, a famous artist who lived during the two previous reigns. I remarked to him that he was giving more attention to his work than had been stipulated for the money agreed upon. He grandly replied, "I do not work for money alone; I work because I love my profession."

Although seemingly living in a world of dreams, the Tehran artist knew how to establish his credentials in an efficient manner according to the Iranian custom. As a guarantee of the quality and meaningfulness of his own work, he simply referred to his deceased teacher. His famous instructor Aga had undoubtedly been the inheritor of a long tradition and very probably the master of a local guild of artisans.

From his book, we may conclude that Benjamin was another person who had learned to love his new profession and did not work for money alone. With evident disappointment, he soon became the reluctant heir to a more recent tradition governing his employment as the first Minister Resident and Consul General. Due to some distant events completely beyond his control, Benjamin's appointment and his substantial involvement in public life in Iran were terminated very abruptly in 1885. This unwelcome event took place immediately after Grover Cleveland and the Democratic Party were returned to power in the White House in March of that year. By this ill-considered decision of the new administration, a promising opportunity for mutual understanding and cooperation between two distant nations was lost.

Percy Molesworth Sykes was a British military officer and sometimes diplomat who entered deeply into the life of Iran over a period of more than thirty years. His extensive involvement culminated in his active command of the South Persia Rifles in action against Qashqai insurgents during the First World War. From the very beginning in the 1890s, he was aware that his role in Iran was highly ambiguous and controversial. He writes,"At first I did not mention that I was an officer travelling for my own amusement, but when I found that I was considered to be employed on some wonderful mission, I revealed the fact, and was not believed, no Oriental ever travelling except for gain or as a pilgrim."

In 1894, Sykes founded the first British consulate for the large region of Kerman province and Persian Baluchistan in southeast Iran. His detailed journal *Ten Thousand Miles in Persia* (1902) is a revealing personal and documentary record of his early experiences. In his lively accounts of his many adventures, Percy Sykes combines uneasily the contradictory qualities of a sympathetic observer, a well-trained military officer, an enterprising government agent, and a decisive man of affairs.

In some ways, Major Sykes became the de facto governor of the Kerman region, ensuring its precarious commercial and political stability with his own small guard of Indian soldiers. In distant Tehran, his numerous activities and recommendations were viewed with considerable interest and some nervous suspicion. One of his roles as consul was to promote Iranian trade with Britain and India. Writing about the contemporary carpets of Kerman with more enthusiasm than knowledge or judgment, Sykes claimed,"These unrivalled products of the loom … are incontestably the choicest the world has ever seen. … The patterns are very ancient, and evidently date from pre-Mohamedan days, as figures are present."

Before long, Percy Sykes was sufficiently expert in carpet knowledge to be able to suggest some necessary improvements to a prominent government leader. He writes about one of his successful interventions:"The Farman Farma introduced some ugly European patterns, but these, at my instance, were given up, and by rigorously insisting on adhesion to the old patterns, as well as by opening out new markets, I have assisted in bringing the industry to a thoroughly healthy condition."

In *The Persian Carpet,* A.C.Edwards conjectures that Major Sykes was objecting in particular to carpets such as the finely knotted Kerman pictorial rug that was later acquired by the Victoria and Albert Museum in London. As indicated by the inscription woven into the carpet, it was made to order at that time for the provincial ruler Farman Farma. The strong European influence on its remarkable design is quite easy to detect. This Kerman rug has an intricate non-traditional design taken from a famous painting by the eighteenth-century French painter Antoine Watteau.

The first major exhibition of the long history of Iranian art was held in London in 1931. Conceived on a very ambitious scale, *The International Exhibition of Persian Art* boldly attempted to survey for the first time the entire artistic heritage of Iran from prehistoric times to the present. The English travel writer Fred Richards was one knowledgeable observer of

Iranian culture who attended the London exhibition. In his book *A Persian Journey* (1931), he describes the recent exhibition and he mentions three factors that had made it possible. In his words, these were the broadmindedness of the present Shah in allowing treasures to leave Iran, modern possibilities of transport, and the tranquility of the country.

Except for these new factors, as the author notes, essentially the same exhibition could have been held more than three hundred years before in the time of the first Queen Elizabeth. Richards was clearly puzzled by the almost complete omission of the art of the last three centuries. Reflecting his familiarity with the Iranian art of that period, he writes in a surprised tone that comparatively nothing of Persian work was seen in the London exhibition which had been done since the glorious reign of Elizabeth's legendary contemporary Shah Abbas. The most famous monarch of the Safavid dynasty, Shah Abbas ruled Iran in the years between 1587 to 1629 from his new capital city Isfahan.

A lengthy contemporary review in the American publication *The Antiquarian* gives a good indication of the strong impression the London exhibition made at the time. We read that "this gorgeous display of rugs, ceramics, miniatures, jewels, and sculptures, so far as pure quality of entertainment goes, eclipses easily any exhibition in which there are only paintings to serve as wall decoration."

The anonymous review continues with a description of some of the unusual features of the exhibition.

> The spacious eighteenth century rooms of Burlington House have been ingeniously adapted to show the fifty centuries of Persian art in an historical sequence. Most ambitious of the exhibits, and the first to strike the eye of the visitor, is a scale reconstruction of the portal of the Masjid-i-Shah (Shah Mosque) of Isfahan. At one-third the size of the original, it stands thirty feet high. ... To heighten the effect, a Persian guard, clad in the splendor of Oriental silks and brocades, stands motionless beside the portal.

The reviewer then describes in admiring detail some of the most opulent of the 2500 objects on display in the galleries of the Royal Academy. He concludes his review with a generous note of acknowledgment to the principal organizer: "And the exhibition is due to American initiative, through its director, Arthur Upham Pope, who is also director of the American Institute for Persian Art and Archaeology, which, with the Deutsche-Persische Gesellschaft and the Association Française des Amis de l'Orient, sponsored the Exhibition."

The substantial influence of Arthur Upham Pope on Iranian art studies in this period deserves some close examination. A near contemporary of A.C.Edwards, he had a much more public career. For almost five decades, Pope worked closely with the highest Iranian government officials in developing and promoting his views on Iranian art. These were definite views which he expressed with a certainty and confidence comparable to the strong opinions of the redoubtable Percy Sykes.

Early in the 1920s, he visited Iran for the first time after a long journey from San Francisco to Isfahan lasting five weeks. Already an internationally recognized authority on Iranian art, he came to Iran with a clear sense of mission. Pope described himself as a pilgrim who was resolved to "tell the Persians how great their art had been in the eyes of the wisest and best of Europeans."

> So the first chance I got ... I gave an address to a group of notables, including Reza Khan and the leaders of Persian society. I spoke with all the fire and fury that I could command to tell the Persians that they had a most glorious history and a tradition of infinite worth and that they had, apparently for the moment, forgotten the key to their own treasure.

It appears this forceful message was received with some enthusiasm by the distinguished group of notables attending. The forgotten keys to the kingdom were soon to be rediscovered and handed over to the American connoisseur.

In *An Introduction to Persian Art since the Seventh Century A.D.* (1930), a book written in preparation for the London exhibition, Pope attempts to describe the unifying features of the historical development of Persian art. Leaving little room for argument, he writes that an art of design had been the constant and primary concern of Persian aesthetic genius over the centuries.

> Though it concerned itself with an art of design, the Persian aesthetic genius cannot therefore be relegated to a secondary rank. For in the same sense both music and architecture are arts of design, proof enough that design of a supreme quality attains a high seriousness and deep meaning that make it one of man's greatest achievements. The arts of design have no immediate appeal to sentiment and make no direct reference to nature, but their very abstractness, their detachment from a specific ideational content or emotional entanglement is a source of tranquil power. Nor are they merely a series of enticing forms. Like the greatest music, they may characterize and reveal ultimate values and give expression to the basal and universal forms of the mind itself.
>
> Great design has the authority of logic. Design bears, indeed, the same relation to beauty that logic does to science and philosophy. It is the proper introduction to art, its indispensable framework and perhaps also its finest achievement.

Pope's great work had behind it the authority of Reza Shah Pahlavi "under whose enlightened rule," he writes, "the old monuments are being restored and new arts encouraged." He also notes in his preface his obligations to the Minister of the Court, Prince Teymurtash, for permission to photograph some of the more important mosques and shrines and to study otherwise inaccessible material.

In one passage, Pope attempts to understand and communicate the undeniable aesthetic values of the famous Persian carpets of the classical Safavid period. Lacking a sense of irony, he writes, "Only when we see a great carpet as a chord of individual schemes co-ordinate and organized, can we realize its full aesthetic worth." Without any discussion, he summarily dismisses from consideration in his comprehensive survey the entire factory production of carpets in contemporary Iran. In his usual magisterial style from which there is no appeal, Pope describes that production as an industry, not an art, which "need not concern us here."

A Survey of Persian Art from Prehistoric Times to the Present (1938-39) is the lasting monument to Pope's industry and his devotion to the great subject that was his life's work. Co-edited with his wife Phyllis Ackerman, the six large, profusely illustrated volumes of the survey involved the collaboration of the leading European and American scholars of Iranian art and archaeology.

With considerable difficulty, Pope attempted to give some structural unity to the many specialized contributions. Explaining his guiding principles, he writes, "[The *Survey*] aims to be comprehensive, systematic, consistent, and organized – in short, to have, as far as possible, the character of the achievement of a single mind, though it essays a task possible only through the loyal co-operation of many."

Pope writes that exceptional care was taken in the choice of the thousands of objects illustrated to ensure their authenticity and for their maximum demonstrative value. Many of them had been seen earlier in the decade on display in the London exhibition. Momentarily adopting an uncharacteristic tone of apology, Pope sadly admits that photographs of some ugly objects were included in the *Survey*. He justifies this necessary but regrettable lapse from high aesthetic standards, writing that these unpleasing objects were included only for their instructive value. He explains, "Sometimes they illustrate degeneration, sometimes a relation to myth or ritual. However far from beautiful, they may be of high documentary value."

In the introduction to *A Survey of Persian Art*, Pope carefully outlines the single-minded ideas that underlie the thousands of pages and the many illustrations of the monumental work.

> Art seems to have been the most fundamental and characteristic activity of the Iranian peoples, the most adequate record of their life, their most valuable contribution to world civilization; and the history of their art throws light upon many problems in the history of human culture. …
>
> The peculiar genius of Persia found its most adequate embodiment in the so-called arts of decoration, those that depend for effect upon beauty of pattern and expressive design. In these Iran attained a mastery that scarcely faltered through the unequalled duration of her cultural history. This sense for decoration illumines all her artistic creation. As a people the Iranians seem to have thought decoratively, for the same canons of lucidity, precision, design, and rhythm are revealed in their poetry and music.

> Indeed, Persian art is especially significant as the most authoritative exponent of the view that the primary purpose of art is not representation but decoration.

The lengthy introductory essay deals with many other aspects of Iranian art in its complex social, historical and religious dimensions. However, this overall characterization of Iranian art throughout history as primarily a non-representational art of decoration is the central unifying idea of the *Survey*.

It is difficult to return from the grandeur of the vision of Pope and his collaborators to the more practical, emotionally entangled human level of A.C.Edwards in *The Persian Carpet*. There is a small connection that appears without comment on the title page. The subtitle *A Survey of the Carpet-Weaving Industry of Persia* seems to be intended as a subtle ironic reference to Pope's more imposing work. Both authors described themselves as pilgrims to Iran, but the similarities in their methods and interests mostly end there.

Edwards was undoubtedly aware of Pope's abrupt dismissal of all contemporary factory production of carpets as industrial products without artistic significance. He was not in a position to reply in kind, but Edwards does allow himself one very pointed, direct criticism of Pope's methods. There had been considerable scholarly interest concerning the precise time and place of origin of the so-called Vase carpets, the large carpets with vase designs that are among the surviving masterpieces of the Safavid period. By some personal method, Pope had arrived at and steadfastly maintained in his *Survey* an opinion that was shared by few others.

With English understatement, Edwards writes about what had become the controversial question of the origin of the Vase carpets: "The reader must not be wearied with another hopeless quest. But I cannot refrain from registering a mild protest against Mr. Upham Pope's surprising and personal *ukase* [decree] that they were woven in the small mountain village of Joshaqan." Pressing home his advantage on this field of battle, Edwards emphasizes that the Joshaqan carpets of the last 200 years were all woven in straightline patterns, "yet Mr. Pope asserts that the Vase carpets – those masterpieces of curvilinear design – were woven in this village."

Adopting his usual empirical method of direct observation, Edwards took the time to visit the Victoria and Albert Museum in London. He compared their famous rose-ground Vase carpet to a large fragment of an eighteenth-century Joshaqan carpet that was also in their collection. Despite what he describes as his best efforts to be objective, he failed to find any similarity in design, color or construction, indeed any "hint of parentage between the two pieces which might account for Mr. Pope's strange whim."

Reinforcing this very firm judgment, there is another eloquent comment by the usually complacent Edwards that may be found by the most attentive readers of *The Persian Carpet*. Slightly concealed in the book's index under the expected heading "Pope, A. Upham," there is one sharp-tongued entry that reads "mistaken attribution of carpets by."

Edwards points out quite convincingly that the skilled dyers, creative designers, planners, draftsmen, and master weavers necessary to produce such carpets were not normally to be found in small mountain villages such as Joshaqan. It is possible to detect a reference here to his own experiences in helping to develop the carpet industry in Hamadan in the 1910s. These unforgettable daily challenges had taught him the great difficulties of the task of assembling in one place at one time all of the artisans with these many necessary skills.

In a tone of exaggerated surprise, Edwards writes, "The monumental *Survey of Persian Art* contains no less than 152 plates of Persian carpets. Of these Mr. Pope has definitely attributed no less than thirty-six to this small village, with four more possibles!" Finally, he closes the argument with some practical reasons for his own preference for Isfahan and the court factory of Shah Abbas in the early seventeenth century as the place and time of origin of the Vase carpets.

With some evident reluctance, Edwards does acknowledge in his book the necessity of addressing another controversial question, the possible symbolic meanings of carpet designs. However, despite his intimate professional knowledge of Persian carpets over a half-century, he has remarkably little to contribute in this direction. Perhaps overly influenced by Pope and the prevailing conceptions of the time, Edwards seems to prejudice his brief discussion by first writing the conventional wisdom that "the Persians are an artistic people who regard design as an end in itself."

From that unpromising beginning, the conclusion that Edwards soon reaches is reasonably predictable.

> The end which [the Persian designers of urban carpets] had in view was delight through symmetry and beauty; but no more. During the years which I spent in Persia, I never heard any reference to symbolism in carpet design.
>
> Some writers, however, have insisted on the mystical significance of certain motives which appear in tribal rugs. Many of these geometric, ornamental forms no doubt possessed meanings when they were first devised, many centuries ago. But it is doubtful if there was any mystique attached to them. It is more probable, I think, that they were intended to represent some common animal, bird, plant or object; and that by reason

2.2 Bakhtiari *Vase Design* *(c.1920, 4.27 x 3.86)*

This brilliantly colored design draws freely on Safavid models in the bold and confident way of Bakhtiari carpets in this period.

> of countless repetition down the centuries they have degenerated beyond recognition. The rugs of Fars are particularly rich in forms of this kind. When I was in Shiraz I tried to find out if any significance was now attached to some of the more interesting of them. I failed.

This is very little better than the similar characterization of carpet designs to be found in J.K.Mumford's *Oriental Rugs*, written fifty years earlier. Mumford does describe the maze of carpet design as a symbol language but one that had been all but lost. He believed the dialects of this ancient language were no longer understood by the weavers of his time.

Edwards experienced complete failure again when he engaged in another earnest search for symbols in carpet designs. Without reporting any successes, he attempted to find survivals of Turkish design elements from the eleventh century in the contemporary rugs of the Afshar, Qashqai and the other Turkish tribes that entered Iranian territory from central Asia at that earlier time. To end what he clearly viewed as the aimless discussion of symbolic interpretations, Edwards concludes with a questionable suggestion. He writes, "A tribal weaver, as she crouches over her horizontal loom, is more likely, I think, to seek inspiration from what she sees than from what she thinks – if, indeed, she thinks at all."

2.3 Qom *Vases and Grapes* (c.1940, 4.69 x 3.34)

Edwards praised the creativity of Qom designers in the 1930s and 1940s. The vases and clusters of grapes have recognized spiritual meanings as external forms that conceal a precious inner essence.

2.4 Afshar *Caucasian Design* (c.1870, 1.73 x 1.29)

This rug recalls the colors and geometry of Caucasian weaving. In the mid-eighteenth century, many Afshar moved from the Caucasus to southern Iran by order of the Afshari ruler Nader Shah.

These apparently hasty judgments require some considerable effort to explain. Edwards was searching for what would now be called signs or emblems which are design elements intended to have clearly understood interpretations. In his brief discussion, he defines symbolism in carpet designs quite narrowly as the use of motives or figures to represent an idea or some form of life or being.

As presently understood, symbols are more ambiguous than signs or representational figures. They may have a wide range of possible meanings, and they often require considerable cultural knowledge for their accurate interpretation. A familiar example is the difference between a street sign and a national flag. The street sign is intended to convey clear information while the flag evokes associations and emotions in more personal ways.

To make a comparison, the symbols of traditional Chinese art have relatively well understood meanings in Chinese culture. There are old lists and manuals that enumerate and classify these symbols and give their standard interpretations. Iranian art and carpet design developed in a very different way, in part reflecting the notable cultural preference for concealment and ambivalence. To understand the symbolic language of Iranian visual art may require from the viewer a much greater degree of creative participation in a complex cultural tradition.

Edwards is certainly correct when he writes that cultural symbols may degenerate beyond recognition after countless repetitions. Over time, cosmic patterns may gradually evolve to become cosmetic designs. However, it is also possible at any time that these culturally significant symbols may regenerate and their original meanings may be restored. With this more optimistic possibility in mind, some viewers and writers will still insist on finding symbolic meanings and spiritual motivations.

The opinions of Edwards on the creative sources and the motivations of the designers of Persian carpets were undoubtedly influenced by his early personal experiences and observations. In the travel journal *Persian Miniatures*, his friend H.G.Dwight records a detailed description of the methods of work of the designers and their assistants who were employed by the new carpet factory in Hamadan in the 1910s.

> Black-capped *mirzas* ["clerks"] sit around a long table, busy over water-colours and sheets of squared paper and samples of dyed wool and pieces wickedly cut out of old rugs. The head of the designing room is a man of forty, perhaps, with a singular face, both dark and pale, distinguished and ravaged. He smokes a miskal of opium a day. But he can take one look at a carpet and reproduce it for you in water colour, with all the brightness and delicacy of the old miniatures. … The other mirzas are younger, some of them no more than twelve or fifteen. The big mirzas paint entire designs, in the exact colours which the weavers are to use – such designs as Persians have always painted, save when some *Firengi* ["foreigner"] desolates them by ordering

2.5 Tabriz *Ideal Garden* *(c.1930, 4.05 x 2.97)*

Edwards appreciated contemporary Tabriz designs. With his focus on aesthetic delight created by symmetry and beauty, he neglected the possibility of symbolic meanings.

> a vast carpet which is nothing but a border around a central desert of pink or blue, empty or flowerless as a billiard board. The little *mirzas* paint the actual working patterns, copying enlarged sections of the design on paper of which each square stands for a knot or a fixed number of knots.

This description makes more understandable the strong opinion expressed by Edwards that Persian carpet designs had reached their final and definitive form in the Safavid period three or four centuries before. In *The Persian Carpet*, he writes that every Persian designer of his time could draw these designs with his eyes shut. This last comment should not be taken literally, but it does have some limited validity. However, it mainly reflects the high value in traditional Iranian education that was placed on accurate visual observation and on extensive memorization and rote learning.

As a quasi-government official who was presumed to be a supporter of the many government reforms of the period, his method of direct questioning in Shiraz and elsewhere was unlikely to be productive. In the context of his time in Iran, folklore traditions and some religious beliefs were seen by many in positions of influence as outmoded cultural relics. They were to be officially devalued when they were not denied or rejected altogether. It is largely these neglected traditions and beliefs that often find creative symbolic expression in Persian carpet designs.

Another factor working against Edwards was the strong cultural preference in Iran for ambiguity and concealment. In response to his numerous questions, he would certainly have experienced the notable reluctance of Iranians to express definite opinions to strangers or to be confined to single, unambiguous meanings. In many circumstances, the simplest answer to a direct question in Iranian culture is often an immediate denial of any special knowledge. If that is unsuccessful in turning aside the unwelcome question, the next expedient may be an assertion of complete agreement with the opinions of the questioner. This is frequently accompanied by an elusive proverb of Sa'adi or an opaque quotation from Rumi or Hafez.

Conversation in Iran has been compared to a subtle game in which the goal is to gather information from others while concealing to the greatest extent possible one's own intimate concerns and opinions. In situations requiring mutual agreement, it is a familiar custom for Iranians to present almost equally the arguments both for and against the actions or decisions they support. This is expected behavior which may occur without the conscious awareness of the participants.

What seems to be indecisiveness or ambivalence to outsiders is better seen as an effective cultural method to preserve the long-term unity of the social group. When a common agreement is eventually reached, no individual will be seen to have been totally opposed to the decision. As a result, no person feels excluded or becomes isolated from the group. For all of these reasons, Edwards was more likely to be successful as a sympathetic observer of Iranian culture than as an objective interviewer.

2.6 Yazd *Binesh Design* *(c.1900, 4.08 x 3.05)*

Binesh patterns often combined European influences and Iranian design conventions. His renowned workshop in Yazd later became part of the Iran Carpet Company.

The surprising judgment that tribal weavers do not think about what they are doing also requires some explanation. Mumford makes a similar observation: "Her fingers seem to know the pattern, and half the time her eyes are not upon the work at all." To all appearances, Edwards was not a serious student of aesthetic theory or art history. Conscious of the importance of his task, he may have done some general background reading when he was writing *The Persian Carpet*. For example, there is some indication he may have read the influential book *Aesthetics and History* (1948) by Bernard Berenson. The author was then a prominent art theorist, recognized internationally as the leading connoisseur of Italian medieval and renaissance art.

Using almost the same words as Edwards, Berenson writes that artists are more craftsmen than thinkers: "The real artist, if at the moment of creation he thinks at all, thinks of little but his craft, the action and arrangement chiefly, and of the skill and mastery he had acquired previously." This opinion reflects Berenson's view that the formal qualities of an art object were more important in determining artistic quality than subject matter and extraneous knowledge.

In his wide-ranging studies of European art, Berenson developed an aesthetics of pure perception and a theory of life enhancement by art. He followed the model of the famous dictum in Walter Pater's influential essay *The Renaissance* (1873): "All art constantly aspires towards the condition of music." Pater criticized the dominant narrative and didactic components of nineteenth-century art.

> In its primary aspect, a great picture has no more definite message for us than an accidental play of sunlight and shadow for a few moments on the wall or floor: is itself, in truth, a space of such fallen light, caught as the colours are in an Eastern carpet, but refined upon and dealt with more subtly and exquisitely than by nature itself.

Pater's view greatly diminished the necessity to examine art works in their various historical and social contexts, and it neglected symbolic or religious interpretations.

Conveniently for Berenson, this aesthetic evaluation of visual art served the contemporary needs of his wealthy Puritan patrons in Boston. They would not have appreciated any pronounced emphasis on the strongly Catholic iconography of the many medieval and renaissance paintings they were acquiring following Berenson's recommendations. Two influential Iranian examples of this phenomenon of purposeful neglect could be mentioned here; the Ziegler Company beginning in the 1870s and the Iran Carpet Company beginning in 1935. Both companies followed similar aesthetic and decorative approaches to the evaluation and promotion of carpet designs, generally ignoring the possibilities of culturally significant symbolic meanings and deeply felt religious motivations.

If Edwards had read more widely in contemporary aesthetic theory, he would have received some confirmation of his approach in the influential work of the formalist critics Roger Fry and Clive Bell. Their doctrine of "significant form" was strongly influenced in its development by the earlier ideas of Pater and Berenson. This view devalued content and context as extra-aesthetic influences which were considered primarily to be distractions from the true artistic qualities of the art object. They were distractions, for example, from the formal relations of lines, shapes and colors that constitute a painting.

In his book *Art* (1914), Bell stated this new position in aesthetics very clearly, perhaps a little too clearly.

> The representative element in a work of art may or may not be harmful; always it is irrelevant. For, to appreciate a work of art we need bring with us nothing from life, no knowledge of its ideas and affairs, no familiarity with its emotions. Art transports us from the world of man's activity to a world of aesthetic exaltation. … In this world the emotions of life find no place. It is a world with emotions of its own.

Briefly stated, no associations from ordinary life are needed to appreciate a work of art.

In *Vision and Design* (1920), Roger Fry employs similar language. He describes a work of art as an expression of emotions regarded as ends in themselves. This approach enables Fry to resolve most of the problems of art interpretation in a remarkably simple way. He achieves this by advocating giving up the attempt to judge works of art by what he calls their reaction on life. This implies that the ethical dimensions of art, if any, are irrelevant to questions of aesthetic merit. However significant they may be in other contexts, the emotions of life can find no place in the rarefied world of significant form.

These closely related conceptions from Pater, Berenson, Fry and Bell were extremely influential in subsequent decades in the interpretation and evaluation of all forms of visual art. They gave the principal justification for the dominant twentieth-century movement to abstract art. Paintings came to be viewed as objects that referred to nothing outside themselves. Color and form replaced representation as the primary sources or carriers of aesthetic feeling. The aesthetic quality of an art object was not influenced by considerations of content and motivation. According to this view, the true subject matter of art was art.

Very probably, these recent conceptions were a decisive influence on Pope's view that the abstractness of the arts of design, what he described so eloquently as "their detachment from a specific ideational content or emotional entanglement," is the main source of their tranquil power. We recall his very definite opinion that the primary purpose of art is not representation but decoration and his claim that the full aesthetic worth of a great carpet lies in its coordination and organization of individual schemes.

We should also recall Pope's disdainful remarks about certain ugly objects to be included reluctantly in the London exhibition and in his *Survey of Persian Art*. Although he is unable to find significant aesthetic qualities in these objects, he concedes at least a possible relation to "myth or ritual" and he admits the possibility they may be "of high documentary value." It is quite evident that his main interests in art appreciation did not lie in these directions.

When he writes about obtaining permission from a government leader to photograph "the more important mosques and shrines," we may assume that Pope is not considering their religious importance in any serious way. Significantly, he does not mention requesting or obtaining permission from any religious authorities. His principal emphasis is decidedly on the importance of these monuments in art history. In a later work, he summarized the historical achievements of Persian architecture as "the triumph of form and color." All of these judgments are direct applications or developments of the doctrine of significant form as the primary and even sole measure of aesthetic interest.

To restore some balance, it may be helpful to refer to the work of another contemporary of Pope and Edwards who pursued a very different path. Beginning with an amateur interest in Indian art, A.K.Coomaraswamy later studied all forms of traditional religious art. He questioned repeatedly the relevance of approaches that were primarily scholarly and aesthetic. His own emphasis in evaluating these art objects was on their methods of communication of cultural meaning and on what he called their witness to the experience of truth.

For Coomaraswamy, the true evaluation of an art object was not primarily in terms of its aesthetic surfaces. A genuine appreciation could not be confined entirely to the limited means of ordinary empirical vision.

> The judgement of an image is a contemplation, and as such can only be consummated in an assimilation. A transformation of our nature is required. It is in the same sense that [the Chinese philosopher] Mencius says that to grasp the true meanings of words requires not so much a dictionary or a knowledge of epistemology as a rectification of personality. ….
>
> Symbolism is a language and a precise form of thought; a hieratic and metaphysical language and not a language determined by somatic or psychological categories. Its foundation is the analogical correspondence of all orders of reality and states of being or levels of reference. ….
>
> It becomes, then, a question of the restoration of significance to forms that we have come to think of as merely ornamental. ….

These ideas presented a much-needed challenge to Berenson's doctrine of pure perception and to the formalist aesthetics of Fry and Bell. Coomaraswamy's approach was diametrically opposed to Pope's magisterial insistence on the primarily decorative qualities of Persian art.

Coomaraswamy rejected decisively the premature aesthetic classification of art objects as beautiful or ugly without an understanding of their original cultural significance. Writing of Christian art objects, he argues they can be judged only according to their expression of the ideas that are their formal basis, and this judgment cannot be made without an adequate knowledge of the ideas themselves. He then extends the same observation to include the full range of archaic, primitive and Oriental art.

This approach to traditional art was the antithesis of the contemporary doctrine of significant form as it was then being developed by Fry and Bell. Coomaraswamy followed closely the words of Mencius when he wrote, "Connoisseurship rightly understood can be achieved only by a rectification of the whole personality, not by the mere study and collecting of works of art." This is a clear response to the primarily aesthetic approach to connoisseurship that was exemplified by Berenson and Pope in two very different areas of art studies.

Directly confronting Fry and Bell and their many followers, Coomaraswamy expressed his concern over the misuse of a key term. He complained, "It is often impossible to understand just what is meant by 'form' as the word is used by contemporary aestheticians." Bell admitted in *Art* that the concept of "significant form" had been introduced in preference to "beauty" and other traditional terms primarily because of its lack of previous mental associations.

Responding to the methods of Fry and Bell in a different way, Coomaraswamy's own wide-ranging studies dealt with the meticulous details and contexts of the different traditions of religious art. This considerable effort was undertaken with the goal always in mind of linking these cultural traditions together in the great synthesis of a common universe of discourse. With their focus on the perception of narrowly defined aesthetic values which were believed to be unaffected by content and context, the followers of the doctrines of significant form did not have to work nearly as hard.

There are many small indications that A.C.Edwards did appreciate the importance of symbolic communication in other contexts despite his failure to discover it in carpet designs. We have noted his criticism of the rug making of the Khamseh as a purely commercial proposition, suggesting strongly that he recognized and appreciated other personal motivations. We have seen his reaction to the yellow bird introduced spontaneously by the young weaver in Hamadan among the flowers of the carpet border she was knotting.

The tolerant response of Edwards indicates he was aware on some level that the woven bird was the symbol of a child's mental freedom. His American visitor H.G.Dwight reached much further in his more exuberant imagination. He viewed the unexpected yellow bird as a poignant symbol of the loss of older values and social priorities. It represented for him a nation's cultural independence that had been thoughtlessly sold to foreign commercial interests.

During Dwight's time in Hamadan, he and Edwards walked the narrow lanes and streets of the city. When they were not reading their rug books, they passed their leisure time by exploring together an unfamiliar world they found endlessly fascinating. On these walks, they examined closely the only feature that broke the monotony of the mud walls lining the residential streets. They studied the intricately carved wooden doorways that opened to the small courtyards before many private homes.

Edwards did not point to the formal aesthetic qualities of these doors, but instead he attempted to understand their symbolic significance to Iranians. He told his less knowledgeable American friend that a door or gateway in Iran was the index of a man's importance in the world. Echoing this perceptive comment, it is very noticeable that a large number of the photographs illustrating *The Persian Carpet* show doorways to private homes, old city gates, and entrances to religious buildings.

Many of the wooden single or double entrance doors to the homes of Hamadan would have communicated some elementary symbolic meanings in another obvious way. Traditionally, there were always two different iron knockers on these doors, one to be used only by men and the other by women. The highly significant forms of these very functional objects communicated unmistakably their intended uses. They conveyed this message by representing symbolically some important differences of the male and female anatomies.

Included among the illustrations in *The Persian Carpet*, there is a photograph of a Kerman doorway that silently illustrates this phenomenon. We can be sure that two high-spirited young men wandering freely through the mud-walled streets of Hamadan in 1914 would have noticed these extraordinary cultural signs with great interest. However, this is an unambiguous folk symbolism that Dwight and Edwards very delicately chose not to point out to their readers except possibly in the coded phrase "the index of a man's importance." At least on this subject, the American and the Englishman both adopted the usual Iranian preference for concealment and ambiguity.

There is a more elaborate indication of the openness of A.C.Edwards to symbolic communication to be found in an anecdote that describes passing through a door or gateway of a different kind. An account of this experience was related by Edwards to another friend living in the Hamadan region. During the First World War, the British army officer F.A.C.Forbes-Leith was posted to the Hamadan area of western Iran. He participated in some dangerous military actions there and in the near regions of Iraq against the opposing forces of the Ottoman Empire. For several years after the war, he lived about fifteen miles from Hamadan. His proven leadership abilities were employed in managing an extensive estate for a wealthy Iranian who preferred to spend his time more entertainingly in Tehran and the cities of Europe.

Major Forbes-Leith wrote about his adventures and observations during a dangerous and eventful decade in the appealing memoir *Checkmate: Fighting Tradition in Central Persia* (1927). In one passage, he repeated for the amusement of his readers the anecdote told to him by the personal friend and fellow countryman who was engaged in the carpet business in Hamadan.

> The automobile has made great strides in this country as a means of transport during the last few years, but until the Russian invasion in 1915, there was only one car in operation, and that was owned by a friend of mine, Mr. A.C.Edwards of the Oriental Carpet Company, Ltd. An amusing incident occurred when he first traversed the short metal road between Enzeli and Kasvin. On arriving at the tollgate, the collector, who had never seen or heard of such a thing as a mechanically driven carriage, found that he had no tariff rate on his schedule of charges for such a vehicle, and was very puzzled as to the correct fee to charge.

> They chatted about the car for some time, and in the course of conversation my friend mentioned that it had the strength of fifteen horses. "Ah," said the intelligent one, "then if fifteen horses are passing through the gate when the machine works, I must charge you the same rate that fifteen horses would pay." My friend protested, but the keeper was adamant and collected his money. On his return, however, my friend had a brain wave. A few hundred yards above the gate he hired a horse at trifling cost, hitched it to the car, and passed through the gate under the power of one horse, for which he tendered payment. The gatekeeper's sense of humour was very much tickled and he accepted the situation and the money.

In this revealing incident, the baffled Iranian gatekeeper and the boastful English resident of Hamadan were able to negotiate a practical solution to their immediate problem. They did this at least temporarily by arriving at a shared metaphorical or symbolic understanding. With some difficulties and hesitations, they were finding a way to communicate with each other. They were learning for the first time how to navigate in an unfamiliar world whose rules were strange to both of them.

Edwards returned to Hamadan in 1948 after a long absence in order to examine the state of the carpet industry there and to revive some old memories. The large carpet factory he had helped to build and manage in the 1910s was then owned by the Iran Carpet Company and continuing to produce carpets. Viewing the once familiar scene with some understandably strong emotions, he stepped aside for a time from his role as an objective surveyor to allow himself some personal observations.

To express his deep feelings, he made use of a predictable but necessary metaphor: "The satisfaction which I feel is that of a person who contemplates a great tree which has grown from a seed which he himself has planted. For there are now a thousand looms in the town, producing some fifteen hundred carpets a year." For the historical record, Edwards was careful to note some of the changes he had contributed to in a major way. When he had first arrived in Hamadan in 1912, he writes with some evident pride, there were no looms in the city to make large carpets.

Reading between the lines of *The Persian Carpet*, there is considerable evidence Edwards would have preferred in some ways to have written a different book. In his introduction, he justifies using the long-established names for the regions of Iran instead of following one of Reza Shah's recent innovations. By a remarkable royal decree, Iran had been divided into ten *Ustans* or provinces identified officially by numbers only. This was another measure among many that was designed to reduce the regional identification of Iranians which remained very strong. Showing again his characteristic verbal restraint, Edwards describes the new system as artificial and hardly likely to endure.

Edwards also feels the need to justify another choice he makes throughout his book and in its title, his decision to continue to use the words Persia and Persian. He gives a conventional explanation: "I have done so because to me, at least, the word 'Iranian' – particularly when

2.8 Hamadan *Eslimi Spirals* (c.1970, 2.20 x 1.39)

*A second Kowsari design is described as an **eslimi** dragon head pattern. This is a reference to the debatable idea that **eslimi** or Islamic spirals derive from Mongol and pre-Islamic dragon designs.*

applied to the products of the weaver's art – does not suggest the antiquity, the elegance or the renown which the word 'Persian' awakens in my mind." As we know, Arthur Upham Pope had made the same choice for similar reasons more than a decade before. This was despite the substantial support for his *Survey of Persian Art* that came from the highest levels of the Iranian government.

In a brief passage later in *The Persian Carpet*, Edwards outlines some of the severe hardships that had been imposed on the Qashqai and other nomadic tribal groups by the harshly enforced settlement policy of the 1930s. With obvious approval, he notes that the recently settled Qashqai had rejected their new life. They had returned immediately to their traditional nomadic ways as soon as Reza Shah was deposed and exiled in 1941.

2.7 Hamadan *Shah Abbassi Pattern* (c.1970, 3.05 x 1.97)

*The factory managed by Edwards in the 1910s was acquired by **Sherket Farsh Iran**. This design created by S. Kowsari is classified by the ICC as an overall Shah Abbassi pattern.*

Visiting the province of Khorasan and the holy city of Meshed in 1948 on his year-long journey, Edwards noticed another visible change that had been made possible by the recent political changes at the national level. Showing less verbal restraint than usual, he writes, "The medley of battered European hats which Shah Riza had stupidly compelled the villagers of Khurasan to wear were being discarded; and the people were resuming their picturesque white turbans."

Shortly after beginning his career in the carpet business in London, young Arthur Cecil Edwards was given some concerned advice by a disapproving uncle. Intending to be helpful, the uncle cautiously warned his inexperienced nephew that he had embarked on a sinking ship. Looking back to his beginnings, Edwards returned fifty years later to this unforgettable metaphor. To conclude his sizeable book and his long career, he responded buoyantly to his uncle's early warning. Amplifying the symbolic image considerably, he wrote: "This luxury ship of slender tonnage has battered and buffeted her way through one economic gale after another." Despite all difficulties, he predicted confidently, this small ship would continue to make her customary landfalls.

It is apparent that Edwards attempted to look beyond the certainties of the moment to see what would have lasting value. In the introduction to *The Persian Carpet,* he feels the need to apologize to his readers for including the many short anecdotes and descriptions scattered throughout the book under the genial heading "Conversation Pieces." He weakly justifies these digressions from the main text as contributing background atmosphere, writing that they were intended to provide relief from the many cheerless pages on the techniques of carpet weaving.

Twenty-five years before the publication of his carpet survey, Edwards had written another book, *A Persian Caravan* (1928). This is a charming collection of tales and personal stories very much in the spirit of these later "conversation pieces." This little-known work showed very clearly that, despite his understandable business motivations, the early and primary interest of Edwards was equally in the human dimensions of carpet weaving and of Iranian culture in general. We have already learned from his friend Major Forbes-Leith that Edwards knew how to tell an amusing story about himself.

"Water" is the title of one of the stories in *A Persian Caravan*. It describes the visit of a European traveler to Kashan after an exhausting thirteen day journey across the desert from Yazd. Following the old Iranian custom, his host in Kashan has ridden out twelve miles from the city to welcome the traveler. Seeing the visitor's weariness, the merchant Seyyid Abbas does not burden his guest with many words. He says only, "Wait until evening." In the late afternoon, they turn off from the main road and suddenly they find themselves in a large walled enclosure. Filled with dusty trees, this unexpected garden is a welcome relief after intolerable leagues of sun-scorched desert.

Seyyid Abbas tells his visitor, "This is Feen." One of the best-known public gardens in Iran, *Bagh-e Fin* was built in the seventeenth century by order of Shah Abbas. It was initially intended to serve as a royal *manzel,* a resting place for the king when he traveled. Located near Kashan on the road to Isfahan, it was restored early in the nineteenth century by Fath Ali Shah Qajar.

The merchant graciously welcomes the exhausted traveler to his city by first showing him the features of the famous garden.

> Seyyid Abbas beckoned to me, and I followed him to another part of the garden. Soon he stopped and pointed to a little stream of water, no bigger than a man's arm, which issued by a broken conduit from a bank of earth. It ran for a dozen yards and emptied into a brimming water-tank. Then Seyyid Abbas, the merchant, turned to me and said: "Sah'b, in the whole of Feranghistan, which you have seen, tell me, is there a stream of water equal to this stream of water?"

The visitor misses an opportunity for meaningful communication by pondering the unexpected question in a very literal way. He thinks of all the great rivers he knows in the whole of *Feranghistan* including the yellow Thames, the ancient Nile, the holy Ganges, the Congo, the Amazon, and Niagara.

The European traveler in the story, probably Edwards slightly fictionalized, is hesitant or unable to respond in a more imaginative way. Perhaps affected by his weariness and the oppressive heat, his mind wandered to the world's greatest rivers and he does not find the appropriate words to answer the question. At that moment, he may not have known that the small stream of water in the royal garden was the result of the great effort necessary to build and maintain a *qanat*. These were the underground channels found in many of the dry regions of Iran that collected the groundwater from distant mountains.

This concealed source of water produced nothing less than a miracle in the *Bagh-e Fin* near Kashan. It was a life-giving *qanat* that made possible a beautiful garden in what otherwise would have been another featureless part of an arid desert. In a central metaphor of Iranian culture, these unseen underground channels acquired far more than an exclusively practical significance. The weary *Feranghi* traveler does not perceive that the concealed *qanats* of Iran and the gardens they made possible were also to be understood symbolically. In Iranian spiritual culture, they were perceived as constant reminders of the hidden source that is the cause of all life.

Edward Browne was an earlier English traveler who was more successful in entering this metaphorical realm on his first approach to Shiraz in 1888. After climbing a final mountain pass, his traveling companion Haji Safar cried out, "Ruknabad! Ruknabad!" They had reached the source of the small stream that Hafez had celebrated five centuries before as better than any in Paradise.

In this famous refuge for poetry and the imagination, Browne did not experience the feelings of disappointment frequently reported by more demanding visitors.

> I saw nothing but the limpid water rushing from its rocky source; heard nothing but its melodious ripple; thought nothing but those thoughts which rise in the mind of one who first stands in the favourite haunt of an immortal

> bard who immortalizes all that he touches. ... One does not love Hafiz because he wrote of Ruknabad: one loves Ruknabad because it was written of by Hafiz.

Unlike the business-minded traveler who was initially unimpressed by the feeble stream of water in the royal garden near Kashan, Browne was no longer acting as an objective observer. His memories and emotions were becoming fully engaged as he came nearer to achieving his long-anticipated goal.

As he approached Shiraz, Browne's primary aim was not to record dispassionately the salient features of the natural scene before him. He had no desire to measure the meager flow of Ruknabad, and then compare it precisely to all other rivers and streams. His strongest desire at that moment and throughout his year-long journey of discovery was more personal. His unwavering ambition was to become an involved participant in a living tradition and a vital culture.

In his account of his stay in Meshed in 1948, Edwards describes the area in the pilgrimage city that was considered by the believers to be sacred. This extensive area is centered around the holy shrine of Imam Reza, the burial place of the revered eighth Imam of Shi'a Islam. Surrounded by a broad circular road, this area and its many impressive buildings dominated the city whose name means "the place of martyrdom." Edwards notes that the sacred precinct was almost a city within a city, containing mosques, courtyards, and religious colleges, as well as caravanserais, baths, shops and dwellings.

The entire area was called *bast*, a protected enclosure or religious sanctuary, a word derived from *bastan* meaning "to enclose." These sacred refuges large and small were found throughout Iran, in remote locations and on busy city streets. They were often marked off by a chain, perhaps hanging across a road or placed in front of a small niche in a bazaar. For the believers, the bounding chains created places of physical safety and spiritual freedom. They were visual reminders in everyday life of the divine protection of *Allah*.

As a gifted observer of people and events, Edwards would have noticed these religious sanctuaries everywhere in his travels during his time in Iran. He certainly understood Iranian culture well enough to know their social and religious importance. "Sanctuary" is the title Edwards chose for one of the stories in *A Persian Caravan*. His story tells of the misadventures of an Iranian merchant who finds temporary protection from his creditors in one of these holy refuges.

A.C.Edwards was a more successful merchant and manufacturer who valued his independence and presumably never needed urgent protection from his creditors. As a result, he held himself both physically and mentally apart from these enclosed refuges for the imagination. During his thirteen years in the carpet business in Iran, he never heard any reference to symbolism in Persian carpet designs. Each day of those thirteen years, he passed by these transitional spaces that represented an invitation to a different kind of experience. Despite his many opportunities, he failed to recognize the true significance of these sacred refuges. Like Persian carpets themselves, they were potential entrances to an ideal imaginative realm located somewhere outside the ordinary world.

3 The Wild Rue

In the 1930s, Sadeq Hedayat was one of the few Iranian writers to take a serious interest in the nation's folklore and traditional beliefs. During his time as a student in Paris in the previous decade, he had published an article *La Magie en Perse* describing ancient Zoroastrian customs. In 1931, he published *Owsaneh (Tales)*, a small work collecting some old folk songs and stories intended mainly for children. The title by itself already indicates the author's interest in things that had been almost forgotten. *Owsaneh* is an old form of the modern word *afsaneh* meaning legends or stories.

In the introduction to *Owsaneh*, Hedayat relates his unusual interest in folklore studies to an important contemporary theme. He comments briefly on the modernization of Iran that was then taking place, and he points cautiously to some of the unrecognized consequences.

> Ideas are gradually changing, and old habits and attitudes are being transformed. ... The only unfortunate aspect of these developments is the neglect and disappearance of a body of popular legends, belief and songs. ... For until now such popular culture has been thought to be unimportant. And not only has there been no attempt to collect them, but they are apparently regarded as being superfluous, and better forgotten.

Hedayat developed this supposedly "unimportant" interest much further in a better-known work first published in 1933. In *Narengestan (The Land of Fascination)*, he brings together a more extensive collection of popular customs and superstitions inherited from past centuries.

Hedayat's uncertain attitude to the materials he includes in *Narengestan* is another demonstration of the familiar Iranian reluctance to express unequivocal opinions. It also reflects the controversies that were being vigorously debated at the time of writing concerning the continuing significance of traditional social values. Seemingly contradicting his earlier introduction to *Owsaneh*, Hedayat writes, "These decayed beliefs will not die out on their own. ... Only their publication would diminish their importance and reveal their insignificance." Despite this disclaimer or perhaps because of it, the book was suddenly removed from sale a short time after publication when it received strong criticisms mainly from religious interests.

By way of comparison, the more familiar literary aims of the eminent Anglo-Irish writer William Butler Yeats were in many ways similar to those of Sadeq Hedayat. At the beginning of his long writing career, Yeats studied the neglected resources of Irish folklore and pre-Christian Celtic traditions. He worked tirelessly with the aim of creating a common symbolic language and a widely-shared national culture following the ambitious model of classical Greek art and literature.

> The Greeks, the only perfect artists of the world, looked within their own borders, and we, like them, have a history fuller than in any modern history of imaginative events; and legends which surpass, as I think, all legends but theirs in wild beauty, and in our land, as in theirs, there is no river or mountain that is not associated in the memory with some event or legend.

In his early years of study and writing, Yeats looked within his country's borders for the sources of an Irish literature that would be able to communicate a unified cultural vision accessible to all. Out of these almost forgotten or disparaged native materials, he sought to create a renewed literature that would "seem the work of a single mind and turn our places of beauty or legendary association into holy symbols."

From this beginning, Yeats later searched for what he called the Great Memory which was his concise description of the universal heritage of symbolic understandings that was common to all cultures. His self-assigned task was to bring the ancient symbols and their meanings back to life in ways that would be found to be meaningful in the modern world. He was motivated by his belief that these neglected symbols from earlier times were still able to communicate meanings more profoundly than any abstract system of ideas.

With this all-embracing goal constantly in mind, Yeats studied the diverse forms of imaginative knowledge in many of the world's cultures and he reworked them in creative ways in his plays and poetry. The varied resources he explored over several decades included folklore and myth, magic and alchemy, spiritualism, Greek philosophy and metaphysics, the Buddhist Noh theater of Japan, and the Hindu scriptures of India.

Equally, Sadeq Hedayat studied many of the same subjects and sources as well as contemporary European literature and he employed them creatively in his writing. In assimilating these many influences, Hedayat worked with one considerable geographical advantage over Yeats. Greek thought, Zoroastrianism, Buddhism and Hinduism as well as Islam and its mystical tradition have been immediate realities in Iranian history. The surrealist novel *Buf-e Kur (The Blind Owl)* completed and self-published in 1936 during Hedayat's time in India is generally considered to be his most important work. The novel brings together all of these diverse influences in a complex, dreamlike way that has defied satisfactory analysis to the present day.

A work greatly admired by Hedayat, *The Wild Rue* (1938), is now considered to be the classic documentary study of Iranian folk beliefs. The author Bess Allen Donaldson was an English resident living in the 1930s in Meshed, the capital of Khorasan province and the most important pilgrimage city in Iran. Most of her information was collected locally in Meshed and the surrounding region. However, as she defensively explains, "since pilgrims come to the 'sacred city' of Meshed from all over Iran, many to remain for the rest of their lives, its population is after all a representative group."

Like Hedayat a few years before, Donaldson thought it necessary in a period of rapid changes to apologize to her readers for her unusual antiquarian interest. With some apparent relief, she writes in her preface, "This book represents the old life, with its fears and superstitions, which, happily, are now beginning to pass away." The author is not completely convincing when she attempts to present herself in this preface as an objective observer who was conducting an unemotional and representative survey of Iranian folklore. As one small indication of her own more progressive and modern views, we notice she is careful to maintain some distance from these outdated beliefs by placing the phrase "sacred city" between quotation marks.

3.1 Bakhtiari *Open Field* *(c.1930, 3.84 x 3.03)*

Often interpreted as signs of European influence, open field patterns have sometimes a spiritual meaning. They may suggest the emptiness required of the traveler who seeks God.

In *The Wild Rue*, Donaldson records a bewildering variety of popular superstitions and rituals dealing with pilgrimages, childbirth, and the evil eye. She describes occult methods of divination and the extensive use of *talism* ("talismans") to ensure health and good fortune, as well as many other folk beliefs and practices. As in the mystical Ireland imagined by Yeats in his early work, every river and mountain in Iran seems in her account to be associated in the memory with some event or legend.

To mention one intriguing example, Donaldson describes the old stone lions of uncertain age and origin that were to be found in many parts of the country. In some regions, they were placed at the graves of men who had lived and died bravely. Following an old custom, these mysterious lion monuments were often visited by childless women. By pouring oil on the lions and by passing under them, the women believed they would be helped to become pregnant and bear a strong male child.

Donaldson also describes some common uses of an old ceremonial cannon in Tehran which was popularly called the "pearl cannon." In the nineteenth century, it had been placed in a prominent position in a public square by Nasreddin Shah Qajar. During Donaldson's time in Iran, the cannon was being used by the hopeful women of Tehran in the same way as the more traditional stone lions and with the same purposes in mind. This brief reference to the pearl cannon may have had a considerable influence on one of her Iranian readers. A fantastic invented history of the various uses of this cannon over several centuries provides the central story of Sadeq Hedayat's late work, *Tup-e Morvari (The Pearl Cannon)*.

The book title *The Wild Rue* refers to the desert plant whose seeds, *esfand*, were burned as an incense in many Iranian homes. Most commonly, the wild rue seeds were burned in order to ensure good fortune by averting the evil eye, the *nazar* or *chashm-e shur*. Donaldson records two of the many incantations that were customarily chanted during the ritual burning of the *esfand*.

> Wild rue, seeds of wild rue,
> Thirty or three seeds of wild rue,
> Crack the eye of jealousy or hostility
> In the neighbour to the right,
> In the neighbour to the left,
> In the neighbour across the way,
> In the neighbour behind the house,
> Whether tall or whether short,
> With large eyes or with small,
> With eyes of green or eyes of black.

In Iranian life, there were numberless small rituals and observances intended to avoid attracting from others the eye of jealousy or hostility. In most circumstances, it was considered potentially dangerous to give or receive praise. Any boasting about possessions or accomplishments was to be strictly avoided. The harmful consequences of the unpredictable *chashm-e shur* were greatly feared. The evil eye could manifest itself at

3.2 Qashqai *Symmetric Pattern* *(c.1970, 1.66 x 1.21)*
Balancing like a mathematical diagram, a small rug displays the seriousness and playfulness of folk art.

unpredictable times and in unexpected ways, threatening to destroy the tranquility of the family and the local community.

The second incantation recorded by Donaldson that sometimes accompanied the burning of the seeds of the wild rue was more conventionally religious. It was intended to invoke the strong protective and healing powers that were associated with the *panj tan*, the "five bodies" or the "five persons."

Wild rue, who planted it?	Mohammed.
Wild rue, who gathered it?	Ali.
Wild rue, who burned it?	Fatima.
Wild rue, for whom?	For Hassan and Hossein.

The "five bodies" is the expression used colloquially in Iran to refer to the members of the holy family of Shi'a Islam. The *panj tan* includes the Prophet Mohammed and his daughter Fatima, and the first three Imams, Fatima's husband Ali and their two sons Hassan and Hossein.

There is a cherished image of the holy family sheltering together under the green cloak of Mohammed at a time of difficulty and danger. The names of the *panj tan* were universally believed to have a strong protective value against the inevitable misfortunes and uncertainties of life. Women in labor prayed fervently to the members of the holy family to ensure a safe delivery and a healthy child. During her time in Iran, Donaldson observed the varied uses of these five revered names in daily life. They were frequently inscribed and worn on rings, and they were commonly displayed on signboards in shops.

In carpet designs, a hand is most often interpreted as a reference to the five persons of the holy family, or to the martyr Hazrat Abbas whose hand was cut off when he attempted to carry water to the wounded son of Hossein at Karbala. Other possible direct references are to the hand of Fatima which is said to represent the whole religion of Islam, or to the hand of Ali who is often described in Shi'a Islam as the hand of *Allah*. More subtly, a grouping of five flowers in any Persian carpet design is often intended by the designer and weaver as a visual reminder of the *panj tan*.

A design element containing twelve flowers commonly refers to the twelve Imams, the first Imam Ali and his eleven descendants. Fourteen flowers grouped together in a carpet design are almost certainly meant to be a symbolic representation and reminder of the *chahardah ma'sum*. These are the "fourteen pure ones"; Mohammed, Fatima, and the twelve Imams. Carpet designs with an element repeated seventy-two times are intended by their designers and weavers to recall the seventy-two martyrs of the faith who died with Imam Hossein at Karbala in the year 680.

Donaldson describes the old trees found in many places in Iran that were believed to be sacred. They were considered to have a special significance because of their associations with important persons and events, and they were often visited respectfully by travelers and religious pilgrims.

> Trees under which saints are said to have sat or slept, or to have had a dream, are numerous, and are considered sacred. Their branches are covered with rags and strings, fragments from the clothing of the pilgrims who have tied them onto the trees to signify some sworn vow or some expressed desire.

In one of the small villages she visited during her journey in 1934, Onera Merritt-Hawkes learned that the old wood of a particular tamarisk tree could not be used except to cook food for a sick person or for a special feast. Each year, the joyful harvest celebrations of this village were always held near this sacred tree. The villagers believed their ceremonial tree had acquired its special powers many centuries before. There was a very old local tradition that their sacred tree had been visited by each of the twelve Imams before they became invisible.

In *The Golestan* of Sa'adi written in the thirteenth century, there is a well-remembered story centering on another sacred tree. It seems that this all-purpose tree could be used in more than one way to bring good fortune. In his characteristic manner, Sa'adi increases the story's effectiveness by relating it as a personal anecdote.

> In the territory of Diarbekr, I was the guest of a very rich man, who had a handsome son. One night he said: "During my whole life I never had any child but this son. Near this place is a sacred tree, to which men resort to offer up their petitions. Many nights at the foot of this tree I besought God, until he bestowed on me this son." I heard that the son was saying to his friends, in a low tone of voice, "How happy should I be to know where that tree grows, in order that I might implore God for the death of my father." The father was rejoicing in his son's wisdom whilst the son despised his father's decrepitude. Many years have elapsed since you visited your father's grave; what piety have you shown towards your parent, that you should expect dutifulness from your son?

This seemingly simple tale indicates there could be some skepticism about many of the popular beliefs in magical powers. Paradoxically, this uncertain attitude to folk beliefs and customs was an essential part of their power over the imagination.

In most cases, folk beliefs should be distinguished from religious beliefs. They are usually viewed in much more personal and pragmatic ways, and they are to be judged primarily by their proven effectiveness in avoiding disasters and bringing good fortune. Despite all skepticism, these popular beliefs do serve some important purposes at the most critical times in local communities. They make the potential accidents and misfortunes of life immediately understandable in direct and humanly meaningful terms.

What folk beliefs helped to achieve was a humanization of the natural world. They permitted a comprehensible internalization of external experiences which is a primary goal of the shared customs of any community. We notice that Sa'adi ends his cautionary tale of a sacred tree with a heartfelt plea to our better natures. He asks for a sincere observance of one of the ordinary rituals that will always define our common humanity.

There is another valuable record of Iranian traditional beliefs from an unlikely source. We have encountered Major Percy Sykes as the British military officer and diplomat giving earnest advice to the government leaders and carpet makers of Kerman in the 1890s. Another aspect of his activities that is now less well known was his profound interest in the popular customs and religious beliefs of Iranians. With the assistance of Ahmad Din Khan who was an employee at the consulate in Kerman, he assembled many of his observations into a remarkable but largely forgotten book *The Glory of the Shi'a World: The Story of a Pilgrimage* (1910).

In this appealing work, Sykes relates the fictional adventures of a pilgrimage made by a prosperous merchant from his home in Kerman to the sacred shrine of Imam Reza in Meshed. The merchant Nurullah Khan was fulfilling a vow he had made during a severe epidemic that had devastated the people of Kerman. At the time of greatest danger for his family, he had made a promise to himself and to *Allah*. If he and his family were to be spared from illness and death, Nurullah Khan had solemnly vowed to hasten to prostrate himself at the holy threshold of the Imam.

When early readers accepted *The Glory of the Shi'a World* as the authentic travel journal of the merchant's pilgrimage, Major Sykes felt it necessary to correct that mistaken impression. He did this by adding an apologetic prefatory note to later printings. In his defense, Sykes stated that his original ambition had been to write a "second *Hajji Baba* which would serve as a true picture of Persia some ten years ago … just as Morier in his immortal work depicted it in the reign of Fath Ali Shah." The problem had arisen because Sykes had originally misrepresented his work as his own translation from an original Persian manuscript.

Despite this poetic misrepresentation of his authorship, Percy Sykes protested his innocent motivations. He claimed it had never been his intention to deceive his readers. He had believed there was a sufficient clue provided in his book for anyone to determine the identity of the true author. For very attentive readers of the first printing, this single clue was to be found in the fictional merchant's slightly disguised claim that he was the grandson of James Morier's famous creation Hajji Baba of Isfahan.

In a characteristically optimistic way, Sykes proceeds to turn around the criticism he expected to receive when his unintentional deception became more widely known. He does this by ending his brief note of apology with a personally gratifying thought. Apparently untroubled by concerns about the evil eye, he concludes irrepressibly, "At the same time, for high authorities to consider that my work must have been written by a Persian constitutes high praise." To some considerable extent, Sykes consoled himself, he had succeeded in his ambition to be considered a second James Morier.

Whatever their powers for good or evil, the local observances of folk beliefs and traditions created meaningful associations and vivid personal memories. They gave a powerful focus to ordinary village activities. When these long-established customs inevitably came into conflict with new values in recent decades, the reaction was often very strong and unpredictable. In the 1960s, Rita J. Wiesinger directed some UNESCO literacy and social programs in Dezful and the surrounding region of southwest Iran. Her book *Light me a Candle* (1973) describes her personal experiences and her sympathetic observations of some of the many changes that were then occurring.

One despairing village woman made an eloquent protest to Wiesinger against the careless destruction caused by the new ways.

> "Our life is becoming harder and our debts heavier. Recently we were told that our lands would be taken away, dwellings destroyed and the ground levelled. It is sad to leave our ancestral homes and our cemeteries. How can the dead be moved? We cannot abandon them as on every Friday prayers must be said on their graves, food offered and *khorma* (dates) distributed to the mourners.
>
> Even our sacred trees are being uprooted. An official came with a tractor to level land on which a holy tree stood. All our women and children lay on the ground to save it but the gendarmes removed them. The man behaved like a *shaitan* (devil), but he said he was an engineer. *Khanum* (lady)! Why can we not continue to live as our forefathers did?"

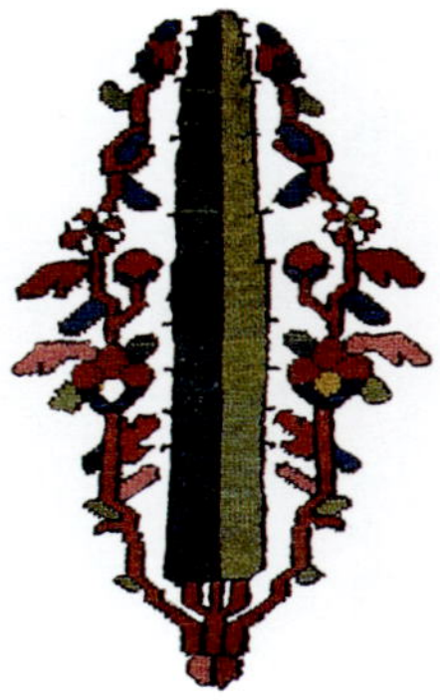

The new mythology of economic development and social progress was forcefully represented by the powerful symbolism of the modern tractor in confrontation with the sacred tree. It was also represented in human form by the gendarmes and the engineer for whom, at least in their official roles, the old values had no significance.

The metaphysical poetry of William Blake written at the turn of the nineteenth century addressed many of the same passionate concerns that Wiesinger recorded in the 1960s. His poetry was the strongest contemporary protest in the English language against the devastating loss of human meaning that he saw occurring in the early years of the industrial revolution. In his philosophy, Blake favored imagination and intuition over the unbalanced supremacy of reason. He criticized demonstration that was blind to all the simple rules of life. For Blake, the enemy of what he called whole vision was a reasoning power that had become divorced from the human imagination.

The universally comprehensible image of the sacred tree uniting earth and heaven seems to be common to all traditional cultures. We recall that even the practical-minded A.C.Edwards found it necessary on one occasion to use the symbolism of the tree to express his thoughts and emotions in the most humanly meaningful way. He compared his satisfaction at seeing the development of carpet making in Hamadan over his lifetime to that of "a person who contemplates a great tree which has grown from a seed which he has himself planted."

In Iranian culture, the cypress tree is often used as a visual metaphor for an ideal of human behavior. Firmly rooted in the earth, the cypress stands perfectly erect, always pointing toward the sky and another reality. Seen as symbols of the soul's journey, the many birds may find temporary rest and shelter in the branches of the cypress tree during their arduous and lengthy ascent to heaven.

We recall the most famous cypress tree of Iranian history that was planted at Kashmar in Khorasan province by the prophet Zoroaster. This event celebrated the final acceptance of the new faith by the Shah. The great tree grew for more than one thousand years until it almost reached heaven. Its violent destruction soon after the Arab conquest was a symbolic act that signaled the presence of new rulers and the acceptance of another faith by most Iranians.

The ancient sacred tree is an essential religious image that occurs very frequently in William Blake's poetry and visual art. In the context of his time, Blake knew that not everyone could appreciate the emotional force and the human meaningfulness of this image. Long before the careless destruction witnessed by Wiesinger in rural Iran in the 1960s, Blake prophesied the devastation that would be produced by the industrial changes he was witnessing. He wrote, "The tree which moves some to tears of joy is in the eyes of others only a green thing that stands in the way."

As a woman from India, Rita Wiesinger was able to talk relatively freely with the Iranian women participating in her programs about their deepest concerns. Her book title came from the words of a peasant girl who told her, "I am illiterate and feel like a woman in a dark room who cannot see. Light me a candle!" Wiesinger describes visiting the home of a local woman in the village of Sharafabad. Beginning their conversation in a very conventional way, her host Farida explained in some detail the usual religious obligations of a devout Shi'a Moslem.

Farida then volunteered to explain the significance of something in her home that was much less conventional. She could see it had attracted the curiosity of her visitor. Wiesinger could not fail to notice the large cross drawn with blue indigo dye that dominated the center of one wall.

> "It is intended to keep away the *kafar jinn*, the infidel spirit. He is malevolent and sends bad luck and death. He frequently assumes the shape of an owl, and lives in dark and dirty places, under trees, at doorsteps, in kitchens and cemeteries. We fear the evil spirit very much and adopt special measures to keep it away. We wear talismans, use charms, burn incense, avoid sleeping at entrance doors and make a cross with indigo on our house walls after saying *Bismallah - Rahmaneh - Rahim*. These words frighten the evil spirit."

In *The Wild Rue*, Donaldson records that the same powerful protective formula was commonly seen written on silver amulets: "In the name of God the merciful and compassionate." Called the *bismallah*, these are the opening words of the *Quran*. In all their variety, these folk beliefs in beneficial and malevolent *jinn* or spirits were universally held in the villages and they

3.3 Bakhtiari *Cypress Trees* (c.1910, 3.47 x 3.20)

The cypress may be imagined as a refuge on the soul journey, a reminder of prayer, an ideal human pointing to the One, or the pole joining earth and heaven.

3.4 Qashqai *Contemplation of Form* (c.1970, 1.97 x 1.08)
A principal motivation of some patterns including this spare geometrical design may have been the mystical contemplation of pure form.

affected almost every activity in the home. Following the community's traditional customs and rules was believed to give some protection against the *jinn* and the many dangers and misfortunes of life.

There is a moving description of the making of one Qashqai carpet in recent times that shows the continuing importance of these common beliefs. The American anthropologist Lois Beck lived and traveled with a nomadic Qashqai family in southwest Iran for more than a year in 1970 and 1971. She describes how the women of the small group she followed carefully planned their major weaving projects for the coming winter. During the rest of the year, they used any spare time available from their other tasks to spin and dye the wool they would need for their weavings.

> By the time women arrived at the winter pastures they expected to have all the yarn in the chosen colors for the one or two major items they planned to weave that season ready. Women plotted out their weavings years in advance and could describe each item in detail and sketch the design motifs in the dirt.

Beck describes the great interest each Qashqai woman she met took in the work of the other women, and she notes the strong competitive spirit among unmarried and recently married women over the speed and skill of their weaving. The men of the local community were expected by the women to take an attentive interest in this culturally important activity. Beck noticed that men and boys who were visiting from other camps would be asked to describe in detail the current weavings of their family members and their female relatives.

In the family with whom Beck was staying, there was one teenage weaver Zolaikha who set up a carpet loom in her home during the winter of 1971. To invoke good fortune and the protection of *Allah* for her weaving, she first recited the *bismallah,* "In the name of God, the most merciful, the most compassionate." She then began to weave a beautiful carpet with the brilliantly colored wool she had prepared very carefully during the summer and autumn months.

Very soon, Zolaikha had to abandon the long-planned project because her mother had contracted a serious illness requiring an operation.

> An item such as a gelim, jajim, or pile carpet was considered pleasing to the eye and hand of the weaver and could not be woven during a period of crisis. Zolaikha began a sugar bag, but visitors, objecting, proclaimed that it was too attractive and not utilitarian enough.

Heeding these objections from her neighbors, Zolaikha then decided to weave a bag so plain and functional that it would not attract either the evil eye or the critical comments of visitors to her home. However, she did not forget the major weaving project she had been forced by unfortunate circumstances to abandon. When she learned that her mother was recovering from her illness, Zolaikha returned immediately to the loom and completed her carpet without delay.

Only a few months later, a distressing event occurred during the spring migration. To her great dismay, Zolaikha's father ordered her to show the carpet she had made with such care and love. Without consulting his daughter, he had decided to offer it to some visitors. They were two Persian merchants who had traveled from the nearby town Kazerun.

> The carpet had come to represent her distress and then her relief; she had woven talismans into it to aid her mother's recovery. She had crafted the item with care, for she had expected it to be part of her dowry.

Despite her obvious strong feelings, the commercial transaction was completed quickly and the beautiful carpet was taken away by the merchants.

A short time later, Zolaikha and her sister Zohreh returned sadly to their regular tasks. They were bravely trying to put the grievous loss of the carpet out of their minds. When they went to collect water at a nearby spring, they happened to see something that disturbed them deeply.

> At the bottom of the gorge, they spotted the two Persians having a picnic with their families. There, under the feet of romping children, was Zolaikha's carpet laid out with food and a samovar. The sisters put their arms around each other, and tears ran down Zolaikha's face.

The dimensions of meaning revealed so affectingly in this small incident are not unique to this isolated experience. To a greater or lesser extent, these personal meanings and sincere emotions are essential components of all tribal and village weaving.

From conception to completion, Zolaikha's dowry carpet became the physical embodiment of her hopes and fears. The careful planning, the competitive spirit, the specialized knowledge of dyeing and design, the religious and folk beliefs, the vivid imagination, the family's material needs, the father's authority and the hopelessly entangled emotions of life – all of these found eloquent expressions in her carpet. These ethical dimensions of carpet making are missing when we read somewhere that a tribal weaver seeks inspiration from what she sees and not from what she thinks. They are missing when judgments of aesthetic value are based exclusively on formal relations of lines and colors or on the coordination of decorative schemes in the completed design.

In *Living Tradition of Iran's Crafts* (1979), Jasleen Dhamija develops the view that simple objects of everyday use can be expressive of a whole way of life and thought. According to Dhamija, craft objects provide a texture to daily activities and they may express the inner life of those who make and use them. She describes the simple *haft-hasht* ("seven-eight") design, alternating upright and inverted v's that form a wavelike pattern. This ancient design is frequently seen woven in textiles, drawn or incised on pottery and carved into wooden tools.

A wooden plough that Dhamija saw being used in a village near Kashan was covered with this elementary repeating design. She interpreted this in a very straightforward way as a symbolic representation of either flowing water or the ploughed furrows of the village fields. At the same time, she recognized that engraving the surface with this common design also served some important functional purposes. The incised pattern strengthened the plough and allowed it to dry evenly.

The same very common *haft-hasht* design was observed by Dhamija on the border of a *sofreh ardhi*, the special decorated cloth most frequently used in village homes for wrapping bread dough and for storing grain and bread. Traditionally, this *sofreh* was woven by the mother of a new bride as a present that her daughter would take with her on her first journey to her new home. It was given with the mother's heartfelt wish that her daughter's family would always have bread.

The *haft-hasht* design of the border signified again to Dhamija the presence of water. The main design of this special *sofreh* included the representation of a tree and birds in flight. This was interpreted by the author in a very simple way as a symbol of growth and an indication that the grain of the new family would be safe. There are other metaphorical interpretations of this design that seem equally possible.

3.5 Qashqai *Sofreh* *(c.1960, 1.36 x 1.23)*

Used in many ways as a functional covering, the ***sofreh*** *acquires over time a metaphorical significance. It symbolizes the daily activities and inner life of Iranian families.*

Jasleen Dhamija played a prominent role in encouraging the development of handcrafts in Iran in the 1970s after a similar career in India. She was unusually sensitive to the importance of the many rhythms she understood were always involved in traditional hand work. In a remote village in northern Khorasan, she watched two Turkmen women working silently and swiftly on a large carpet.

> After a while I just listened to the rhythm of the fingers raising and releasing the warp threads, as if they were playing on a giant harp. The room was filled with the sound of the weaving and we were absorbed in its rhythm. I looked at the faces of the women weavers – so calm, so full of repose and confidence. … They too were absorbed in the rhythm of their work, in the flowing cadence that they had created and unconsciously absorbed.

3.6 Quchan
Salt Bag
(c.1960, 0.61 x 0.39)

These textiles were used to store valuable possessions such as salt. A narrow opening and reversing designs echo the psychological desire to create a protected space.

It is a common observation that the quality of carpet weaving may be judged by listening to the rhythms of the work. This reassuring and restful quality of repetitive hand work is what Dhamija found lacking in industrial societies where there is more often a disturbing dissonance with natural human rhythms. She writes, "In the skillful use of the hands and the soothing rhythm of the work (which requires a concentration of the mind), the play of imagination, and total involvement, we get a feeling of completeness and strength which flows from deep within."

Jasleen Dhamija was one of the contributors to the volume *A Survey of Persian Handicraft* (1977), a major government-sponsored publication edited by Jay Gluck and Sumi Gluck. This impressive book with many illustrations followed the model of Arthur Upham Pope's *A Survey of Persian Art* which was republished in the same year in a third edition of sixteen volumes. One article, "Namad Felt Mats" co-authored by Dhamija with Niki Keddie and Khosrow Pir, describes in considerable detail the production of the traditional *namad* in Fars province. The namads are the sturdy felt mats with simple designs that have a variety of uses. They are frequently placed under more valuable pile carpets, and they are often used in Iranian homes for their warmth in winter.

When the Qashqai nomads moved in the spring migration to their summer quarters in the mountains of Fars province, they supplied wool from the spring shearing to the settled namad makers living in some of the villages along their route. Half of the wool provided would be used to make namads for the Qashqai families with the other half serving as payment to the villagers for their work. When the Qashqai returned to their winter quarters in late autumn, they collected the namads they had ordered months earlier. With its simple annual rhythms, this trade established some important commercial and personal connections between the nomadic and sedentary people of the region.

To conclude her own book, *Living Traditions of Iran's Crafts,* Dhamija returned to a description of this craft as it was practiced in the regions of Mazanderan and Semnan. She counted thirty-eight rhythms that were involved in the full cycle of namad making, beginning with the preparation of the wool. Almost everyone in the community became involved in some way in one or more of these many activities. She observed that even very young children contributed their labor at one important stage of the lengthy process. They participated in the common task by adding the colored wool that formed the simple designs.

3.7 Qashqai
Women's Celebration
(c.1970, 1.74 x 1.06)

Dancing in a circle to celebrate a marriage, the Qashqai women enclose a protected space free from all evil spirits. The dancers imitate the divine pattern by turning in the direction of the stars.

The final stages of the work on the larger namads were the most physically demanding. Three or four men moved the namad back and forth with their feet for an hour or more. Together, they called out repeatedly *Ya Ali, Ya Ali* in deep resonant voices. The older workers told Dhamija stories of namad makers they remembered who had entered a state of ecstasy in response to the insistent rhythms of the work. In former times, they said, these workers had abandoned this world by calling out in unison *Ya Hu, Ya Ali* ("Oh, He! Oh, Ali!"). For these inspired workers, namad making became much more than a practical activity undertaken for strictly economic reasons. In their imaginations, it became a *zikr Allah* which is a "remembrance of God."

3.8 Khamseh
Random Pattern
(c. 1930, 1.93 x 1.56)

The freely scattered elements of the field design suggest the stars of the night sky.

The many technical requirements and the economic motivations of namad making did not prevent this ordinary activity from sharing in the most significant cultural values. In the 1950s, the Danish anthropologist Fredrik Barth conducted extensive field studies of the nomadic Basseri tribe which was part of the Khamseh Federation of five tribal groups in Fars province. In the initial stages of his ethnological research, Barth grew increasingly doubtful of its value or potential interest.

After many months of observations, he remained disappointed by his inability to find in Basseri life what he could describe as significant ritual activities. The few rituals he was able to observe seemed to him to be unconnected to each other, and he could not relate them in significant ways to important features of the social structure. In addition, Barth found that the Basseri were generally uninterested in religion as it was preached by the Persian mullahs with whom they had occasional contact. Unlike other Iranian tribal groups, they were seemingly indifferent to metaphysical problems.

Barth then had a key insight that completely changed his evaluations of the ordinary customs of everyday Basseri life. He came to realize that "the very forms of an act which reflect the technical imperatives may also be vested with central and crucial meaning in a symbolic system or context." After a period of resistance, it gradually became clear to him that all their activities in their camps and during migrations could be seen as having the most significant meanings for the Basseri in a shared symbolic framework.

He had begun his field studies with the common preconception that practical activities of fundamental economic importance could not also have supreme ritual value. Barth would later describe this as a naive assumption. As his understanding of the structures of Basseri nomadic life increased, he eventually abandoned this opinion.

He began to see symbolic and ritual meanings in places and practices he had not previously considered.

> This value is revealed in the way the migration cycle is used as a primary schema for the conceptualization of time and space, in the fact that many nomads, after the external disturbance of enforced sedentarization, resumed migratory life in spite of economic costs, and finally, in the emotional engagement of the participants in the migration. … the participants respond, not to the utilitarian aspects of the activities – to good pastures and potential butterfat – but to the movement and its dramatic form – to the *meanings* implicit in the sequence of activities.

Fredrik Barth came to understand that his mainly external and objective descriptions of economic and social arrangements had missed the more important personal truths.

Barth accepted the idea that the ordinary customs of the Basseri should be seen in an entirely different way. Within a more sympathetic and comprehensive cultural understanding, he admitted these customary practices could be transformed into a description of the most central features and beliefs of Basseri life. Their customs may have had primary and essential economic motivations but they could also reveal the meanings and inner values that made up their imaginative life.

These important observations and interpretations among the nomadic Basseri have influenced many later anthropological studies in Iran and elsewhere. They contradict or at least strongly qualify the overly simple view expressed by A.C.Edwards that the rug making of the Khamseh was a purely commercial proposition lacking personal and cultural significance. To partially defend Edwards, we have now seen that one trained ethnologist from Denmark with a much greater opportunity to observe very nearly came to similar conclusions about all aspects of the nomadic life of the Basseri tribal subgroup of the Khamseh Federation.

We should not forget the larger social context during the unsettled period of their observations. Both Edwards and Barth were surveying and writing shortly after a time of great dislocations in the lives of the nomadic tribal communities in Iran. Fredrik Barth's hard-won final conclusions and Jasleen Dhamija's perceptive observations should be kept in mind whenever hasty or preconceived judgments are sometimes made about the primary motivations behind tribal weavings and all Persian carpets of the modern period.

The *haft-hasht* design that occurs so frequently in tribal and village craft work is also found in the borders of most Persian carpets if we accept slightly or even heavily disguised floral variants as examples. Reciprocating design and counterchange pattern are two technical terms in textile studies for patterns in which a basic element reverses regularly in direction. Such a design can create a feeling of motion. It may also create the perception of a continuous oscillation between what is perceived as foreground and background. The reversing "v" pattern of the *haft-hasht* design is the simplest example of a reciprocating design.

Perhaps influenced by her knowledge of folk symbolism in India, Dhamija's interpretation of the *haft-hasht* design as symbolizing flowing water seems much too restrictive. More fundamentally, the design may represent the flowing of time in natural and human-based rhythms, and it has other possible meanings. The borders of Persian carpets are generally made up of many reversing designs. These oscillating designs act to impose an elementary rhythm on our perceptions analogous to breathing. We should recall that the rhythms of traditional Iranian music are strongly based on the primary rhythm of breath.

The oscillations of the *haft-hasht* design in tribal and village weaving have another important significance in folk beliefs. They are confusing to the *jinn,* the malevolent spirits. In the villages and tribal areas, it is a well-known fact that the *kafar jinn* with evil intentions find the intricate zigzag patterns of the borders difficult to cross. This implicit cultural metaphor is probably the most important reason for the use of these patterns on the *sofreh ardhi,* the cloth for bread dough described by Dhamija. In the same way that a *talism* guards the tranquility of the home or a hanging chain declares an area is enclosed or *bast,* the constantly reversing reciprocating designs of the border of a Persian carpet create a protected space.

In *The Persian Carpet,* Edwards turns his attention to explaining what he calls the tenacity and immutability of the border convention. In contrast to some borderless Chinese and Indian carpets, he writes categorically that no man has yet seen a Persian carpet without a border. Characteristically, he favors a straightforward practical explanation and he does not look for a possible symbolic interpretation.

> The Persians regard the border as a necessary framework to set off the ground pattern. Their designers would maintain that without it the attention is distracted from a steady contemplation of the main design.

He then describes the basic elements that in his opinion must be present in every border design. These are a middle band with one, two or three narrow guard bands on each side.

According to Edwards, the guard bands should have patterns which are short, insignificant repeats in order not to detract from the importance of the middle band which is the border proper. Also characteristic of Edwards is his description of the repeat patterns of the minor borders as being insignificant. It should be noted that simple reciprocating or counterchange designs, often floral or geometrical variants of the *haft-hasht* design, are the most common patterns for these guard bands.

There may be more significant cultural reasons for the persistence of border designs than simply as a neutral frame for the ground or field pattern. The function of the border surrounding the field of a carpet is not restricted to permitting a steady contemplation of the main design. Its primary function is to produce in the mind an imagined separation of outer and inner. This is a fundamental duality encountered repeatedly in all aspects of Iranian private life and public culture.

In the traditional home, there was always an interior space, the *anderun,* which was reserved for the exclusive use of the immediate family. This protected private area was considered distinct from the *birun,* the more public space of the home where visitors would be received. We cannot forget the two Persian families having their picnic on Zolaikha's lost carpet so heedlessly laid out with food and a samovar. To some extent, the families had created an *anderun* on their new carpet, a protected private space that excluded Zolaikha and her sister Zohreh.

On the philosophical and psychological levels, there is a corresponding division of ordinary activities into the internal, the *baten,* and the external, the *zaher.* The *baten* is the realm of the personal and intimate where sincerity and free expression are possible. The *zaher* is the less predictable realm of the external world where maintaining appearances becomes important and guarded behavior is appropriate.

The private world of the home has an unusually strong resonance in Iranian culture. With all its cultural associations, the home expresses the strong desire of individuals and families to be in an ideal protected world, the enclosed garden of the *baten* or personal realm. The phrase *bi khane,*"without a home," has an equally strong resonance in the Iranian imagination, conveying a solitary and empty existence. The many religious sanctuaries called *bast* ("enclosed") to be found in all parts of Iran were another reflection of this psychological desire for a protected refuge.

Every Persian carpet reflects and constantly reinforces these fundamental cultural understandings. The conventional border and field form of Persian carpet designs visually displays the strong separation in Iranian culture between outer and inner experience. Protected by the intricate border, the field design creates in its viewers the feeling of sanctuary or refuge from the perils of an unpredictable world. Stepping with the right foot over the border onto the field of the carpet is a movement in the imagination from *birun* to *anderun,* from *zaher* to *baten.*

There are some other important rhythms involved in the making of many Persian carpets. These human rhythms are not described by Dhamija, but they certainly deserve to be recorded and remembered. We may find a passing mention of them in *Persian Lions, Persian Lambs* (1965), the insightful travel journal of the American academic Curtis Harnack. His appealing book records the ordinary events and observations of his year in Iran where he taught English at the University of Tabriz.

Harnack lived near the showroom of *Sherket Farsh Iran*, the Iran Carpet Company, which was located in the main business district of Tabriz. On his usual route to the university, he had often stopped for a few moments to admire the beautiful carpets temptingly displayed in their show window. One day, Harnack decided he could resist the temptation no longer. With the assistance of one of his students, he set out to buy a carpet from the company as a permanent souvenir of his time in Iran.

After examining the extensive selection in the company's showroom, he boldly asked the manager if he could visit their Tabriz factory to see how some of their carpets were made. Normally, the carpet factory was closed to foreign visitors without valid business reasons or special arrangements. That domain was effectively an *anderun* intended to be kept strictly private in almost all circumstances. However, according to long-established Iranian customs, it is very difficult to refuse a definite request from a *mehman*, a respected guest or visitor, or from an honored teacher.

Later on the same day, the persuasive American professor was being shown around the factory by its manager. Harnack immediately knew he had not prepared himself sufficiently for what he would see. Young children were working diligently on large carpets that were suspended on sturdy looms twelve feet high. To the visitor, the small workers seemed to be like birds. They were all perched on tall scaffolding before their half-completed carpets. Glancing around the room, he thought that many of the children appeared to be considerably younger than the legal working age of twelve years.

Harnack was surprised and deeply moved to find that an atmosphere of gaiety prevailed among the children in the carpet factory. He watched in fascination as the young carpet weavers tied knots so quickly their fingers were a blur. As they worked, the children were singing.

> First a row of little girls would burst forth with: "Pass me the blue, oh the blue, pretty blue; pass me the blue, pretty blue, oh, the blue," and down from the spools above came the blue yarn. Then another phalanx of children, boys and girls mixed, would start up with: "Now send me the black, now the black; oh, send me the black, yes the black," and finally in a kind of chorus, they would all join in: "Now the blue, now the black, now the red; oh, send the black, now the red, now the blue," and the yarn would vibrate through the air in front of the loom, as faster and faster they worked, buoyed up by their singing, making it a game or a race, until they broke down in torrents of laughter – or the supervisor came by and stood sternly below them, scanning the quality of their labor.

In unpromising surroundings, the birdlike children had created a lofty playground for themselves. If only in their imaginations, the beautiful carpets they were knotting had become their enclosed garden.

After watching the children's work and their play for some time, Harnack then turned to the company official showing him around the carpet factory. He told the manager that he had seen enough. Communicating only with himself, Harnack criticized what he called the devil's logic that had made carpet weaving the best or the only alternative for these children. At the end of the long day, the visitor turned away reluctantly from his original intention. He had decided he would not buy a carpet during his time in Iran.

In his preface to *A Survey of Persian Handicraft*, Jay Gluck recalls the growing interest in viewing folk craftwork as art in Iran in the 1960s. Surprisingly, some of the young artists returning from the art schools of Paris and New York were among the first collectors of the creative folk art of the Iranian villages and tribal groups. Influences from folk art began to appear very noticeably in their own art, introducing native and traditional elements into the abstract international styles they had developed in their studies. In this period, *Khane Iran* ("House of Iran") opened in Tehran in the basement of a leading modern art gallery. It quickly became the principal meeting place in the city for artists and others who had become interested in traditional handcrafts.

An important event occurring at the same time was the highly praised renovation of the interiors of the Shah Abbas hotel in Isfahan. This project was completed following the creative ideas of Mehdi Ebrahimian, a young artist from Isfahan who had recently returned to Iran after completing art studies in Paris. Not satisfied with the limited resources that were easily available, Ebrahimian carefully researched what was still known about the traditional techniques in metal, glass and plaster work. When necessary, he reinvented some old craft methods that had been ignored and lost in recent decades.

Ebrahimian salvaged the elaborate wood-framed doors and windows from old buildings that were then being hastily demolished to make way for new construction. He was able to restore and use some of them again, and they also served as models for his more contemporary designs. In the following years, Mehdi Ebrahimian's ingenious approach to cultural renewal became very influential in Isfahan and throughout Iran. His sensitivity to cultural precedents and his modern inventiveness showed to many Iranians that it was possible to combine traditional methods and values with current ideas in a beautiful and meaningful synthesis.

Jay Gluck's principal mentor in developing his own interest in Persian art and handicrafts was the famous American authority Arthur Upham Pope. In 1958, as Gluck was about to travel to Iran for the first time, Pope gave him some memorable advice. Two decades after his completion of the grandiose *Survey of Persian Art*, he said to the younger man, "Search for the soul of the country, look for the folk arts, the traditional artcrafts." By giving this belated advice to the impressionable young man, Pope seemed to be admitting he had neglected this important task in his own work.

Because of his close connections with Pope, Gluck was later to be given some useful assistance in his work in Iran and some very similar advice. These came from an even more prominent source, Mohammed Reza Shah Pahlavi.

> In an audience with His Imperial Majesty came the next admonition, "Leave Tehran and see the villages," as His Majesty spoke animatedly and affectionately of the artistic and indominatable soul of his people. He summed up the material value of art when his gaze swept the *khatam* marquetry walls of his study, "A people who can do this, can do anything they set their hearts and minds to."

Jay Gluck did proceed to follow this earnest advice from these two eminent individuals, helping to open up new areas of study of Iranian folk crafts. However, the turbulent history of the two years immediately following the publication of *A Survey of Persian Handicraft* has given another interpretation to the Shah's last statement, an ironic meaning that was certainly not anticipated or intended by him or by Gluck.

A short introductory essay written by Pope was published posthumously in the new *Survey*. Consistent with the grand style he employed throughout his career, the brief essay has an ambitious title, "The Significance of Persian Handicrafts." Pope returns to some of the central preoccupations that were so evident in his major work four decades earlier. As before, he begins his discussion in prehistorical times. He describes the patterns inscribed and painted on the pottery dated to c.3500 BC that had been found in recent decades near Susa in southwest Iran.

Although the various simple designs that appear on this ancient pottery apparently depict natural phenomena, they are viewed by Pope in a more ambitious way. He interprets these designs as a symbolic visual language intended by their creators to communicate universal concerns.

> They were symbolic appeals to the infinite powers for help by sympathetic magic, all showing want for water, with water birds and running clouds, water accumulation on the mountains with pools and reeds, all conceived and drawn with great emotion, much as they still are today in the woven goods of Kurdistan, Khurasan and Azerbaijan, among others.
>
> These decorated vessels were the product of the whole community – their interest, beauty and communicability were products of the common mind. In various forms, they were the basis of all art and although elaborately expanded and developed, these arts had their nourishing roots in the general character of the human intelligence, its experience and needs, and resources and emotional response to figures and patterns.

The impressive sweep of these ideas over more than five millennia and the majestic sweep of the Shah's gaze across the elaborately decorated walls of his study are much too grand for the modest approach taken in this book. However, it might be argued that a common culture is not necessarily or primarily the expression of the common mind, at least not in the ways this elusive concept was understood by Pope.

The culture of a whole community may be better understood as a conversation in many languages and forms of expression. It is built up out of the full complexity of the socially-conditioned reactions of individuals to their human and natural environments. Like the young Qashqai weaver Zolaikha, the true participants in a community are those who respond in their own uniquely varied ways to their personally and culturally meaningful opportunities for creative expression.

This responding to social experiences in some considered form is an ethical responsibility of every mature individual. These responses are essential to create or renew the sense of the connectedness of experience, and they are the fundamental basis of art. In the most important ways, the patterns of Zolaikha's carpet and even those of her community were created or recreated by her emotional and intellectual responses to her experiences. They were the products of her uncommon mind.

There was at least one rhythm in Iranian life that A.C.Edwards learned to appreciate during his early years in Hamadan. Trained to assess and act on any likely business opportunity, he used this predictable annual rhythm for the commercial advantage of his carpet enterprise.

> Every woman will contrive to finish at least one or two rugs before the feast of the New Year, which is at the vernal equinox: for its sale will bring in a few *tomans* to the household at a time when each member of the family must have something new to wear. This is the season which gladdens the heart of the trader, for the rugs come pouring in from the villages and he can quickly fill his stores with the wares of his choice.

At the spring equinox, the Iranian New Year or *Nouruz* is greeted with a long-anticipated celebration that involves the whole community.

The arrival of *Nouruz* or "the day of renewal" is the most joyful event of the year in Iran. Beginning at the spring equinox and taking place over a two week period, there are many small rituals that every family attempts to observe during *Nouruz*. It is a time to thoroughly clean every room of the house, to receive guests in great numbers, and to return their visits. It is a time to burn the *esfand*, the wild rue, whose acrid smell permeates the home and causes the *kafar jinn* with harmful intentions to flee.

Following an old custom, merchants may borrow some of the best carpets from nearby homes to display on their storefronts. This tradition symbolizes in a natural way the recognition of the social obligation to share and it is a revelation of a significant part of the concealed inner life of Iranian families. For this brief interval at the beginning of each year, there is much less separation allowed between inner and outer experience. After months of concealment on a loom in the *anderun* of an Iranian home, many carpets emerge to see the full light of day and begin their long journeys to other homes in Iran or in distant countries.

Nouruz is a time recognized by all for the forgiveness of any misdeeds and misunderstandings. Each year, it provides a welcome occasion for a healing of enmities and a renewal of old friendships. In his brief description, Edwards stops well short of the profound metaphorical meanings of the simple customs of the *Nouruz* celebrations. Wearing new clothes and displaying the best carpets in public locations at the New Year signal the promising beginning of a more hopeful and abundant life. These personal and social gestures indicate a willing abandonment of the misfortunes and unhappy memories of the past.

When these specially selected carpets were removed temporarily from their usual places of confinement and displayed openly before everyone, they acquired some different significances. At *Nouruz*, they revealed the inner spiritual wealth of Iranian life that was carefully concealed at other times of the year. If only for a brief time, the beautiful carpets on display for all to see became recognized public symbols of the complete renewal of personal and community life.

Even in the towns and cities, flowers and green plants are seen everywhere at this special time of the year. Every fruit tree is in abundant blossom. At the end of the bleakness and hardships of winter, the plants are covered again in leaves and flowers. They wear their beautiful new garments as proudly and joyfully as the people. If we choose to observe, we cannot fail to notice that the busy animals and all nature are eagerly joining the flowering plants and trees to greet the sudden arrival of spring.

The period of celebration begins at nightfall on the Tuesday evening before the spring equinox. This is marked by the celebration of *Chahar Shanbeh Suri*, the Feast of Wednesday (literally, "redness Wednesday"). In a much-loved tradition that has Zoroastrian roots, Iranians of all ages take turns in leaping over a small fire of *boteh* which is a desert thorn bush. At the same time, they each recite a short verse addressed to the fire. "Take from me my yellow color and give me your red color." "My troubles and my age I cast into your flames; give me your warmth and brightness in return." "Our paleness yours and your redness ours."

The dominant fields of very many Persian carpet designs are colored in a vivid blood red. In Iranian homes, these carpets may serve as reminders throughout the year of this cherished moment of new beginnings. They may recall these fervent wishes expressed by everyone at the time of celebration when winter ends and spring begins. This is the joyful moment when everyone wishes for themselves and all others the redness of vigorous health and the renewal of abundant life in the year to come.

This time-honored fire ceremony and all the Nouruz observances had a transcendent significance in Iranian life. They were intended to achieve nothing less than a transformation of consciousness in all who participated. These common rituals during the days of renewal revived the normal conversations of the community. They represented a turning away in the imagination from the constrained life and seemingly endless privations of winter. They signaled an abandonment of all the harshness of their lives in the year that has ended and a resolute turning from illness to health. They encouraged in each individual a turning away from social separation to a willing union with others.

3.9 Qashqai *Complex Design* *(c.1960, 3.10 x 1.75)*

Completing this carpet has given a lasting form to a weaver's skills, knowledge and imagination. That permanent unity created through constant effort may be the most significant meaning.

The shared observances during *Chahar Shanbeh Suri* and *Nouruz* demonstrated the possibility at any time of a turning by everyone toward an idealized vision of human behavior. The small fire of the *boteh* thorn bush was large enough to burn away everything that was no longer needed. The alchemy of its flickering red flame magically transformed matter to spirit. While it burned, all substance became essence. At the very beginning of the time of renewal, everything was and was not. *Yeki bud, yeki nabud*. In the light and heat of that small flame, all perceptions were magically transformed and imagination became real.

At that single moment separating day and night, every family and the whole community willingly joined in the celebration. All were eager to experience this transformation from matter to spirit in their own lives. Each year, the celebration of *Chahar Shanbeh Suri* and *Nouruz* renewed in the participants a fuller perception of ordinary reality in its human meaningfulness and truth. The earth turned once more, and everything came into balance again at the spring equinox.

4 The King's Threshold

In her extensive travels throughout Iran in 1934, Onera Merritt-Hawkes was seeking far more than an aesthetic appreciation of the monuments of Iranian culture. She did describe the famous shrine of Shah Ni'matullah Vali Kermani (d.1431) at Mahan near Kerman as the most beautiful in the country. By an old convention, the founder of this religious order of itinerant dervishes was called a Shah, but his kingdom was not an earthly one. The rule of Shah Ni'matullah and his successors in Mahan was confined to a spiritual realm.

Like many travelers before her, Merritt-Hawkes commented admiringly on the fine architecture of the shrine. After a long period of neglect, it had been restored in the nineteenth century by order of Nasreddin Shah Qajar. She also commented in the conventional way on the great beauty of the surroundings. When she visited in July, the well-kept gardens were brilliantly lit by the flame-like flowers of the numerous pomegranate trees.

The interest of the English visitor very soon turned from the beauty of the architecture and the gardens of the Ni'matullah shrine. In other words, she turned her attention away from the entrancing physical beauty of aesthetic surfaces as seen by empirical vision. In her brief time there, she was more interested in learning about things that were less visible. She was attempting to understand the ways of life and the personal motivations of those who had been drawn to the shrine to visit for lengthy periods or to live.

Founded more than five hundred years before, the influence of this well-known Sufi order had reached as far as India. Of the several hundred members in 1934, only about thirty were living at the shrine when Merritt-Hawkes visited. The others were engaged in moving about the region and country for months and years at a time. In their restless wanderings, they carried to every village and town a simple message of the unity of God and the world. One dervish of the order had returned recently from western Iran after a journey that had lasted a full year.

At the time of her visit to the shrine, there was some excitement about the recent arrival of the latest recruit to the Ni'matullah order. He was a thirty-six year old man from a prominent Bakhtiari family who was a close relative of the current minister of war. He gave a poignant reply to her indelicate question, "Why should a man in such a position become a dervish?" Without hesitating, he answered in what seemed to Merritt-Hawkes a very direct way. He said, "In the world there is no freedom. In the world there is no peace; here there is perfect peace. In the world there is no real honesty; here there is God's honesty."

The poignancy of this reply comes from our more complete knowledge of the dangerous historical context of this chance meeting. In 1934, Reza Shah turned his attention to breaking the remaining political power of the Bakhtiari. In recent times, their large tribal group had become the wealthiest and most influential in Iran. The leaders of the Bakhtiari had dominated or played decisive roles in the central government for most of the two decades preceding the *kudetta* (coup d'état) of 1921.

The numberless carpets made by Bakhtiari weavers in this period showed a remarkable variety of boldly creative designs. They were an obvious material sign of this new-found prosperity and they gave a clear indication of the increasing social confidence of the tribal group. The great numbers of Bakhtiari carpets woven from roughly 1900 to 1930 may be seen as a reflection of the growing economic and political influence of their leaders regionally and at the national level.

Almost certainly, the recent recruit encountered by the English visitor had some more urgent motivations he was not able to mention in any direct way. In all probability, he was seeking a sanctuary at the Ni'matullah shrine as far removed as possible from the lethal dishonesty to be found in contemporary Tehran. Like some other Bakhtiari leaders, his relative Sardar Assad who was minister of war was not able to find a safe refuge for himself in that turbulent period. In the same year, he would suddenly lose his prominent government position and then he would lose his life.

The remote shrine of Shah Ni'matullah had welcomed all visitors since its founding in the early fifteenth century. Some weeks later, Merritt-Hawkes was less successful in gaining entry when she attempted to visit the mosque of Fatima in Qom. Dedicated to the memory of the sister of Imam Reza, the eighth Imam, this beautiful mosque is recognized as one of the holiest shrines of Shi'a Islam. Seeking official permission to view the interior of the mosque, Merritt-Hawkes traveled some distance from Qom to visit the secluded home of the treasurer of the shrine. She was received graciously by this prominent religious leader in his beautiful garden but he did not consent to her request.

The venerable shrine leader thought it was necessary to give his English visitor some explanation of his decision. From his personal experiences, he knew there were many possibilities for misunderstandings and misrepresentations in that difficult period for those who defended the traditional role of Shi'ism in national life. He was also careful to make an important distinction when he said, "I very much regret I cannot allow you to see the inside of Fatima's shrine, but I want you to understand that it is not because we are fanatical, but because we are deeply religious."

Merritt-Hawkes could not help wondering to herself if her distinguished host was one of the mullahs who had been so rudely humiliated by Reza Shah six years before. Despite her curiosity, she wisely avoided mentioning this delicate subject. Instead they passed the time by talking about a less difficult but still controversial topic. She mentioned her interest in Sufism and her recent visit to the Ni'matullah shrine near Kerman. The religious leader told her, "He was a great saint, a great teacher, but his followers ...."

On the subject of the followers of Shah Ni'matullah, his voice trailed off and he failed to complete his thoughts. His choice to remain silent was understandable since he was aware that any words he used could be misinterpreted in that uncertain time. His silence was still eloquent in communicating his disapproval of their undisciplined ways and their questionable religious orthodoxy.

Choosing his words very carefully again, the religious leader continued, "I am glad you have seen the beautiful shrine of Mahan. We have been a nation of artists and we may be again. Our Shah is great." It was probably not apparent to the inquisitive visitor but it seems likely the Shah being referred to by the shrine leader was intentionally left slightly ambiguous. Like many others in the disordered context of that period, he found it more convenient to talk about the aesthetic qualities of the Ni'matullah shrine than to mention in any serious way its spiritual and religious significance.

During her time in Tehran in the 1890s, the English writer Gertrude Bell observed with great interest the simple routines and rituals of the dervish who was living at her garden gate. Her description of the holy man's modest activities included a significant metaphor that was familiar to her from classical Persian literature. She made some imaginative comparisons to the very different way of life of a more prosperous neighbor who also resided close to her gates. Nasir al-Din Shah Qajar (Nasreddin Shah) was living nearby in the royal splendor of the *Golestan* palace.

> Before our garden gates there dwelt a holy dervish. He too was a king - in the realms of poverty - and over the narrow strip of wilderness he bore undisputed sway. He levied pious alms for taxes, his palace was a roof of boughs, four bare poles were the columns of his throne, and the stones of the desert his crown jewels. His days were spent in a manner which differed little from that of his neighbour and brother sovereign. The whole long summer through he had collected the surrounding stones and piled them into regular heaps. His futile religious exercise was almost completed, he was putting the finishing touches to a work which winter winds and snows would as surely destroy as the winter of ill-fortune will scatter the other's wealth. But the dervish was untroubled by thoughts of the future; he labored to the glory of God in his own strange fashion, and though his jewels needed neither locks nor seals nor men-at-arms to guard them, their human interest lent them a value unattained by the Treasure of the King.

This description of the daily activities of the impoverished dervish reads unmistakably like a passage from the works of Sa'adi or Hafez.

Throughout Iranian spiritual culture, there are many signs of this very old recognition of a fundamental similarity of the apparently different roles of the king and the dervish. A proverbial saying expresses the cultural understanding of the source of this similarity: "The dervish should be given his rights; he holds them from God like the Shah." Until recent times, it was commonly believed that neglecting the modest needs of the holy dervish who chose to live at the threshold of the home or at the garden gate would bring lasting shame and ill fortune to the household.

There are numerous centuries-old stories of encounters between kings and dervishes, often with the king being required to wait uncomfortably at a humble threshold. While the king waits impatiently, the dervish takes all the time necessary to complete his ordinary religious observances. There are many other proverbial stories that recognize this duality of prince and pauper in a different way. They tell of Iranian kings who disguised themselves as itinerant dervishes in order to be able to travel freely and learn the true state of affairs in their country.

An ode written by the famous Shah Ni'matullah in the fifteenth century refers to this surprising cultural duality. In the translation by Edward Browne, the poem begins, "King and beggar are one; foodless and food are one, are one." Reversing ordinary perceptions completely, the poverty of the dervish was the same as the wealth of the king. The material poverty of the holy wanderer and the emptiness of his life in ordinary terms were to be seen as indications of a spiritual wealth.

In his travel journal, Browne describes one unusual privilege of the Sufi dervishes that was widely accepted in Iranian culture at the time he made his observations. He writes that the wandering dervish had the unquestioned right to "enter any assembly and to go wherever it seemeth good to him." In a culture that carefully defined social limits and protected boundaries in most circumstances, only the king or the king's messenger possessed the long-established right of the dervish to cross all thresholds.

We can be sure the repetitive religious exercises observed by Gertrude Bell at the garden gate of her home in Tehran were not considered to be futile activities in the mind of their practitioner. The holy dervish was learning or performing the very old art known as geomancy or divination by geomancy. One form of this mystical practice studied the patterns of points and lines that had been drawn or arranged on the ground. The purpose was to discover concealed patterns and hidden connections which were then used to give advice or to make predictions of forthcoming events.

In *The Wild Rue*, Bess Allen Donaldson describes a related form of *raml* or geomancy as the science of reading the future by means of the positions taken by pebbles thrown upon the ground or from lines drawn upon the sand. Donaldson also records the traditional folk belief that the understanding of *raml* dated originally from the prophet Daniel in ancient times. According to these common beliefs, Daniel had received his instruction in this sacred art directly from the angel Gabriel.

In *A Year Amongst the Persians*, Edward Browne described the secret initiation of one seeker after occult wisdom that involved similar practices. During forty days of solitude and mental concentration, the novice in this mysterious art "spends the greater part of this time in incantations in the Arabic language, which he recites within the area of the *mandal*, or geometrical figure, which he must describe in a certain way on the ground."

The obsessive interest of the dervish in the recognition of hidden patterns and their mystical interpretations that was witnessed by Bell in the 1890s had very old roots. In *The Republic*, Plato explains the primary metaphysical significance of geometry and its fundamental importance in spiritual education. Geometers make use of the visible forms in order to recognize the true realities that can be seen only by the mind. This deeper perception was literally a re-cognition or a remembering since it was believed that knowledge of geometry was innate. According to the philosophy of Plato, this knowledge was acquired before birth when the human soul was still directly in contact with the world of ideal forms.

The repetitive geometrical exercises of the dervishes with stones and lines were a contemporary expression of this early view of geometry. Using the most humble materials, they were intended as a rigorous training of the mind. Ideally, they would enable the mind to see not only geometrical patterns but all physical forms and relations in terms of the eternal patterns of the cosmos. The traditional designs of Persian carpets may be interpreted as another manifestation of this metaphysical understanding of geometry. At least in their earliest origins, these intricate designs reflected this ancient mystical attempt to discover the unchanging universal patterns behind all changeable appearances. They were an attempt to express the divine patterns controlling human destinies in a visible material form.

In his first days in Iran in 1887, Browne met an itinerant dervish who was willing to respond to some of his many questions. The holy wanderer patiently explained to the inquisitive visitor some of the simpler cultural meanings of the common signs of his chosen way of life.

> The true *arif* or adept, he informed us, was distinguished by four external signs: the *tabar*, or axe, which serves to protect him during his wanderings in the desert from ferocious beasts; the *kashkul*, or gourd slung on chains, in which he receives alms; the *taj*, or felt cap embroidered with texts, which crowns his head; and the *gisu*, or long locks, which fall over his shoulders.

The *taj* of the dervish is literally a crown like the royal crown, but one whose jewels are carefully embroidered texts from the *Quran*. Together with the *kashkul* and the *tabar*, the bowl for alms and the two-edged axe, they may have been received by the novice dervish from the *shaykh*, the head of his order, as external signs of a new life. His *gisu* or long hair indicated the willing abandonment of the normal concerns and attractive illusions of this temporary world.

The bowl and the axe belonging to the dervish were intended to serve much more significant purposes than the merely practical ones of holding alms and slaying wild beasts. The rounded horizontal shape of the *kashkul* has been described as symbolizing the passive, receptive feminine quality, and the linear vertical form of the *tabar* represents the active, outward male aspect of all activities. Both qualities of this primary duality of male and female were brought to a unity in the person and the way of life of the wandering dervish.

Many dervishes were immediately recognizable from their *khirqah*, the patched woolen cloak they often wore. These tattered garments were received as a gift from the *shaykh*. They had been passed down from earlier dervishes as a principal sign of their profession. The many patches were a visible representation of the great age of these cloaks, and they were an unmistakable sign of the acceptance of material poverty. The patches also indicated the inheritance of a very old spiritual tradition, the *silsileh* or chain of succession that could be traced to the founder of the dervish order. Some orders traced their chain of inheritance back as far as Ali, the first Imam.

Another familiar symbol of the dervish in former times was the animal skin that he wore or carried. The animal skin or *pustin* could be the pelt of a sheep, a gazelle or a lion. Very often, a small prayer carpet would be carried instead as a substitute for the *pustin*. This small carpet belonging to the dervish was then understood as a symbolic representation of the traditional animal skin. There were very few other material possessions. According to a common proverbial saying, a dervish who owned more than could be covered by his animal skin or prayer carpet was in a state of forgetfulness of God. In a profound parallelism, ownership of the animal skin by the holy wanderer visibly signified that the dervish was himself a possession of God.

In *The Glory of the Shi'a World*, Percy Sykes describes in considerable detail the greatly increased activities of the itinerant dervishes in the period just before *Nouruz*, the Iranian New Year celebrated at the beginning of spring.

> Dervishes pitch tents outside the houses of the great and recite prayers for their prosperity. It is customary to make them a handsome gift; but if this be not done quickly, they blow their horns at intervals during the night and, by rendering sleep impossible, loosen the purse-strings of the rich Khan or merchant. Indeed I have never forgotten the awe with which I regarded a dervish at Mahun, who possessed a beautifully inlaid axe of a great age, a begging bowl on which the combat of Rustam with the White Div was carved, and a very fine lion's skin. While I was gazing in wonder at these articles, *Ya Hu* was pronounced like a lion's roar and my heart became like water.

The usual symbols of the dervish were present in this scene in an impressive way. He possessed a beautifully inlaid *tabar* of great age, a very elaborately decorated *kashkul* and a fine *pustin* which was a rare lion's skin.

The ram's horn is a familiar element in carpet designs, and it was another commonly seen possession of the holy dervishes in former times. Used here with such good effect by the itinerant dervish of the Ni'matullah order at Mahan (locally pronounced Mahun), it was also understood as a cultural symbol of the constellation Aries and a reminder of the renewal of all life each year at the spring equinox.

The exclamation *ya hu* ("Oh, He!") spoken so forcefully was the *zikr Allah* of the holy wanderer, his "remembrance of God." These short phrases were repeated constantly by the novice dervish as a spiritual exercise. They were intended to change his state of consciousness.

4.1 Yazd *Kashkul and Tabar* (c.1900, 4.92 x 3.47)

*At the center of this noble design are concealed representations of the **kashkul** and the **tabar**, the bowl for alms and the two-edged axe of the dervish.*

The endless repetition of the *zikr* enabled the dervish to enter a state of self-abandonment and forgetfulness of this world. In this mental state, there should be nothing present to the mind of the dervish except the remembrance of God.

Other commonly heard remembrances invoked the revered memories of the first three Imams, *ya Ali, ya Hassan, ya Hossein*. The remembrance *ya haqq* ("Oh, Truth!") pointed to the Real behind all appearances and to the truth of the revelation of Islam. The most common *zikr Allah* was the *ya hu* that Sykes heard pronounced with such heart-stopping fury. This *zikr* was often shortened to the one word *hu*, and sometimes even to the single letter *h* (pronounced *heh*). Going one step further, the members of some Sufi orders practiced what was called the silent *zikr*, performed with the breath alone.

All foreign travelers in Iran in the nineteenth century could have described similar observations and experiences, but by the 1930s these wandering dervishes were only rarely seen. The first dervish met and interviewed by the always observant Onera Merritt-Hawkes lived a quiet life with his books and flowers in a small shrine near Shiraz. He supported himself by accepting modest alms from any visitors who came to see him. In a poetic way, this solitary dervish explained to her the essence of his beliefs.

> "The past and present are one. Now is eternity, and death is but an incident in life. … A blade of wheat, a petal of a poppy, the love of men and women, all are part of God. The Moslem says that there is no god but God, but we say there is nothing but God."

Impressed by the atmosphere of peace in which he lived, the visitor described his calmness as a serenity which was not empty, but creative.

Later, in the less serene atmosphere of the Shiraz bazaar, Merritt-Hawkes reacted very differently to the loud undisciplined dervishes she encountered. She writes with uncharacteristic impatience and intolerance: "There I sympathized with the right of the police to cut their long hair, to make them give up their long coats, their little embroidered caps and the loose cloth that is twisted around the head and hangs down behind."

In the lively bazaar, the English visitor had a chance encounter with some of the few remaining representatives of the *qalandari*. These were the wandering dervishes who had shown their rejection of the ordinary world by their careless appearance and their objectionable behavior. They did not recognize the many boundaries and social restrictions that were accepted without question by all other members of the community. A common figure in the poetry of Hafez and Rumi, the *qalandar* or *rend* was the rogue or scoundrel who protested against the hypocrisy and corruption of the world by a rejection of ordinary standards.

These outspoken reprobates ridiculed the pretensions of the quieter Sufi ascetics and they mocked what they saw as the arrogant claim of these ascetics to a special possession of spiritual knowledge. The *qalandari* dervishes were often called *malamati*, the blameworthy. They were accused of selling their few possessions including even their prayer carpets to buy forbidden wine. The *malamati* justified their scandalous behavior by saying they preferred honest sinful behavior to concealed hypocrisy.

The outwardly blasphemous conduct of these unruly dervishes was believed by them to be in conformity with the inner meaning of the religious law. They pointed to the passage in the *Quran* where the Queen of Sheba tells King Solomon that kings destroy a city when they enter it. The incorrigible *malamati* were to be found in the *kharabat*, in empty deserts and ruined places. They were also found in wine taverns and in all places of ill repute. The *malamati* said they had been destroyed in the material world by allowing God to enter their inner beings. They accepted their ruinous fate without complaint, knowing that stones must first be crushed in a mortar in order to be transformed into healing medicines.

Their torn garments were symbols of their desire to escape from the veil and prison of the material world. The word es-cape is a reminder of this ancient and universal human desire. Its original meaning was to throw off a cloak. By their misconduct, the *qalandari* dervishes sought to throw off forever the deceptive cloak of this transitory world. They believed that only when everything had fallen into ruins would there be revealed the *ganj*, the hidden treasure and eternal values they were seeking.

These practices were imaginative metaphors for the experience of ecstasy, the state of mystical intoxication of the dervish on the spiritual journey to union with the One. In this poetic logic that purposefully defied the rigid rules of conventional behavior and ordinary logic, the *rend-i kharabat* or villain who lived in devastated places free of all attachments to the world came to represent the true lover and sage.

4.2 Qashqai *Lion of **Allah*** *(c.1950, 1.95 x 1.40)*

Small signs of life on the withered tree suggest rebirth and renewal. When seized by the divine vision, the traveler will die to this world and awaken to a new consciousness.

The dramatic design of the Qashqai carpet is a violent portrayal of the dervish in the state of forgetfulness and self-annihilation who has been seized by the divine vision. The lion of *Allah* is a common metaphorical description of Ali, the first Imam of

Shi'a Islam. Here the powerful lion of God has seized the innocent, defenseless lamb. The helpless creature has been caught in a moment of unawareness and self-forgetfulness.

The lion has carried the lamb some distance up the cosmic tree to reach the next stage of the spiritual journey. The withered tree in a featureless plain is a sign that the unsuspecting lamb, or the dervish that the lamb represents, has been wandering in a barren desert. The tree itself is another symbolic representation of the holy dervish. In a frequent poetic comparison, the impoverished dervish is *bi-bargi*, "without means," and the withered tree is *bi barg*, "without a leaf."

However, we also notice a very significant detail in the design; the apparently dead tree is beginning to bear leaves. According to a treasured *hadith*, a traditional saying attributed to the Prophet, we learn, "The faithful person engaged in *zikr Allah*, remembrance of God, is like a green tree in the midst of dried-up trees." In a familiar image of Sufi poetry, the tree sheds its leaves in the autumn, passing through material and spiritual poverty in order to emerge in full glory in the spring. The brilliant blood-red ground of the design is another bold representation of the new life of the dervish at the long-anticipated time of complete rebirth and renewal.

There is a memory of these dervishes and their beliefs to be found in many Persian carpet designs, meaningful references to their ancient way of life that have not been fully acknowledged. There are many designs that include unmistakable realistic images of the *kashkul*, the *taj*, the *tabar*, the ram's horn, or the sword of the dervish that recalls *Zulfiqar* (literally, "two-edged"), the famous sword of Ali. The animal skin of the dervish, the *pustin*, is also portrayed realistically in many carpets; for example, in the finely knotted small Isfahan rug illustrated (c.1970).

There are many more carpets whose design is based on the animal skin in less realistic and more stylized ways. Although rarely noticed, the animal skin may be considered to be the principal design element in many of these carpets. The carpet illustrated is dated to c.1870 and is believed to have been made in Ravar, an old carpet-making city north of Kerman. It has a central field in undyed grey wool that almost certainly represents a stretched animal skin. With this interpretation, the carpet design must then be seen as a symbolic reminder of the simple life of the dervishes and their all-consuming desire for self-annihilation and union with God.

The Ferdows carpet shown was made in the Khorasan oasis town formerly known as Tun. It was made c.1970, at the same time as the Isfahan rug and a full century later than the Ravar carpet. As seen in this example, there is one immediately recognizable feature of many Ferdows carpets of this period. They were knotted entirely with undyed wool in the natural shades of white, brown, grey and black. This was very often intended as a sign of a meaningful connection to Sufism, a slightly concealed reference to the undyed wool cloaks worn by the wandering dervishes. In this carpet, the central field in white wool reinforces this interpretation. It is a stylized but clear representation of a stretched lamb skin, a symbol which recalls the materially impoverished life of the dervish.

4.3 Isfahan ***Pustin*** *(c.1970, 1.67 x 1.10)*

The central image of the intricate pattern is an animal pelt or skin, the pustin that was one of the few possessions of the wandering dervishes.

4.4 Ravar *Animal Skin* *(c.1870, 2.09 x 1.32)*

The field in undyed grey wool is more than a neutral background for the elaborate medallion. It symbolizes the animal skin of the dervish and the practices of Sufism.

4.5 Ferdows *Lochak Toranj* (*c.1970, 3.06 x 2.00*)

Many modern Ferdows carpets were woven entirely with undyed wool. The conventional ***lochak toranj*** *or medallion and corners description of the design avoids possible spiritual meanings.*

As seen in the Ferdows carpet, very many carpets have the so-called *lochak toranj* design. This is the familiar "medallion and corner" design which is the most commonly recognized pattern of Persian carpets. Probably intentionally, the neutral medallion and corner description used in Iran conceals the original meanings of this well-known design which are derived from the ideals of Sufism. In the Iranian way, the common term for these designs avoids all potentially troubling questions of deeper motivations.

Very often, these patterns may be more meaningfully described as having animal skin designs in the central field. A significant aspect of the symbolic meaning of the *lochak toranj* design is the mental reversal of background and foreground that is required for the viewer to see the animal skin. With frequent repetition over several centuries, this source of the medallion and corner pattern in Islamic mysticism may have been forgotten by many and purposefully concealed by others. However, it seems apparent that this very common *lochak toranj* design was originally a visual expression of one of the core symbolic images of Sufism.

In its origins, the medallion and corner design was intended as a visualization of the animal skin in an idealized form. It was a representation of a primary visual symbol of the way of life of the wandering dervishes. When the animal skin as the representation of the dervish is acknowledged as the main design, the central medallion then acquires a profound spiritual significance as well. It may be seen as the heart of the Sufi mystic or the essence of his inner nature. On the arduous spiritual journey to union with the divine, the dervish has endlessly polished his inner essence until it becomes a flawless mirror capable of perfectly reflecting the One.

Following the logic of this interpretation, the central medallion in Persian carpet designs does have transcendent meanings. It becomes an indication of the mystical embodiment of the cosmic pattern by the spiritual traveler. The central medallion should be seen as an earthly reflection through the dervish of the divine unity. It is a symbolic representation and material vision of the divine pattern descended to earth. This interpretation accounts for the extremely elaborate medallions of many carpet patterns. In their intricate medallions, these carpet designs present sublime visions of the goal of the spiritual seeker which is a complete union with the One.

In many other carpets, the animal skin of the dervish is represented in less obvious forms, often as an element of the design. In his discussion of Qashqai weaving in *The Persian Carpet*, A.C.Edwards describes their designs as rectilinear, and he writes that this is a feature common to all tribal carpets. He draws special attention to two design elements that appear repeatedly in Qashqai weavings. He then makes a potentially significant observation: "The first is merely a geometrical figure. The second appears to be something more: the conventionalisation, perhaps, of a stretched lambskin, a turtle, a crab or a beetle."

This speculation is as far as Edwards takes the matter, and he then continues in a more characteristically cautious way. Immediately, he denies the possibility there could be any remaining symbolic meaning to the intriguing figure in Qashqai carpets resembling a stretched lambskin. In justification of this hasty opinion, he writes, "But its form has undergone a change through constant repetition; so that today even those who reproduce it constantly are unaware of its significance."

One of the illustrations in *The Persian Carpet* shows a Tabriz carpet dated c.1930 with a design that contains an unmistakable *kashkul* and an obvious dervish sword in the pattern. Ignoring these highly significant details, Edwards may have been unaware of their presence or their significance. More likely, he did notice them but he was unwilling to be drawn into what could have become a possibly controversial discussion of Sufism. Instead, he describes the carpet pattern unhelpfully as merely an ingenious design in which Persian and Chinese motives have been cleverly combined.

In another place in his book, Edwards repeats the conventional explanation of the origins of the medallion and corner design as having evolved from fifteenth-century designs for embossed leather covers for copies of the Quran. He was aware that others had made the same observation; for example, Pope in *A Survey of Persian Art*. However, neither Pope nor

Edwards go further to reveal the primary source of this design in the animal skin of the dervish. We should remember it was during the fifteenth and early sixteenth centuries that the images and concepts of the philosophy of Sufism exerted their most profound influence on the development of the many forms of Persian art.

It is difficult to summarize the ideas of Islamic mysticism since it is not a well-defined doctrine with explicit rules and rigidly fixed beliefs. It is more a way of spiritual seeking. The dervish living a tranquil life in the small shrine near Shiraz told Merritt-Hawkes that there is nothing but God. In the fewest words, he had expressed the essential idea of Sufism. In this metaphysical philosophy, everything in the world perceived by the physical senses is to be seen as an emanation from the One, the hidden source of all. The constant goal of the Sufi mystic was to go beyond himself to attain a complete union with the concealed source called the Real. Expressed differently, the spiritual traveler sought a total forgetfulness of self and a personal annihilation in God.

The word Sufi is commonly derived from the Arabic word *suf* meaning wool, an indication of the total simplicity that the dervish way of life required. The practice of Sufism is called *tasawwuf* which is most plausibly translated to mean originally "to wear a woolen cloak." As in the earlier Christian monastic tradition, the undyed grey or white wool cloaks worn by the wandering dervishes indicated both material poverty and spiritual wealth. Until recent times, these cloaks remained the principal visible sign of the ancient way of life of the itinerant dervishes.

In Sufism, the five external senses are believed to have their complements in five internal senses identified as common sense, imagination, intelligence, memory, and active imagination or intellect. Spiritual practices were concerned mainly with the development of the inner sight of these internal senses. External forms such as carpets were not to be ignored in their rituals. They were to be used by the followers of Sufism primarily as reminders of the true reality, the concealed reality which was to be found in the unseen world that can be apprehended only by the five inner senses. Every object perceived by the physical senses in the material world was considered to be a symbol that was to be conceived by the inner senses in its true nature.

The profound symbolism from Sufism that can be found in Persian carpet designs is not confined to the obvious visible signs of the dervish life; the *kashkul* and the *tabar*, the sword, the animal skin, the ram's horn, and the *taj*. Perhaps the most common and most easily recognized symbol of the philosophy of Sufism that occurs in carpet designs is the double square which is also called the eight-pointed star. This is the elementary pattern consisting of two interlocking squares.

The fundamental meaning of the double square is the interpenetration of matter and spirit, the primary duality that the Sufi mystic learns to see as a unity. In many traditional cultures, the square by itself is recognized as a basic symbol of human presence and identity. A central medallion with sixteen or thirty-two points is produced in a simple way by a repeated doubling of the double square. The limit of this process is the circle, the universal symbol of the wholeness and perfection of the divine unity.

4.6 Kerman *Qurani Design* (c.1960, 3.95 x 3.15)

The familiar design had originally a religious significance. It derives from decorated covers in leather, wood and metal made in Timurid and Safavid court workshops for copies of the Quran.

The dual nature of existence is frequently seen represented in carpet designs. It is expressed again by another very common symbol of the dervish. Like the *tabar*, the sword of the dervish cuts through the duality of matter and spirit. The sword of the holy wanderer is a reminder of *Zulfiqar*, the famous double-edged sword of Ali who was the first convert to Islam and the first Imam of Shi'a Islam. The balance or left-right symmetry of the designs of prayer carpets is another symbolic expression of this fundamental duality of the seen and unseen, of substance and essence. This is also true of very many patterns such as the double square formed in some way by doubling or reflection from simpler patterns.

Chehel sutun or "forty columns" is the common name for a famous building in Isfahan that was built in the royal enclosure for Shah Abbas in the late sixteenth century. Its open *eyvan* or reviewing platform has only twenty columns that are visible to the eye, unless we follow an old custom and also count their reflections in a water-filled pool in front of the building.

In *The Persian Carpet*, A.C.Edwards retells this common observation. Once again, he shows the less imaginative side of his character by calling this traditional method of counting the forty columns a fanciful explanation. Consistent with his usual preference for more prosaic understandings, he writes, "The probable explanation of the discrepancy is that there were twenty pillars on the west side of the building which was destroyed by fire during the reign of the last Sefavi king, Shah Sultan Hosain."

By a long-established tradition, *chehel* or forty has been conventionally used in Iran to represent any large but indefinite number. Edwards must have known something that almost every child knows. In the famous children's story, Ali Baba is said to have encountered forty thieves. Edwards would have known that *chehel minar* or "forty pillars" is a very old term used to describe the ruins of Persepolis. In *The Wild Rue*, Bess Allen Donaldson records the common oath "by the forty lamps of Imam Reza." In a predictably literal way, she relates the popular oath to a huge candelabra that could be seen in the holy shrine in Meshed dedicated to the eighth Imam.

It may be that the number forty used in these ways had originally a more subtle significance. Forty is a doubling of the number twenty which, like the square, is an ancient primary symbol of human identity. For this elementary reason, twenty was used as the base of some early counting systems. Despite the conventional explanation, forty is not only an indefinite large number commonly heard in Iranian colloquial speech. From what Edwards would have called a more imaginative or even fanciful viewpoint, it becomes a symbol with an interpretation that is comparable to the primary meaning of the double square.

In an Islamic culture deeply interested in number symbolism, it is not likely that the number forty was chosen arbitrarily. It represents a completeness or completion by doubling, and it serves as another concealed reminder of our dual human nature and of all dualities. Seeing an object and its mirror image as in the *chehel sutun* in Isfahan, seeing the double square or any pattern formed by reflection or doubling, the mind should be led to ask the great question. What is the true nature of reality? Between the material object and its reflection, between the substance and the essence, which is real? The symbolism of the number forty suggests the unity of matter and essence is the true reality.

4.7 Kashan *Double Square* *(c.1960, 4.07 x 3.16)*

This tile design focuses on the double square, the primary symbol of the duality of matter and essence that we learn to see as a unity.

The Sabzavar carpet made c.1970 by the Iran Carpet Company is a creative version of a garden design that is seen in some classic Safavid-era carpets. The ancient city Sabzavar in Khorasan province is located on the main pilgrimage route from western Iran to Meshed. In all probability, this unique design was developed at the Tehran College of Art. It combines numerous elements from the philosophy of Sufism in an original way. In both obvious and disguised forms, the double square symbol is a prominent design element in the border and also in the field.

The border design draws insistent attention to the theme of repeated expansion and contraction. This is a reference in Sufism to breathing, the most fundamental process of life. As a spiritual exercise, the cycle of inspiration and expiration in breathing is experienced as a model for a continual mental expansion and contraction. It may also be a subtle reference to *ya hu*, the most common *zikr* that requires both inspiration and expiration. The border design acts in an elementary but forceful way to establish a breath-based rhythm which subtly influences our subsequent perceptions

Instead of a more conventional medallion, the center of the Sabzavar carpet depicts a *hoz mahi*, a pool of water containing fish. This is an essential feature of the ideal garden in Iranian culture. In the four directions from the center, there are stylized animal skins in undyed wool which are conceived in the shape of an elongated double square. The realistically drawn fish and crabs in the *hoz* are a discordant element in the design until we interpret them as subtle reminders of another level of existence. To the receptive mind, they may suggest the primary theme in Islamic mysticism of the invisible being made visible.

When it is very still, the pool of water at the center of an Iranian garden functions as a mirror that reflects the sky. This is intended to recall the unending effort of the Sufi mystic to make his heart like a polished mirror. His heart, the primary symbol of his inner nature, will then reflect only the beauty and truth of the One. The smaller pools of water in the centers of two of the four stylized animal skins reinforce this primary meaning. We recognize that these pools of water and the central *hoz mahi* are all drawn to suggest elongated double squares, the most widespread symbol of the philosophy of Sufism.

Among the many puzzling elements of the field design are the numerous vases drawn in what appears to be the Khotan style of eastern Turkestan. The vase is a common design element in Iranian art that has numerous symbolic meanings in Sufism. Like any external form, the vase serves as a container or *zaher*. What it contains metaphorically is the interior meaning, the true significance or *baten*. The emptiness of the vase is its primary symbolic meaning. It is intended to recall the constant goal of the dervish to achieve a state of emptiness or self-annihilation, completely liberated from the distractions and snares of the material world. From that receptive emptiness, the most beautiful flowers may grow. In that creative emptiness, we may rediscover our origin in the divine.

Another less well known interpretation makes a profound connection between the vase form and the *zikr Allah* of the dervish. As the wind blows gently across the mouth of the empty vase or as we breathe across it, the deep resonant sound *hu, hu, hu* is heard repeatedly, at least in the imagination or by the inner senses. This constantly repeated sound is heard in Sufi mysticism as a *zikr Allah*, a remembrance of God.

4.8 Sabzavar *Hoz Mahi* *(c.1970, 4.20 x 3.02)*

*The medallion is a **hoz mahi**, the fish pool of Iranian gardens. In the dark stillness of night, the motionless pool reflects the sky and brings the cosmic pattern to earth.*

4.9 Isfahan *Tile Design* *(c.1900, 2.77 x 1.47)*
Every repeated tile pattern may be infinitely extended. By finite means, they allow viewers to contemplate the unbounded.

The Isfahan carpet illustrated made c.1900 seems at first glance to have a pleasing repetitive design with relatively few colors. The most basic observation of the predominance of red and blue suggests, perhaps first at the subconscious level, an oscillation between earth and heaven. This primary theme, the duality of matter and spirit, is already suggested by the repeated alternation of red and blue in the narrow border.

The central field is a subtle example of a tile design, a regular interlocking pattern that fills the field. Since it can be mentally extended indefinitely in all directions, such a tile design may always be seen as a representation of the infinite by finite means. The necessary key to the interpretation of the carpet pattern emerges from a focused concentration on the repeated elements of the field design.

We recognize that the design of the field of this Isfahan carpet combines two of the prime symbols of Sufism and the way of life of the dervish. These two elements are the animal skin and the double square, combined here in a deeply meaningful way. In the Sabzavar carpet, the animal skin is drawn in the stylized form of an elongated double square. In the Isfahan carpet, the field design is made up entirely of subtly drawn animal skins colored in red. In the center of each one, we find the double square in the color blue. If we need to be reminded, this blue is a reflection of the sky or heaven in the polished mirror that is the symbol of the inner essence of the dervish.

We notice the double squares are drawn in a way which suggests to the receptive mind that they are about to double again. This dynamic image does have a precise symbolic interpretation in Sufism. Represented by the animal skin, the dervish has taken into himself or has learned to reflect all of nature. This reflection or personal embodiment of the cosmic pattern is the transcendent goal of the wandering dervish. It is symbolically expressed here by the double square representing a unified vision of the duality of matter and spirit.

One of the most familiar design elements seen in Iranian textile patterns is the *boteh*. This is literally the desert thorn bush burned in the celebration of *Chahar Shanbeh Suri*, the Feast of Wednesday which marks the end of the old year and the beginning of *Nouruz*. This association gives the *boteh* design some profound imaginative connections with the Iranian ideal of personal and community renewal at the spring equinox. It makes some significant historical connections with the ancient Zoroastrian reverence of fire and its transforming properties. And there may be some other compelling reasons why this simple and very recognizable image occurs in so many forms in every variety of Iranian visual art.

After many centuries, the *boteh* design has developed a great variety of connotations and symbolic meanings in Iranian culture. Merritt-Hawkes gives a vivid description of the source of one of these familiar interpretations.

> The grey-backed crow is everywhere, making its ugly noises, but I always liked to see them sit on the top of the cypresses until they bend over, looking like the designs on Paisley shawls. There are folks who say that the design is a folded hand, but watch a garden with cypresses and crows and you'll know.

Despite this impressive visual evidence, her preferred explanation does not seem to be completely convincing. We should be aware that the crow like the owl is almost always considered to be a bird of bad omen. In Iranian folk beliefs, the crow is most often seen as an unwelcome messenger who brings bad news.

However, the image of the cypress tree which is bent by the wind does have other culturally significant symbolic interpretations. Like the ideal man, the erect cypress tree joins heaven and earth, constantly pointing toward the One. When it is bent over by the unseen wind, this is most commonly understood as a symbol of submission. It is then seen as a reminder of the obligation of prayer in Islam, a word originally meaning submission. In Byzantine Christian art, there are some very similar earlier images showing cypress trees bent in homage or submission to the cross.

4.10 Sarouk
Boteh *Design*
(c.1970, 2.02 x 1.31)

*The **boteh** pattern has the same form as the **kashkul**. Both may be imagined as visible containers of an invisible essence. Their shapes express the possible unity of outer form and inner meaning.*

The elegant design of the Sarouk rug was very probably intended as a meditation on the spiritual significance of the *boteh* pattern. Among the smaller *botehs* in this original design, our attention is forcefully drawn to the very large single *boteh* that completely dominates the field. The shape of this elaborate *boteh* suggests clearly the characteristic rounded form and small opening of the *kashkul*, the begging bowl which was a primary sign of the materially impoverished way of life chosen by the holy wanderers. This spiritual interpretation is reinforced by the presence in a highly stylized form of the head of a *tabar*, the two-edged axe of the dervish.

A significant feature of the unusual design of the Sarouk rug is the presence of one of the most meaningful Zoroastrian symbols. The narrow openings of the *boteh* and the *kashkul* have a natural symbolic meaning as the point of intersection of outer and inner experience. At the opening in this remarkable design, there is a well-drawn representation of a fantastic bird which may be identified to be the mythical *Simorgh*. As recorded in various episodes of the *Shahnameh* of Ferdowsi, this mystical bird was viewed in ancient Iran as a national symbol of protection and a sign of divine grace.

In Sufi poetry, the meanings of the Zoroastrian image of the rarely seen *Simorgh* evolved to become primarily a mysterious symbol of the elusive divine essence. It became a frequent poetic image of an unearthly being located somewhere outside and above the created order. In this suggestive design, the *Simorgh* or the divine essence that it may represent both shelters in and protects the narrow opening to the *kashkul*.

At a very fundamental level, the characteristic folded shape of the *boteh* suggests both *zaher* and *baten*, container and contained, to the receptive mind. Its form alone should recall for the spiritual traveler the possible unity of outer and inner experience. In the visual art inspired by Sufism, this form is often intended as a constantly repeated visual reminder that every external object may enclose an inner essence. Every *boteh* in a repeated design may be experienced as a repetition of a *zikr Allah*, a reminder of the divine unity behind all appearances.

Reinforcing this mystical interpretation, the folded shape of the *boteh* may be viewed as a dynamic image. Seen in this way, its shape seems about to create an enclosure. In this interpretation, the *boteh* is about to enclose (*bastan*) a protected area that is considered sacred (*bast*). The folded hand interpretation rejected so hastily by Merritt-Hawkes may have some value. Like a folding hand or like the human mind, like the dervish on the mystical path, the *boteh* shape visibly strives to grasp emptiness or essence.

4.11 Semnan *Forty-four Tiles* (*c.1920, 2.68 x 1.39*)

Bounding chains surround and protect forty-four animal skins. That mystical number and the eight-petaled flowers recall the double square. The enclosed ***botehs*** *represent the divine essence.*

This compelling image forcefully drives the receptive viewer to reach a spiritual understanding. In the unsuspecting mind, the *boteh* form spontaneously creates an imagined movement between active and passive, between container and contained, between external and internal, between motion and rest. When we contemplate the *boteh* form in a spiritual way, we are striving to unite these primary dualities. We are contemplating an image that brings these dualities and all others to a unity.

There is another spiritual interpretation of the *boteh* design as it appears in some carpet designs that also connects the form intimately to the philosophy of Sufism. The brief phrase *ya hu* was the most common *zikr Allah* repeated endlessly by the dervish. It was frequently abbreviated to a repetition of the letter *h*, the final letter of *Allah*. In *Mystical Dimensions of Islam* (1975), Annemarie Schimmel explains the deep symbolic significance that was attributed to this letter in Sufi mysticism.

> The divine essence itself is called *hahut* (derived from the *h*, the letter of the essence), and [the thirteenth-century Sufi philosopher] Ibn Arabi is said to have experienced the vision of the divine essence in the shape of the word *hu*, "He," luminous between the arms of the letter *h*.

The *hahut* is sometimes referred to as the "chapter of *h*," the sublime description of the divine essence as it is revealed to the spiritually aware through the letter *h*.

Spoken repeatedly with an outward breath as a remembrance of God, the letter *h* alone will produce a state of breathlessness. This is to be understood as the physical form and the symbol of the emptiness the dervish seeks on the soul journey in preparation to receive the divine. In Sufi mysticism, it is this receptive emptiness of the spiritual traveler that is the primary symbolic significance of the vase form and the *kashkul*.

In the Arabic script used for the Persian language, the usual form of the letter *h* written alone resembles the *boteh* design. Written in this way, it also resembles unmistakably a carpet knot. The logic of this image leads to the interpretation of the making of a Persian carpet as the repetition many times of a *zikr Allah*, each knot corresponding to a "writing" of the letter *h*. Constantly repeated by the weavers, these "letters" inseparably join the weft threads and the warp threads. They join horizontal and vertical, another duality that may be seen as representing the duality of matter and spirit. The carpet knots are formed between the horizontal weft threads, and they surround the vertical warp threads.

In a common image of Persian poetry, the hidden warp and weft threads of a carpet may sometimes be seen as an image of the concealed source or the divine essence. The thousands of warp threads are a multiplicity that is brought to a unity by the *zikr*, the numberless silent repetitions of the letter *h* that create the carpet. Like the dervish endlessly repeating his *zikr Allah*, each warp thread is caught repeatedly between the arms of the letter *h*.

The Isfahan carpet illustrated made c.1930 has at least one very unusual feature that seems to reinforce this interpretation of the tying of a carpet knot as a *zikr*. In the four corners of the design, stylized animal skins are represented in undyed grey wool. By now, we recognize this as an important clue, a likely indication of a significant connection to Sufism. There is another very unusual feature of the pattern that is easy to overlook. It is the presence of realistically drawn carpet knots in the four corners of the field design. For some reason, the four knots shown incongrously in the pattern are drawn to resemble the letter *h*.

This inconspicuous design element in the Isfahan carpet brings our attention to the concealed symbolic meaning of the repetitive motions involved in the knotting of any Persian

4.12 Isfahan *Carpet Knots* *(c.1930, 2.17 x 1.40)*

The unusual knots depicted in the four corners of the field may have been intended as reminders of the carpet's unseen structure.

carpet. In an obvious material way, the many knots that make the carpet do create finally a visible physical unity. This very ordinary activity repeated countless times in the making of a carpet may acquire a corresponding mystical significance. For the followers of the ideals of Sufism, any repetitive activity that frees the mind from distractions may function as a *zikr Allah*. It may inspire the forgetfulness of self that enables the spiritual seeker to enter a state of ecstasy and achieve union with the One.

Both materially and spiritually, the making of the carpet may lead in this way to a unifying vision. For those who have remained open to spiritual understandings, the making of a Persian carpet is an activity that creates a unity of matter and spirit. With this interpretation, the completed carpet then becomes the visible symbol of that unity. The design of the Isfahan carpet reinforces this fundamental understanding. The tying of each knot of the carpet is a constantly repeated activity that functions ideally as the repetition of a *zikr Allah*. When accompanied by an abandonment of self, the act of tying each knot becomes a remembrance of God.

The profound human concerns and motivations that found an expression in the poetry, visual art and philosophy of Sufism were certainly not unique to the Islamic world. They are universal preoccupations that have inspired different creative expressions in other religions and cultures. In the personal life of William Butler Yeats and in his literary career, many close parallels can be found to these primary concerns. These suggestive parallels may help us to gain a wider perspective on the ideals expressed by the followers of Islamic mysticism.

In his play *The King's Threshold* first performed in Dublin in 1904, Yeats deals with some of these fundamental human concerns in ways remarkably similar to those of Sufism. The verse play is set in pre-Christian Celtic Ireland of the seventh century. The central character is the disaffected chief court poet Seanchan (pronounced Shanahan) who has resolved to remain defiantly at the king's threshold. He is determined to fast until death to protest his recent exclusion by the king from the council of the state.

The king calmly explains his decision to Seanchan. He says that he had listened to the advice of the other members of his council, the bishops, soldiers, and makers of the law. They had long thought it "against their dignity for a mere man of words to sit amongst them … and share in their authority." Initially, the king is confident the former court poet will be able to overcome his disappointment and even admit the reasonableness of the decision to exclude him from the affairs of the nation.

In reply, Seanchan insists the poets have always had the right to sit at the king's table. It was an ancient right that dated from the establishment of the world. Now, he is determined to exercise another well-recognized privilege in the ancient Celtic world, the right to starve himself to death on the threshold of the person who had wronged him. The king protests that Seanchan's death in this way would bring him lasting shame. Asking for understanding, he explains again to the former court poet that he cannot change his decision. His rule would be in question if he gave way.

Despite all entreaties from the king, Seanchan's resolve does not weaken. Unwilling to compromise on his fundamental right to sit at the king's table, he replies, "When did the poets promise safety, King?" At the core of his being, Seanchan knows that poetry must serve deeper and more lasting human purposes than the temporary preservation of the king's rule. Before he dies, the poet has a final thought that helps to reconcile him to his fate: "The man that dies has the chief part of the story."

From his early studies of Celtic sources and Irish folk traditions, Yeats sought to create a national literature which both noble and beggar man would share. In his words, he envisioned a universally shared literary and visual culture that would unite market cart and sky. By whatever chain of transmission, there seems to be a common origin to the ancient themes he explored in *The King's Threshold* and the dual roles of king and dervish in the long history of Iranian culture.

In the fifteenth century, the brutal Moghul conquerer Timur expressed his understanding of this primary duality in some very meaningful ways. Despite the unparalleled magnificence of his court and the unprecedented scale of his ambition, he decided he would be buried very humbly at the feet of the Sufi shaykh who had been his close companion and spiritual adviser for many years.

During his rule, Timur had sent the Sufi leader Shah Ni'matullah and his numerous followers away from his capital Samarqand to extensive lands he granted near the remote town Mahan in Kerman province. He was certainly motivated by the practical difficulties and possible dangers of controlling the many thousands who were devoted to the holy man and his teachings. However, Timur justified this decision in a more acceptable way by saying that two kings could not exist at the same time in one city.

Shah Ismail, the founder of the Safavid dynasty (1501-1722) in the early sixteenth century, recognized this cultural duality of king and dervish in a different way. He said that the famous painter Bihzad was half his kingdom. Bihzad was the eminent Sufi leader and artist from the Timurid city of Herat. He was renowned for his miniature paintings which were often inspired by the visual imagery of Sufism. Shah Ismail appointed Bihzad as the head of the new *kitabkhana* in Tabriz, the first Safavid capital. The *kitabkhana* was the important cultural institution that combined the royal library and the workshops for all artists and artisans connected with the court.

The Safavid kings were descended from Shaykh Safi al-Din, a prominent fourteenth century Shi'ite and Sufi religious leader in the Azerbaijan region. As a symbol of their dynasty and their inheritance from Shaykh Safi of a religious authority to rule, they made a significant use of the familiar *boteh* form. Prominently displayed on their tall ceremonial turbans, they wore a jeweled aigrette made in the *boteh* shape. This beautiful *boteh* was originally intended by the Safavid kings as a primary sign of the dual nature of their sovereignty. It gave a visible expression to one of the principal ideals of Shi'a Islam and Sufism. This key symbol of Safavid rule communicated the fundamental unity of the seemingly different roles of the king and the religious leader.

The large Tabriz carpet displays many of the symbols of the way of life of the wandering dervishes that was rapidly passing into memory. Very prominent in the design are realistic depictions of the *kashkul* and the *tabar*. The many empty vases are indications that the dervish has become empty in preparation to receive God. In two places, there are representations of the *taj*, the dervish cap or crown, paired with the royal crown drawn in the style of the Qajar monarchy. Significantly, the symbol that identifies the dervish is closer to the center of this design, above the symbol that represents the king. In a profound imaginative reversal, it is the king who stands at the threshold in this majestic pattern.

The sublime gold-colored field of this carpet is a transcendent representation of the animal skin, the royal domain of the dervish that is only large enough to cover all of his few possessions. In this design, the golden field is a symbolic representation of the state of mind of the spiritual seeker who has been completely transformed by a final alchemy of the human spirit and the divine grace. The dervish has reached the goal of the mystical journey; he has become an embodiment of spiritual wisdom. He sees beyond the changeable appearances of material form. The enlightened dervish sees only the pure eternal light of the divine essence.

In all its forms, this duality of the king and the dervish is universally comprehensible since it presents a theory of mind and its levels of consciousness. Neither king nor dervish can be excluded from a full understanding. The acceptance of their complementary roles in Iranian spiritual culture reflects a profound recognition of the requirement for a mental balance of the practical and the imaginative, of matter and spirit, of earth and heaven, of outer and inner meaning, of form and content, of cosmos and psyche.

The king's vision is reality, while the dervish sees only the Real. The cultural acknowledgement of their common enterprise is a symbol of the reconciliation of their competing visions and of all dualities. In their ideal forms, one cannot exist without the other. The Persian carpet is the meeting place of king and dervish. It is the place where they recognize they share a greater common vision. The poet, the dervish, and the imagination have always had the right to cross all thresholds, even the thresholds of the king's palace and of the mind. The Persian carpet is a way that Sufi philosophy has found to exercise this ancient right.

4.13 Tabriz *King and Dervish* *(c.1920, 4.86 x 2.98)*

Eslimi *spirals recall the turning dance and the many* ***kashkuls*** *and containers enclose an inner essence. The crown and* ***taj*** *reveal that king and dervish share a common vision at the divine threshold.*

5 The Golden Door

By common agreement, the most famous Persian carpet in the world is the Ardebil carpet exported from Iran to England by the Ziegler Company in 1891. As a result of a public subscription campaign supported by William Morris, it was acquired two years later by the South Kensington Museum (now the Victoria and Albert Museum) in London where it may be seen on permanent display. An acknowledged masterpiece of the Safavid period, this very large carpet was originally made for the shrine of Shaykh Safi al-Din in Ardebil, an ancient city near the Caspian Sea in a mountainous region of the province of Azerbaijan.

Shaykh Safi (d.1334) was the leader of an important Sufi order who won converts to Shi'a Islam among the Turkish tribes of the region in the fourteenth century. His descendant Ismail gained power initially in Azerbaijan, and then he extended his rule throughout Iran beginning in 1501. To help unify the country under his leadership, Shah Ismail forcefully established the beliefs of his followers as the national religion of Iran. In this period, the shrine of the famous ancestor who had given his name to the Safavid dynasty became increasingly important as a religious and pilgrimage center.

Originally one of a pair, the Ardebil carpet was completed in 1540 during the reign of Shah Tahmasp, the son and successor of Shah Ismail. A lengthy inscription gives some valuable information about the making of the carpet, and it also raises some puzzling questions.

> I have no refuge in the world other than thy threshold.
> There is no place of protection for my head other than this porchway.
> The work of a slave of the Holy Place, Maqsud of Kashan in the year 942.

This is the poetic translation of the inscription that appeared in many contemporary publications at the time the purchase was being completed by the museum.

The work of a slave of the Holy Place, *amal-i bandah-i dargah*, may be translated less romantically but possibly more accurately as the work of a servant of the court. The porchway, the place of protection for the head of Maqsud of Kashan, is the *dargah*. This word may be translated, very literally, as "the place of the door." This should be understood as the king's door or threshold, but the usual meaning is the royal court. The year of completion recorded in the inscription, 942 according to the Islamic calendar, is now considered to be a misreading for 946 or 1540.

Both the religious and secular meanings of the word *dargah* may have been equally intended in the unusual inscription on the Ardebil carpet. Because of their inheritance from Shaykh Safi of a religious authority, the Safavid Shahs combined in their persons the two roles of secular rulers and spiritual leaders. The famous carpet design inseparably weaves together contemporary aesthetic, religious and political motivations. Perhaps most significantly in the social contexts of 1540, the Shaykh Safi design displays in a barely concealed way the dual roles of king and religious leader claimed by Ismail, Tahmasp and their successors as the foundation of their authority.

Briefly described, the field design of the Ardebil carpet represents the interior of a mosque. It depicts two large lamps suspended from a great central medallion representing the majestic dome of the mosque. The design has been interpreted as an earthly vision of

5.1 Tabriz *Shaykh Safi Design* *(c.1930, 5.76 x 3.96)*

The famous carpet from the Shaykh Safi shrine in Ardebil has been copied countless times since the 1890s. This reasonably accurate version is one third the size of the sixteenth-century original.

the symbolic marriage of the sun and the moon. The two lamps are united in the complex medallion from which they hang. The many small flowers in the field design are set against a deep blue field suggesting the countless stars in the cosmic pattern of the night sky.

This compelling image has been interpreted as a metaphorical portrayal of the union of all masculine and feminine qualities in the divine essence. The mystical union of male and female, active and passive, and of every duality in the One is the great theme of the philosophy and religious vision of Sufism. The goal of the holy wanderer on the spiritual journey is to experience an all-embracing vision of this divine unity. This sublime destination is the transcendent theme represented in the Ardebil carpet and in the poetry and visual art inspired by Islamic mysticism. Through overcoming the many challenges of his role in supervising all aspects of the making of this carpet, the master weaver Maqsud of Kashan may have found a dual place of protection at the royal and divine thresholds.

The complex historical circumstances and the methods of working that gave rise to the Ardebil carpet and many other Safavid masterpieces require some close examination. The art historians T.W.Lentz and G.D.Lowry have analyzed the many contributing factors in their wide-ranging survey *Timur and the Princely Vision: Persian Art and Culture in the Fifteenth Century* (1989). Their research traces in considerable detail the foundations of Safavid art which they attribute mainly to the cultural achievements of the Moghul ruler Timur (d.1405) and his immediate successors in the fifteenth century. These major achievements in artistic expression became possible as a result of Timur's extensive conquests and his ruthless accumulation of almost boundless wealth.

By compulsion or voluntarily, many leading artists and craftsmen moved to Timur's magnificent court at Samarqand beginning in the last decades of the fourteenth century to find employment for their skills. Drawing on many sources, they helped to develop a sophisticated visual language that celebrated the public values of the new elite. Their major works certainly expressed the profound religious ideals of Islam, but they were also intended at the same time to give a permanent expression to a highly idealized vision of the power and grandeur of the Timurid rulers.

Lentz and Lowry describe the adoption of older Persian literary and artistic traditions by Timur and his successors. This came about mainly through the institution of the *kitabkhana*, the royal library and workshops (literally, "house of the book"). They consider the establishment of this central institution as the single most significant step in the cultural development and social legitimation of the Timurid dynasty in the fifteenth century. The *kitabkhana* served several important cultural purposes. It was mandated to collect and preserve what remained of the written and visual records of the past. The many artists and skilled artisans of the royal workshops worked in close proximity to each other, and they collaborated extensively on major projects.

Coming from different regions of the newly established empire, these artists and artisans developed a remarkably uniform artistic vision in all known forms of literary and visual art. Their principal goal was to express in different material forms this unified religious vision which was derived from Islam and the metaphysical philosophy of Sufism. Working separately and together, they achieved a technical mastery and aesthetic refinement in many areas of artistic expression that had never before been seen.

The *kitabkhana* system of the Timurid courts in Samarqand and Herat was later to be adopted by Shah Ismail in his capital city Tabriz after he had consolidated his rule. It was further developed there and in the new capital Qazvin by Ismail's successor Shah Tahmasp. It was this complex combination of factors at the *dargah* or royal court of the young dynasty that resulted in the design and making of the monumental Ardebil carpet and the many other supreme artistic achievements of the early Safavid period.

The profound ideals of Sufism and Shi'a Islam do not require masterpieces on the scale of the Ardebil carpet for their full expression. The Tabriz carpet illustrated made centuries later is believed to be an imaginative depiction of the holy shrine of Shaykh Safi in Ardebil. As an image of the final destination of the Shi'a pilgrim, this carpet undoubtedly expressed the most deeply felt personal meanings to the designer and the weaver, and later to its owner.

The pool of water in front of the shrine is always seen in Islam as a religious symbol of the spiritual purification needed before entering the holy place. When the water is perfectly still, the pool becomes a mirror that will reflect both the shrine and the sky without any distortion. The ever-flowing fountain in the pool is another constant reminder to the pilgrim of the essential spiritual message: there is a hidden source concealed behind all appearances. The two streams of water that mysteriously flow from the pool are growing larger as they leave the shrine. In this carpet design, these small streams from the sacred source seem to be sufficient to make the desert bloom.

The tents of the pilgrims in this Tabriz carpet are erected in front of the shrine, a place of perfect safety after the physical and spiritual perils of the journey. Beyond the shrine, the distant horizon line and the sky represent the boundaries of experience and perception. The horizon is seen symbolically as another divine refuge, doubling the message of the protected sanctuary that is to be found at the holy shrine. The ruins seen in the four corners are the most puzzling features of the design. They may be interpreted as images of the *kharabat*, the devastated places where the dervish on the spiritual journey knows the greatest treasures may be found.

Pilgrimages were often undertaken at times of personal and social difficulties in order to seek the healing interventions of the holy persons of Shi'a Islam. Following an old custom, this carpet may have been made as the permanent personal record or memorial of such a pilgrimage. We may imagine that each time the Tabriz carpet was viewed by its owner became the occasion of another pilgrimage. The carpet would have inspired in its viewers a new spiritual journey in the imagination.

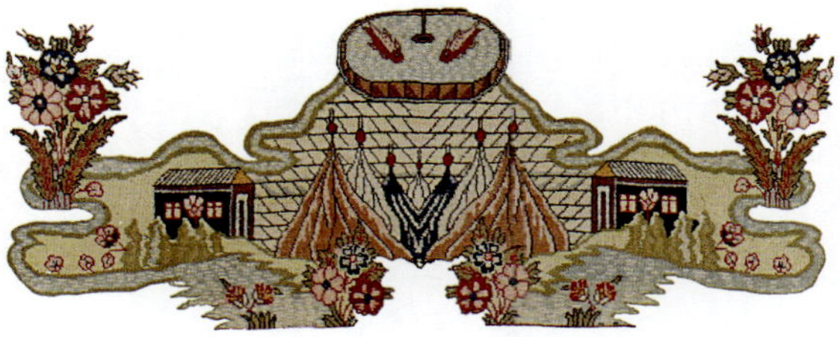

The second Tabriz pictorial carpet presents one of the central images used to communicate the ideals of Sufism. The story of Joseph and Zolaikha is referred to briefly in the Bible and told more fully in *Yusuf*, the twelfth *sura* of the *Quran.* It was later elaborated by many Iranian poets and storytellers, culminating in the very imaginative mystical version of Abdul-Rahman Jami written in the late fifteenth century. The most prominent poet and philosopher of his time, Jami was the renowned head of an important Sufi order. He was also the principal figure in the *kitabkhana* of the royal court of Herat which had by then succeeded Samarqand as the major center of Timurid culture.

In the well-known story, some traveling merchants rescued Joseph from the deep well where his envious brothers had cruelly abandoned him to die. The *Quran* records that the misfortunes of the young man did not cease after his miraculous rescue. When he was restored to health, the merchants who had found Joseph then sold their prize into slavery in Egypt for a few pieces of silver.

The dramatic scene depicted in the Tabriz carpet shows Zolaikha, the wife of his new master Potiphar, at the crucial moment when she first becomes overwhelmed by the beauty of Joseph. In an almost didactic way, the carpet design portrays the five physical senses of taste, touch, smell, hearing and sight that form the boundaries of Zolaikha's world. As

5.2 Tabriz *Pilgrimage Carpet* *(c.1920, 2.95 x 1.96)*

Light cascades down the multi-colored tiles of the façade to the threshold. The awestruck pilgrims approaching the shrine are given an intimation of the divine light.

5.3 Tabriz *Joseph and Zoleikha* *(c.1920, 1.52 x 2.10)*

Zoleikha is imprisoned in the transient world experienced by the outer senses. With Joseph as guide, she will discover the inner senses and divine illumination needed to perceive the eternal.

he plays the lyre, the steady gaze of Joseph looks far beyond these limits. His unwavering gaze is directed away from the many beauties of the transient material world that may be perceived by the physical senses.

In this thoughtful design, Joseph looks instead to the sky where he sees only the beauties and hears the harmonies of an eternal world. Striving to ignore Zolaikha's infatuation and all earthly temptations, he looks toward the divine realm that can be perceived by the mind and the inner senses. Confined to the dark world experienced through her physical senses, Zolaikha does not realize that the visible beauty of Joseph is only a pale reflection of the celestial beauty. Acting as a spiritual guide, Joseph will eventually lead Zolaikha to this deeper understanding.

The Greek temple seen in the distance is a very suggestive element of the design. It may serve the viewer of this carpet as a visual reminder of the profound influence Platonic and neo-Platonic philosophy has had on the development of Islamic mysticism. Another more mysterious element that invites speculation and interpretation is the prominently displayed symbol of Sufism in the design, the impressive lion skin rug that lies at Zolaikha's feet.

The influence of Greek philosophy on Sufism and Islamic traditions has been continuous, profound and controversial since the earliest days in the ninth and tenth centuries. Pythagoras, Plato, Socrates and Aristotle were commonly cited in Sufi poetry and prose, not always with great scholarly accuracy. Much of the influence of their ideas on the philosophy of Sufism is known to have come through the works of Plotinus, the third-century neo-Platonist who lived and taught in Alexandria and later in Rome.

After his death in 270, the life's work of Plotinus was compiled in *The Enneads,* mainly by his student and follower Porphyry. Centuries later, this major work in six volumes was to become the most thorough source of Greek metaphysical philosophy that was widely available in the Islamic world.

During the initial development of the beliefs and practices of Sufism, the single most widely-read text on Greek philosophy was a small work misleadingly titled *The Theology of Aristotle.* This treatise had become known to Islamic scholars in an Arabic translation as early as 840. Commonly called the bedside book of the Sufis, this very influential work was a summary of the philosophy of Plotinus that had been written by Porphyry as an introduction to *The Enneads.*

An account of the experience of religious ecstasy that was quoted very frequently by the philosophers of Sufism provides another significant example of the often unacknowledged influence of Plotinus on Islamic mysticism. Most commonly attributed by these authors to Plato, this sublimely poetic description of the state of spiritual ecstasy also derives directly from *The Enneads*. These well-known examples illustrate the general pattern. To a great extent, knowledge of the ideas of *Aflatun, Aristou* and *Sohrat* (Plato, Aristotle and Socrates) entered Islamic philosophy and culture initially through the neo-Platonic philosophy of *Lohman* (Plotinus).

The Enneads may be described as the supreme guidebook for those on the spiritual journey. Like Joseph as shown in the Tabriz carpet, Plotinus encourages the seeker to look constantly toward the true home of man which may be found far above the cloud and fog of earth. In his philosophy, this celestial home is our true native land to which we can return if we are inspired and guided by love.

> But how is the ascent to be begun? Whence comes the power? In what thought is this love to find its guide? The guiding thought is this: that the beauty perceived on material things is borrowed.

Plotinus gave a famous command to those who were beginning the soul journey: "Cut away everything!" What must be cut away is all the multiplicity of the external world. Only then, when all distractions are abandoned, will the spiritual seeker be able to rediscover the pure unity of self in relation with God.

Analysing the perception of beauty, Plotinus writes that "in visible things, as indeed in all else, universally, the beautiful thing is essentially symmetrical, patterned." Centuries before, Plato and Aristotle had found the primary elements of beauty in order, symmetry and limit. Following closely the philosophy of Plato, Plotinus argues that the beauties of symmetry and pattern must themselves derive from a remoter principle.

> We hold that all the loveliness of this world comes by communion in Ideal-Form. All shapelessness whose kind admits of pattern and form, as long as it remains outside of Reason and Idea, is ugly by that very isolation from the Divine-Thought. And this is the Absolutely Ugly: an ugly thing is something that has not been entirely mastered by pattern, that is by Reason, the Matter not yielding at all points and in all respects to Ideal-Form.
>
> But where the Ideal-Form has entered, it has grouped and coordinated what from a diversity of parts was to become a unity: it has rallied confusion into co-operation: it has made the sum one harmonious coherence: for the Idea is a unity and what it moulds must come to unity as far as multiplicity may.

It is not possible to summarize adequately the philosophy of Plotinus or to describe its profound influence on Persian art in any simple way. However, this brief passage presents one formulation of the core idea from Platonism and neo-Platonism which is the participation of material form in the Ideal-Form.

A material thing becomes beautiful by the extent it borrows from or participates in ideal form. An object remains ugly and shapeless when it has not been completely mastered by pattern derived from reason and idea.

This profound concept was to be elaborated through the beliefs and practices of Sufism. In Islamic cultures, it would find creative expression in philosophy, literature, architecture, music, painting and textiles. In all their bewildering variety, these objects and designs carry a common message and express a single guiding thought. The beauty to be perceived on material things is borrowed. Like the beauty of Joseph, the visible beauty perceived by the physical senses is to be comprehended in its true nature as an emanation from the hidden source.

Many of the historical controversies surrounding the role of Sufism in Islam may be summarized in an examination of the career of Mansur al-Hallaj. Born in southern Iran (c.860), Hallaj traveled widely as a religious teacher throughout Iran and as far as India and Central Asia. He was severely criticized during his lifetime for his unorthodox beliefs and teachings, culminating in his execution in Baghdad in 922.

Hallaj earned the enmity of the religiously orthodox by speaking against some of the accepted obligations of Islam. He is reported to have taught that the pilgrimage to Mecca was not necessary for the believers, claiming instead this obligation could be performed while staying at home. According to some later accounts, these heretical views were announced at the time as the official reason for his execution.

As a spiritual guide, Mansur al-Hallaj is best remembered for the bold statement *ana'l-haqq*, translated variously as "I am the Real," "I am the Truth" or "I am the Creative Truth." Since the Real was one of the names of God, this assertion was commonly interpreted to mean that Hallaj was blasphemously claiming "I am God." Whatever the detailed historical reality, the spiritual seeking and martyrdom of Hallaj were to become in the following centuries major themes of Sufi poetry and visual art. His life became seen as a symbolic representation of the endless conflict between all-embracing love and the narrow rules of religious law.

Reversing our ordinary understanding, Mansur al-Hallaj is always depicted as joyfully welcoming his fate. Like the moth attracted to the flame, he is frequently shown dancing unafraid to the gallows. In the thirteenth century, Jalaluddin Rumi employed this familiar image of the moth and candle, writing in his poetry that the moth sees the flame as a door or a window. This very significant poetic image was intended by Rumi and other writers to recall the events of the martyrdom of Hallaj. For every martyr to divine love, the gallows of Mansur became a representation of the final threshold. It was to be crossed with joy by the spiritual traveler to arrive finally at the supreme goal, complete union with the One.

For the practicing Sufi mystic or for anyone strongly influenced by the ideals of Sufism, there may be a subtle reminder of the fate of Hallaj in the making of any Persian carpet. The frame that supports the warp threads as the carpet is being made is called the *dār*. This is the same word that is used for the frame of any door or window, and it is also the commonly used word for the gallows. The completed carpet removed from the loom may always be seen metaphorically as a door or window that has been removed from its original frame or *dār*.

Extending Rumi's poetic metaphor, the Persian carpet may even be seen as an image of the golden door framed by the *dār-e Mansur*. In another imaginative reversal, the fatal gallows became a common visualization in Sufism of the threshold of the divine king. It was the frame through which Mansur al-Hallaj passed to achieve a joyful union with God. In imagination, the considerable efforts and personal sacrifices necessary to make the carpet may recall the willing sacrifice of his life by Mansur. For the Sufi mystic, every traditional Persian carpet when completed and removed from its *dār* may still serve as a concealed reminder of these spiritual meanings.

Performances of music and dance were other major sources of controversy among the followers of Sufism. The theoretical understanding of music in Islam as reflecting the celestial harmonies of the cosmos was derived directly from Greek philosophy. For some of the Sufi orders, their musical performances known as *sama* ("audition" or "hearing") became the principal means used by their members to enter the state of ecstasy or divine intoxication. These musical concerts by the Sufi dervishes were often accompanied by an elaborate ritual dance intended to symbolize the expression of the divine harmonies in an earthly human form.

Despite recurring controversies in past centuries, this ritual performance became the best known and most widespread cultural expression of mystical Islam. The music and the whirling dance were traditionally performed before or about the *gotb* (literally, "pillar" or "axis"), the *shaykh* or head of the dervish order. As developed in the spiritual practices and the transcendent poetry of Jalaluddin Rumi in the thirteenth century, the *sama* acquired a profound symbolic significance.

Until recent times, members of the dervish order established by Rumi have performed the *sama* as their most significant ritual observance. They have followed the disciplined instructions for these performances that Rumi laid down in the thirteenth century. These are described by Annemarie Schimmel in *I am Wind, You are Fire* (1992), her detailed study of his life and work.

> The dervishes, solemn in their long black cloaks, walk three times around the *meydan*, the place where the master stands, to kiss his hands. Then, as the character of the music changes, they cast off their black cloaks, symbols of the spiritual body, the transfigured person at the time of death and resurrection in Love, an ever-newly enacted return to the Fountain of Life. Beginning with the hymn in honor of the Prophet, ... it ends with a long, sonorous prayer and the deep call *Hu*! ("He!"), the acknowledgment that He is the One who gives life and death; who is the Living from whom everything comes and to whom everything will return.

For Rumi and his followers, this rhythmic dance is experienced as an earthly reflection of the entire universe which is eternally busy with dancing, whirling, and stamping its feet.

In the controlled movements of the dervishes about the *gotb* in the *sama*, there is a moment of revelation when they become aware of themselves as an embodiment of the divine harmony. At that critical moment, microcosm becomes identified with macrocosm. For the participants in the sacred ritual, the material and transient become united with the divine and eternal. The performance of the *sama* recreates in a human form the movement of the stars and planets about the fixed pole of the heavens. The whirling dance imitates the great dance of creation about the One.

The philosopher Ibn Sina (d. 1037) is one of the major figures in organizing the Greek philosophical heritage in a comprehensive way and making it available to the Islamic world. A contemporary of Ferdowsi, he later became very well known to the Western world as

Avicenna. Sometimes strongly critical of the Sufis in his writings, he suggested their asceticism was often not praiseworthy since it was undertaken with the hope of reward. He does write in praise of the *arif*, the true mystic or gnostic, who sincerely abandons all ambition and selflessly pursues spiritual goals.

The great extent of Ibn Sina's work synthesizing all past knowledge and also his personal fame throughout the Islamic world inevitably attracted envious responses and some strongly opposing views in their turn. During his lifetime and in the following centuries, the works of Avicenna served as a convenient foil in Sufi poetry and prose for criticisms of what was seen as the excessive influence of Greek philosophy on Islamic religion and mysticism.

The main objection of the critics to the pagan philosophies of Plato, Aristotle and Plotinus was their neglect of God and the *Quran* as the true sources of all knowledge. Greek metaphysical philosophy emphasized instead the Platonic ideal forms or the emanations from the One as the genuine reality underlying all experience. In the more religiously orthodox philosophies of the critics, their extensive borrowings from Greek thought had been so thoroughly assimilated that its profound influence on their own works was seldom fully acknowledged.

Other major sources of Sufi mysticism were to be found in the revelation of the *Quran* and the long-established traditions of Islam. Every part of the *Quran* has been given numerous mystical interpretations, often of great complexity. One brief passage, the *ayat al-nur (The Verse of Light*) in the *sura al-nur* (*The Chapter of Light)* has been a primary inspiration for the spiritual explorations of many Sufi mystics.

God is the Light of the Heavens and the Earth;
His Light is like a niche containing a lamp,
The lamp is a crystal,
The crystal like a shining star;
It is lighted from a blessed tree,
An olive tree, neither of the East nor of the West
Whose oil would flare
Though fire does not touch it;
Light upon Light;
God guides to His Light whom He will,
For God makes parables for men,
And God is All-knowing of all things.

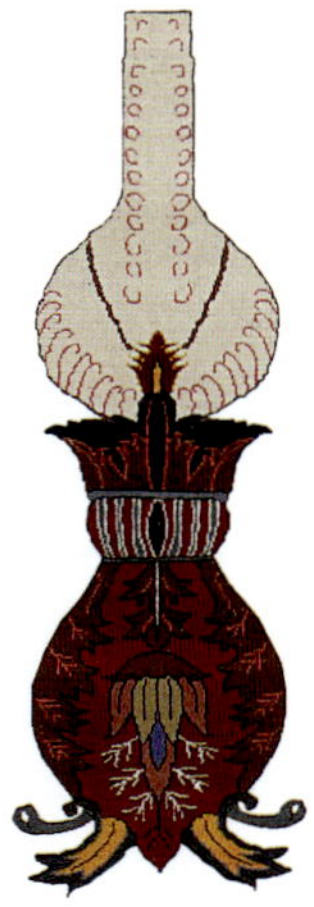

In his detailed commentary on the verse of light, *Mishkat al-Anwar (The Niche for Lights)*, the prominent Sufi philosopher Abu Hamid al-Ghazzali (d. 1111) developed a general theory of the nature of symbols. He then employed this intricate metaphysical theory to give an ingenious explanation of the concealed meanings of this cryptic passage from the *Quran*.

In his philosophy, Ghazzali was frequently concerned with questions of conformity of the various systems of thought to the religious laws revealed in the Quran. In *Tahafut al-Falasafe (The Mistakes of Philosophers)*, he criticized Ibn Sina (Avicenna) and others who had given priority to the methods of Greek philosophy and had sought to apply its ideas to analyze

Quranic teachings. Ghazzali continued the attempt to show that the ideals and practices of Sufism could be made consistent with Islamic orthodoxy despite their undeniably strong connections to Greek thought.

In *The Niche for Lights,* he wrote that light may be understood as an expression for that by which things are revealed. Ghazzali is careful in his metaphysical philosophy to recognize there are two distinct types of light which should not be confused. These two lights are the phenomenal and the divine, and they correspond to very different ways of seeing. He describes their similarities and one fundamental difference.

> Thus you see that just as everything is manifest to man's Sight by means of light, so everything is manifest to man's Insight by means of *Allah;* for He is with everything every moment and by Him does everything appear. But here the analogy ceases, and we have a radical difference; namely, that phenomenal light can be conceived of as disappearing with the sinking of the sun, and as assuming a veil in order that shadow may appear: while the divine light, which is the condition of all appearance, cannot be conceived as disappearing. That sun can never set! It abides for ever with all things.

Directly and indirectly, the philosophy of Plotinus is a principal source for this passage. It follows very closely similar images and ideas from *The Enneads.*

The five physical senses are compared by Ghazzali to *Lights* through whose agency every sort of existing thing is manifested, including objects both of sense and of imagination. Applying his understanding of communication by symbols to the *ayat al-nur,* he presents a profound exposition of the mystical meanings of the verse of light. His interpretation is based on an intricate parallelism between the five classes of Spirit which are the five physical senses and the five symbols *Niche, Glass, Lamp, Tree,* and *Oil.*

The sublime poetic vision of the *ayat al-nur* is given a most moving expression in the Kurdish Quchan carpet illustrated. The Kurdish people of the Quchan area in northern Khorasan are the descendants of a group that was moved from western Iran in the seventeenth century by the Safavid rulers Shah Tahmasp and Shah Abbas. They were transferred to that distant location to serve as a security barrier against the great dangers posed by Turkoman raiders from the north. The Quchan Kurds have maintained many of the traditions of their original homeland, a region that has been for many centuries one of the strongest centers for Sufism and other mystical beliefs.

The compelling design of the Quchan carpet is an image of the soul's journey to the One. We immediately recognize that the design is an emotional portrayal of the ascent of the spiritual seeker to union with God. Like the twisting vines and the leaves constantly seeking the light of the sun, the soul birds in the pattern are shown rising to the divine light. Guided by this essential light, they are flying away from the distractions and lesser beauties perceived by ordinary light and the physical senses.

Represented by the restless birds, the spiritual pilgrims in this design seek to go beyond the material forms and shadows that may be seen by means of phenomenal light. They strive for the total vision that becomes possible only with the pure eternal light of the divine

essence. This ineffable light is symbolized here and in the *Quran* by the light of a beautiful crystal lamp contained in a niche. While experiencing the endless difficulties and many disappointments of the soul journey to complete understanding, the spiritual travelers do have some consolations. They may find a sustaining hope in the wisdom revealed in the *ayat al-nur*: "God guides to His Light whom He will."

The unusual Baluchi carpet from Afghanistan has an intriguing design directly inspired by another passage in the *Quran* that has been given a sublime mystical interpretation. The *sura al-isra'*, the chapter of *The Night Journey*, begins, "Glory be to Him who made His servant go by night from the Sacred Temple to the farther Temple." These few words were later to be extensively elaborated in Sufi poetry and Islamic tradition. Frequently retold over the centuries, this short passage was expanded to become the beloved story of the miraculous night journey of the Prophet Mohammed to the heavens and the Divine Presence.

In Sufi philosophy, this majestic ascent called the *mi'raj* (literally, "ladder") became the supreme model for the spiritual journey. Escorted by the archangel Gabriel, the Prophet ascended into the heavens mounted on the *Buraq* ("mount"). This fabulous creature was an unearthly being most often pictured with the head of a woman, a winged camel's body, and a peacock's tail. Unlike Moses, Mohammed showed his greater merit by not fainting when he was granted his vision of the Divine.

In a poetic image that occurs frequently in Islamic mysticism, the fatal gallows of Mansur al-Hallaj was compared to the heavenly creature that transported Mohammed. In a profound metaphor, the *dār-e Mansur* became the mount that allowed the martyr Hallaj to ascend joyfully to the heavens. The mysterious design of the Baluchi carpet recalls all of these meanings. It portrays the mystical *Buraq* seemingly in readiness to carry the spiritual traveler on a new ascent to union with the One.

5.4 Quchan **Sura** *of Light* (c.1930, 3.15 x 1.89)

Represented by restless birds and twisting grape vines, all of nature is shown rising to the invisible light symbolized by the crystal lamp in the niche.

5.5 Baluchi ***Buraq*** (c.1960, 1.98 x 1.09)

The most famous pilgrimage is the ***mi'raj****, the night journey of the Prophet. The* ***buraq*** *is the unearthly creature on which Mohammed ascended to the divine presence.*

During the Safavid period (1501-1722), there were many periods of major conflicts between the followers of Sufism and the advocates of an orthodox Shi'ism. Under the erratic rule of Shah Sultan Hossein in the 1690s, there was a final period of severe persecution of the Sufi orders. The remaining dervishes in Isfahan were compelled to leave the Safavid capital, and all the familiar signs of Sufism were banished with them. Sufi practices including the repetition of *ya hu* or any other *zikr Allah* were strictly prohibited.

A remarkable decree from the intolerant Shah ordered that all jars and vases in Isfahan were to be concealed from public view or destroyed. This was ordered since these containers were commonly seen as prominent symbols of the practices of Sufism. Even more, blowing across their mouths could produce the forbidden sound *hu* which was identical to a banned *zikr*. The sight of a jar or vase during that troubled time would have been a proscribed reminder of the Sufi remembrance of God.

In Islamic mysticism, the vase form has taken on a primary significance. It symbolizes the creative emptiness of the mystical consciousness. In the Iranian visual art that is inspired by Sufism, the vase image is frequently intended as a concealed representation of the way of life of the dervish. On the spiritual journey, the followers of Sufism must cut away everything from the material world. The vase form is to be seen most meaningfully as a symbol of the enlightened dervish. It serves as a reminder to all spiritual travelers that their primary goal is to empty themselves in preparation to receive God. Free of all material substance, the empty container will enclose only spiritual essence.

Whatever the true time and place of origin of the famous Vase design carpets of the Safavid era which was a controversial subject in the 1930s and 40s, we may safely conjecture they were not made in Isfahan during this unsettled period. It should be noted that Shah Sultan Hossein has not been forgotten in the popular imagination of Iranians. He is given principal credit for the subsequent collapse of the Safavid dynasty and for the long period of violence and chaos that ensued. Since the time of his now legendary misrule, a comparison to the misguided Shah has been one of the harshest insults that could be used to describe any ruler or government official in Iran.

There was another important chain of transmission of the ideals of Sufism over the centuries. This was through the many guilds of artisans that were active in every major town and city in Iran. To maintain the proper frame of mind, an apprentice craftsman in one of these guilds would often perform his tasks while constantly reciting his *zikr Allah* or while repeating specially selected verses from the *Quran*. Like the dervish orders, the Sufi guilds of artisans often traced the inheritance of their special skills and the related spiritual knowledge back through a chain of initiation or *silsileh* to Ali, the first Imam, in the earliest years of Islam.

In *Islamic Art and Spirituality* (1990), Seyyed Hossein Nasr describes how the members of these craft guilds, the *asnaf* or *futuwwat*, thought of themselves as the heirs of very old traditions.

> Through this spiritual and institutional link, which still survives in many Persian cities such as Yazd and Kashan, the masters of the guilds become initiated into the mysteries of Sufism and learn the metaphysical and

5.6 Isfahan *Phenomenal and Divine Light* *(c.1970, 2.16 x 1.29)*

In white and black, the paired designs express the duality of sight and vision. The dominant medallions and the signature Habib meaning friend of God indicate there is only ***Allah****.*

> cosmological doctrines that underlie the symbolism of Islamic art. The rest of the members of the guild in question emulate the methods, techniques and symbols involved without necessarily understanding all of the more profound levels of its meaning, although on their own level of understanding the work does have meaning for them. … It is, moreover, because of this depth of expression, innate to the symbols and images transmitted from the master to the craftsman who study and work with him that often a work produced by a so-called uneducated craftsman has more profundity and intelligence than what many a so-called educated onlooker has the capability to understand.

In the light of these ideas, we may recall the Tehran artisan performing the traditional plaster and gilding work in the 1880s for the resident diplomat S.G.W.Benjamin. He established his credentials with his employer in the traditional Iranian way. He simply mentioned the respected name of his teacher who was almost certainly the master of his guild.

When he referred to his locally famous instructor, the artisan was communicating much more to Benjamin than a mere technical mastery of the necessary skills of his profession. As his American employer quickly recognized, the artisan was more interested in giving a material expression through his work to the deeply meaningful spiritual values he had assimilated during his lengthy apprenticeship. In ways that would now be difficult to reconstruct in any precise detail, it is this chain of inheritance of techniques, methods and symbols through Sufi guilds of artisans that primarily accounts for the philosophical and spiritual meanings that may be found preserved in traditional Persian carpet designs.

If there is a single image that over the centuries has provided a focus for Shi'a Islam in Iran, it is the golden door of the tomb of Imam Reza in the holy shrine in Meshed. To stand at this threshold is the constant dream and the ultimate goal of the Shi'a pilgrim. In *The Glory of the Shi'a World*, Percy Sykes describes in great detail the many stages of the pilgrimage of the fictional Kerman merchant Nurullah Khan up to the moment when he is finally within the precincts of the shrine.

> At last, thanks be to Allah, we moved forward and again prostrated ourselves, rubbing our faces on the threshold of the Golden Gate, one of the marvels of the world. We then rose, overjoyed to be inside the *haram* [sacred precinct], and, approaching the grating round the tomb, shook it, with prayers and entreaties to His Highness the Imam, and kissed it. We also kissed the lock, and you must know that every pilgrim, after handling and kissing the lock on his own account, and that of his dead relations, must do likewise on behalf of his living relations and friends, whose petition to visit the Shrine in person is thereby placed before His Highness. …
>
> The richness of the Shrine is unspeakable. The price alone of the door facing the foot of the tomb is worth the revenue of seven kingdoms, as it is of pure gold. The floor is inlaid with the choicest slabs of coloured marble from Shandiz, and the walls are covered with tiles in white, blue, and gold, like the work of China. Above them there is glass facet work of such beauty that how can I represent it?

The incomparable wealth of the shrine and especially the dazzling riches of the tomb chamber have been accumulated from the donations made by countless pilgrims over many centuries. They are reminders and symbols of the much greater spiritual wealth that the religious pilgrims have carried away with them on their return journey.

There are many small rituals the pilgrims conventionally observe as they approach their goal. Finally, after circling the holy tomb three times, the ecstatic pilgrims pray fervently to *Allah* to accept their praises. They pray that He will bind them anew to His chosen people, the followers of Imam Ali and his successors. The merchant pilgrim quietly concludes his account of this overwhelming religious experience with a few meaningful words. Nurullah Khan writes, very simply,"Thus, at last, was fulfilled the great desire of my life."

The golden door at the foot of the tomb of Imam Reza has such a deep inner significance in Shi'ism that it would be unlikely to be seen represented in carpet designs in any easily recognizable way. A possible exception may be found in the finely knotted Isfahan carpet illustrated. It has a very realistic design drawn in a most unusual three-dimensional perspective. Surprisingly, the design depicts an actual golden door, a double door beautifully painted in the European-influenced Qajar style of the nineteenth century.

Judging from the obvious quality of the door and its very elaborate frame or *dār,* the viewers of this carpet have found themselves in a well-decorated room in a prosperous Iranian home. This impression of material wealth is strongly reinforced by a significant element of the design. We cannot fail to notice the precise border of the fine Isfahan carpet whose edge is just visible on the floor of this imagined room.

Written very elegantly on the golden door carpet, there is a lengthy inscription that immediately points the disoriented viewer in a different direction. It is a moving poem and a prayer that completely reverses the meanings of these ordinary perceptions. In a few words, it asks us to leave this entrancing world of physical comfort and material prosperity for a very different world.

> Oh, God! May your kindness open a door before me
> That will show the way of escape.
> May your grace release me from the desires of both worlds.
> Take everything from my heart except your remembrance.

The verse ends with the sole remaining desire of the spiritual traveler. Free of all encumbrances, he prays that his heart or inner essence will reflect only the divine.

Perhaps the most intriguing detail in the design that subtly echoes this spiritual interpretation is one of the easiest to overlook. It is the disordered state of the fringe of the Isfahan carpet shown in the pattern. This is an intricate detail that was undoubtedly very difficult to draw and knot convincingly. In a room that is otherwise apparently in perfect order, this one discordant design element is an important clue that reinforces the profound spiritual meaning of the design. The disordered fringe seems to indicate the door has been opened recently. Has the fervent prayer for a way of escape from the desires of both worlds been answered? The design suggests that someone has already crossed the threshold. Or is there another explanation? Has there been a strong current of air from a hidden source flowing under the door?

5.7 Isfahan
Golden Door
(c.1970, 1.75 x 1.09)

Wishing to be released from this world, the sole remaining desire is to achieve union. Entranced by beauty, we may pass through the welcoming threshold to a new consciousness.

Like the religious pilgrim standing before the golden door in the holy shrine of Imam Reza in Meshed, the viewer of this design is encouraged in a highly symbolic way to leave all transitory wealth and all material forms behind. If only in imagination, we are invited to open the golden door and step through the threshold. The receptive viewer is invited to become a spiritual pilgrim who willingly abandons everything. Like Mansur al-Hallaj approaching the fatal gallows with joy, the one remaining desire of the pilgrim is to journey past the divine threshold to the different reality on the other side of the door.

Another very different image of a golden door is represented in a unique Baluchi carpet from Afghanistan. The scene depicted is a view of the courtyard of a mosque seen from the *eyvan* or entranceway. In a significant reversal, the viewer of this image stands in the precise position of the door to the mosque. The golden hue of the carpet is an emotional representation of the golden glow of dawn and early morning.

For the spiritual traveler, the return of the sun after the darkness of night is to be seen as a reassuring sign of the divine presence. During the long night, the beautiful lamp above the niche has shone through the darkness with its timeless message of welcome. The sunrise is the primary symbol of the return of human consciousness to a renewed awareness. The return of the sun each morning is also seen as a daily reminder to every person of their responsibility to continue in their own lives the divine act of creation. The majestic sunrise is ideally experienced each day as a *zikr Allah,* a reminder of God's presence.

Attempting to read the design of the Baluchi carpet, we notice a very significant detail that is reminiscent of the Isfahan carpet showing the golden door. A modest carpet with a simple animal skin design is shown at the mosque entrance as the single evidence of recent human presence. This small detail indicates that someone has been able to find temporary shelter and a place of safety at the threshold of the mosque. During the night, the religious pilgrim has found a welcoming place of refuge on the spiritual journey.

This ordinary experience depicted so movingly in this Afghan design should remind us of some older words inscribed on another carpet.

I have no refuge in the world
other than thy threshold.
There is no place of protection for
my head other than this porchway.

These entrancing words were inscribed by the master weaver Maqsud of Kashan on the famous Ardebil carpet more than four centuries before. They describe what still remains a living reality. The Baluchi carpet from Afghanistan indicates in the most direct way the survival of the timeless ideal represented on a much larger scale in the Ardebil carpet. The religious pilgrim has discovered the true sanctuary and peace that may be found in this world only at the divine threshold.

5.8 Baluchi *Mosque Courtyard* *(c.1960, 2.08 x 1.67)*

The empty courtyard reflects the creative emptiness needed to receive God. The peaceful courtyard and threshold invite all to participate in the shared vision.

The very finely knotted small carpet from Nain may be seen as the depiction of the vision of the religious pilgrim who has crossed the threshold and entered the mosque or shrine. By completing those few steps, the pilgrim has moved symbolically from outer to inner meaning, from the container *zaher* to the contained *baten*. He has willingly abandoned all external forms to dwell in the divine essence. The shelter and refuge for the traveler is now provided by the dome of the mosque which is to be conceived as an image of the sky or heaven descended to earth.

The creator of this carpet design was the well-known Fatollah Habibian (d.1994), a lifelong resident of Nain. By many knowledgeable observers, he was considered to be the outstanding Iranian artist of his time working in this form of expression. Some words of Plotinus may be helpful in analysing our strong response to this most beautiful design.

> And we must recognize, that even in the world of sense and part, there are things of a loveliness comparable to that of the Celestials – forms whose beauty must fill us with veneration for their creator and convince us of their origin in the divine, forms which show how ineffable is the beauty of the Supreme since they cannot hold us but we must, though in all admiration, leave these for those.

We may believe with Plotinus that ideal form has entered a material thing. From a diversity of parts, it has rallied confusion into cooperation to make one harmonious coherence.

The dome design of this Habibian Nain carpet may be seen to have a carefully calculated purpose. It is intended to set up in the imagination of the viewer an intense oscillation between the realms of matter and spirit. Repeatedly it creates a reversal in the mind between earth and heaven, an involuntary oscillation between sense and essence that will continue until we learn to see the two realms as a unity.

The Habibian design remakes the material earth into a polished mirror which reflects the divine harmonies of the cosmos. This is the difficult metaphysical task of the Sufi dervish who is on the spiritual journey to union with God. In a profound metaphor, the dervish must endlessly polish the mirror of his heart until it becomes free of all flaws. Only then will his heart or his inner essence be able to reflect the One without any distortion. By contemplating the carpet design, we will eventually leave the world of sense and part to achieve union with the One.

The design of the Nain carpet refers at the same time to the *hasht behesht*, "the eight paradises." This is the usual name for the beautifully decorated eight-sided entrance rooms that were found frequently in traditional Iranian architecture. In the language of Plotinus, these rooms were beautiful because they participated in or modeled the Ideal-Form. Like the eight-pointed double square that occurs so often in the visual imagery of Sufism, they were reminders of the dual nature of existence. They were material forms intended to recall constantly the final goals of the spiritual pilgrims, their liberation from all material concerns and their arrival at the eight doors to Paradise.

5.9 Nain *Mosque Dome by* ***Habibian*** *(c.1970, 2.50 x 1.65)*

Earth and heaven have become inseparably unified in this dome design. In imagination, the cosmic order has descended to the material world.

It is unlikely that Percy Sykes personally observed all of the holy sights in Meshed that he described in such great detail. During the time he was in Iran, the sacred shrine of Imam Reza was not open to non-believers. In *The Glory of the Shi'a World,* he does test the limits of tolerance of that period by including an amateur drawing of the tomb chamber and even an indistinct photograph of the golden door.

In his preface, Major Sykes is careful to avoid a potential diplomatic incident that might have occurred after he openly admitted his authorship of the book. He does this by acknowledging he relied entirely on the assistance of Ahmad Din Khan for his extensive descriptions of the shrine interiors and the rituals performed by the Shi'a pilgrims. In a brief note, the readers are informed that Khan was an employee of the British consulate in Kerman.

Some decades later, during the reign of Reza Shah Pahlavi, there was a period when this holiest of Shi'a shrines in Iran was in imminent danger of being opened to foreign visitors as an aesthetic experience. One of the visitors to Meshed during this period was the travel writer Ella Maillart. She undertook an extensive journey in Iran and Afghanistan in the summer of 1939, eloquently described in her travel journal *The Cruel Journey* (1947). At least for a short time, she was seeking to escape mentally and physically from the growing threat of war in Europe.

In her book, Maillart recalled some troubling personal experiences that had occurred in Meshed on an earlier journey to Iran only two years before when she entered the very center of the shrine of Imam Reza. Accompanied by four guards provided by the shrine authorities, she slowly retraced the same steps taken before her by the Kerman merchant and all pilgrims.

> Four warders having taken me in tow, I was asked to imitate their gestures. We then entered the humming crowd of pilgrims, the huge crowd that moved like a stream, the crowd that wailed, chanted and prayed all at the same time. … We reached the tomb-chamber.
>
> Like my neighbours I had kissed a great silver door …, then a dark door of carved wood; like them I pressed my forehead against a wall of pink marble. Beyond that I could no longer imitate them. They were in a trance: they looked but seemed to see nothing. I, I was still able to observe details. The tomb, under a canopy in one corner of the room, was surrounded by a silver railing and covered with a pall of blue satin. … The silver bars were caressed, kissed and clasped in an outburst of adoration that devoured the whole being of the pilgrims: they were partaking of the holiness of the saint. … They were not looking at this world: carried away by passion they had approached and touched something greater than themselves.
>
> I had no place there. To observe them as I did in a relatively cold way was indiscreet, sacrilegious even. This must have been the greatest moment in their lives, a moment during which wondrously they went beyond themselves. Who was I to scrutinise them as I did?

5.10 Yazd *Mosque Carpet* *(c.1910, 4.85 x 2.96)*

The lengthy inscription indicates that this carpet was dedicated to a religious purpose. It was made to be donated to the principal mosque of Yazd.

> Instead of looking through me as most of the pilgrims did, two bearded veterans, watched me, saw me for what I was: they were so hurt, their faces expressed a pain so acute that I felt sorry.

Although she could not share their emotions, Maillart was deeply moved by the sincerity and fervor of the pilgrims. She was able to observe details, but she was not able to go beyond herself to experience the all-embracing unity of a total religious experience. Unlike the ecstatic pilgrims she pretended to imitate, she continued to look at this world. She could not go beyond ordinary sight to achieve genuine spiritual vision. Feeling completely out of place, she recorded that she then left the tomb chamber and the shrine with undignified haste.

Two years later in 1939, Ella Maillart was once again in Meshed. Remembering her earlier experiences, she was content this time to tour only the outer precincts of the holy shrine. In particular, she focused her attention on the intricately decorated exterior of one famous building. She attempted to understand the aesthetic power of the mosque of Gohar Shad and the strong effect that its "happy proportions, good colours and lasting harmony" had on her imagination.

This well-preserved masterpiece of Timurid architecture was built in the early fifteenth century on the orders of Gohar Shad, the wife of Shah Rukh who was the son and successor of Timur. One decade after Maillart, another prominent traveler agreed with her opinion of its compelling beauty. In *The Persian Carpet*, A.C.Edwards recalls his visit to the shrine precincts in Meshed. He describes the Gohar Shad mosque as the noblest building in the sacred enclosure.

Seemingly unable or unwilling to view this five-hundred-year-old monument of Islamic religious art on its own terms, Ella Maillart hastily retreats in confusion. Once again, she flees from an intractable problem. This time she takes refuge in some very familiar contemporary values, the closely related values of aestheticism and tourism.

> So far I had always fallen in love with robust three-dimensional art – the Tower of Kabus, the charioteer of Delphi, China's Great Wall, the purity of Vezelay, the solidity of the Parthenon, the deep-rooted joy of Romanesque Tournus, the Trimurti of Elephanta cave. What had I to do, then, with an Asian mosque, a lidless box whose inner surfaces alone are seen, shining with paint and lacquer?
>
> I knew that Gohar Shad was "good" and it was casting a spell on me. Nevertheless, I still preferred the turquoise and ultra-marine glazes I had seen in Samarkand.

We should notice that Maillart is borrowing uncritically the language and methods of the recent aesthetic theory of significant form to account for the powerful sensations the monument had produced in her. In her quest to determine aesthetic values, there is no reference to irrelevant factors such as spiritual content, religious meaning or social context. However, we cannot fail also to notice she is having remarkably little success in applying the currently fashionable ideas to her immediate problem.

5.11 Meshed *Shrine Carpet* (c.1970, 2.91 x 1.97)

The carpets in the shrine of Imam Reza are woven in its own factory. The number 2152 is an inventory number used for record keeping that indicates the order in which this carpet was made.

To end her unfocused and inconclusive musings, Maillart could do no better than to include a quotation of questionable relevance from a familiar source. Somewhat predictably, she quotes a lengthy passage from Pope's *Introduction to Persian Art*: "The arts of design have no immediate appeal to sentiment and make no direct reference to nature; but their very abstractness, their detachment from a specific ideational content or emotional entanglement is a source of tranquil power." Despite her earlier opportunities to observe for herself the overwhelming power of the pilgrimage experience and despite the evident emotional entanglement she was undoubtedly experiencing before the Gohar Shad mosque, Maillart could not break the stronger spell that had been cast on her and many others by these hypnotic words.

When Arthur Cecil Edwards visited Meshed in 1948, he took some time from his tireless carpet surveying to renew his admiration of what he called "the incomparable buildings of the Shrine enclosure." Looking ahead a few years, he makes a significant but somehow disturbing prediction about the consequences of some planned improvements to the holy precincts.

> When the railway reaches the city, and when the shops which at present obscure the sacred Shrine are removed and the area is laid out as a garden (which is what the Shrine officials plan to do), Meshed will doubtless become a place of pilgrimage, not only for pious Moslems, but also for many thousands who will wish to pay homage to its majestic monuments for their own sake.

Motivated by their appreciation of art for art's sake, many thousands of tourists would soon be traveling to Meshed on the new railway. And they would be coming primarily to pay homage to the sacred shrine's aesthetic values.

For those curious travelers who would need more information about the numerous architectural landmarks of the holy city, Edwards mentions favorably a volume with which we have become familiar. He recommends *The Glory of the Shi'a World* by Major P.M.Sykes as a useful travel guide. Reflecting the limited values of his time, he describes this fictional account of a sincere religious pilgrimage as a"valuable and amusing book which every visitor to Meshed should read."

Several months later, in the spring of 1949, Arthur Upham Pope led a small group of writers, scholars and Persian enthusiasts on a journey to Iran sponsored by the Asia Institute of New York. The American writer Robert Payne described his personal experiences and observations during this journey of discovery in his travel journal *Journey to Persia*. Before falling asleep on the long flight from Paris to Tehran, the eminent tour leader told the eager young visitor why he should be traveling to Iran and what he could expect to see when he arrived.

> It is worthwhile to go to Persia, if only for the sake of a blue wall – the *ivan* of the mosque of Meshed. It is utterly glorious. Ah, everything in Persia is glorious! Think of the Achaemenian Empire! How splendidly they built! I envy you – to see Persia for the first time, that is the glorious thing!

5.12 Meshed *Grille Design by* ***Saber*** *(c.1920, 3.98 x 3.10)*

A subtle lattice design recalls the silver grille enclosing the tomb of Imam Reza. To bind themselves to the saint, pilgrims attach locks or tie pieces of cloth on which they have written fervent prayers.

These few words are very revealing of the approach that had produced the thousands of pages and the many illustrations of *A Survey of Persian Art* ten years before. There is an almost complete emphasis on empirical vision and pure perception or on the immediate emotional response to color, abstract form and aesthetic surfaces.

In a short passage, this is all summarized by Pope's borrowing three times the essentially religious word glorious. He used it to provide a concise description of narrowly defined aesthetic values that were believed to be common to sacred and secular monuments. In his brief description of the coming changes in Meshed, A.C.Edwards made a similar careless error. He casually misused the religious word homage to mean an aesthetic appreciation alone of a majestic religious shrine.

It is very possible that Pope was being consulted at that time by the national government on the planned changes outlined by Edwards. These renovations involved extensive clearances intended to enhance the beauty of the shrine enclosure and to improve its accessibility to pilgrims and visitors. Although unmentioned by Edwards, we may be reasonably certain there was a more concealed motivation in promoting these major clearances within the sacred enclosure. Very probably, the Iranian government of the day was equally interested in improving accessibility to the shrine precincts for the police and military during the frequent times of political and religious unrest.

According to the usage of the time, the holiest shrine of Shi'a Islam in Iran is misnamed the mosque of Meshed. This monument presumably to the art of its builders and decorators is recommended by Pope to the fortunate first-time visitor for the visual beauty of its *eyvan* or entrance. He hastens to mention the much earlier constructions of the Achaemenians which should also not be missed by the novice traveler in Iran. Then the eminent tour guide fell asleep on the long overnight flight from Paris to Tehran.

The sublime perceptions of the humblest religious pilgrim at the threshold of the shrine were evidently well beyond the grasp of the connoisseur. One decade earlier, Ella Maillart found she could follow the instructions of her guides at least initially as she entered the shrine. She could imitate the gestures of the pilgrims up to a certain point, but this soon became impossibly difficult. However accurate and well-intentioned her imitations, Maillart eventually realized her performance was meaningless. She could not go beyond her limitations to penetrate to the inner meanings of a religious experience. She finally admitted to herself she had no place there.

There was another way to approach the shrine that remained closed to these distracted travelers, the self-forgetful way of the true pilgrim. To enter the holy Shrine of Imam Reza, to enter into the comprehensive imaginative vision of the followers of Imam Ali, to stand humbly before the golden door of the tomb, to partake with one's whole being of the holiness of the saint, to pay sincere homage with every breath to the hidden source of all – ah, that would be glorious!

6 The Vision of a Whole People

When she was gathering her materials in Meshed for *The Wild Rue*, Bess Allen Donaldson collected information from every segment of Iranian society. She describes her collecting methods in the preface.

> The educated and the wealthy, as well as the illiterate and the poor, have made their contributions, and although most of the information has been provided by women, yet there is much that men have added that has been of value.

In deference to the progressive spirit of the times, Donaldson is careful to maintain some critical distance from the many folk beliefs she records. However, she does make an earnest attempt to explain their undeniable power.

> The uninformed mind turns very naturally to something tangible in times of need. They are surrounded by fears; fears of sickness and death, fears of drought and even crop failure, fears of famine and flood, fears of evildoers and their wiles, fears of husbands and their relatives, and all kinds of fears of the supernatural, and in their ignorance they have but sought the help of some "magical power" in strange objects or symbols.

Despite this conventional explanation and the quotation marks cautiously placed around "magical power," the informed mind of the author herself seemed to fall firmly under the spell of these folk beliefs.

In the first paragraph of *The Wild Rue*, Donaldson follows the custom of her time in Iran by lavishly praising the current ruler, Shah Reza Pahlavi. She writes that his many reforms have countered "superstitious practices and outworn ideas" and they "bespeak the progress and enlightenment that His Majesty earnestly desires for his people." With the passage of time, these outdated words from the 1930s may now be read in a very different way. They represent the author's superstitious attempt to avert one contemporary form of the evil eye. In her own terms, she is invoking the magical powers of words to protect the tranquility of her home.

The book that resulted from her prodigious collecting efforts proved to be far more than a catalogue of superstitions and outworn ideas or a lengthy inventory of the concealed powers to be found in strange objects and symbols. More significantly, Donaldson presents an appealing portrait of the imagination and creativity of the members of a national community in confronting each day the uncertain pleasures, the many hardships and the constant challenges of their lives.

Everywhere in Iran, traditional beliefs and local customs have always been used in personally meaningful ways to comprehend and sometimes to resolve the most difficult present-day problems. We do not think any less of the young Qashqai weaver Zolaikha for adding *talism* to her carpet in the winter of 1971, talismans that were intended to help her mother recover from a serious illness. We recognize our own vulnerable humanity in that natural gesture, and we want to believe that the magical power of the talismans helped to protect Zolaikha and her family from all harmful influences.

We admire Zolaikha's sincere recitation of the *bismillah,* the first words of the *Quran,* before beginning to weave. By observing that simple ritual, the young weaver dedicated her efforts to a religious purpose. Through her carpet at every stage from its conception to its completion, Zolaikha discovered and expressed her own personal meanings. At the same time, she participated in and renewed the shared meanings of her family and community.

In a period of great changes and some personal difficulties, her weaving gave a stable balance to all her activities. Like the sacred tree of a village, the carpet slowly taking shape on her loom provided a central focus that enabled a resourceful young woman to unify her many experiences. Her dedication to weaving this carpet symbolized to everyone some major transitions in her life. Wherever her dowry carpet is to be found today, we want to believe it continues to bring the good fortune, health and happiness that Zolaikha imagined for her mother and herself during the long winter when she wove it. That is the imagined world in which we all desire to live.

Another portrait of the creative enterprise of the Iranian community may be found in a vivid description by the English traveler Fred Richards. On some days in 1931, he was a fascinated and attentive observer of the many activities in the Isfahan bazaar. This opportunity to observe occurred in the same year he witnessed another major exhibition of Iranian creativity. In distant London, he attended the grandiose *International Exhibition of Persian Art* organized in meticulous and exhaustive detail by Arthur Upham Pope and his collaborators.

Richards begins his sympathetic description of the vibrant life he found in the Isfahan bazaar with a key observation or, perhaps more accurately, he begins with a significant non-observation.

> One may spend day after day in the main bazaar, or in the narrow and winding tributary bazaars which connect them, and never hear a child crying. The boys have powerful enough lungs, when every day at noon the call for prayer comes from the minaret of the neighbouring mosque; for it is the duty then of these little mites of five and six upwards to come to the door of their father's or employer's stall, and cry at the top of their squeaky little falsetto voices, like the yodellers by the running waters of the Living River [*Zayendah Rud*], the noonday prayer to Allah – "singing for their lunches" as it is called by the profane. Combine with these hundred shrill cries, the clang of the blacksmith's anvil, the hammering of the coppersmiths, the planishing of the brass-workers, the tap-tapping of silversmiths, the whining of beggars, the braying of donkeys, the roaring of protesting camels grudging to be loaded, the murmur of hundreds of voices, the shuffle of a thousand feet, and the result is a curious harmonious combination of noises difficult to describe in words.

The English visitor heard a hundred shrill cries in the crowded bazaar and countless other jarring sounds of human activities, but one familiar sound was strangely absent. He never heard a child crying.

In his account, Richards frankly admits his inability to find words to describe the curious harmony of competing sounds he experienced in the bazaar. Still less is he able to explain it to himself or his readers. However, he gives the strong impression that he found the bazaar's entangled human qualities of more compelling interest than the refined aesthetic qualities of the more formal exhibition he attended during the same year. Unlike the dynamic display of spontaneous life in Isfahan so eloquently described by Richards, Pope's great synthesis of the history of Iranian art made a very different impression on him. It was presented silently and almost motionlessly in the impressive galleries of the Royal Academy in London.

The compulsively observant traveler immediately follows his description of the many sounds in the lively bazaar with a pointed comparison. As if they needed reminding, he recalls for his readers the discordant harmonies and clashing sounds of a more familiar world known only too well from their daily lives.

> Strangely enough, this great chorus of conflicting noises in the bazaar has not the unpleasant ear-splitting effects of the machine-made. It is the strident klaxon, the screaming siren, the roar of the aeroplane engine, the starting throes of the motor-cycle, and the clanking of machinery that jangle the air and jar the nerves.

Fred Richards is attempting to compare the very different cultures of traditional and modern countries. One is an understandable world constructed on a normal scale. Its social coherence or harmony is an expression of a common vision of responsible human activity. The other is an artificial world with limitless ambitions that does not have and may never have those human qualities.

We remember the natural human rhythms found everywhere by Jasleen Dhamija in her studies of the making of folk crafts in India and Iran. No matter where we may look, these comprehensible rhythms are not to be found in the new age of machinery so accurately described by Richards. However, the absence of crying children and the curious harmony of sounds and activities he observed in the Isfahan bazaar may not be so very difficult to explain as he believed. They may come primarily from the countless ways that traditional craft work in Iran follows the repeating patterns and natural rhythms of human life. This unplanned harmony may come from the concealed and visible ways that craft work establishes meaningful connections between the artisans and their communities.

In his early studies of William Blake, a young W.B. Yeats criticized admiringly one of his subject's obsessive preoccupations. He described the constant efforts Blake had made in his poetry and visual art to express his ideas in what Yeats called a single shining image. Strongly influenced by this example, Yeats attempted by his own efforts to create a unified Irish literature and a national cultural identity that would seem in his words to be the work of a single mind.

These personal efforts to create a common national literature by introducing new models and reworking traditional sources in a modern way did not have the results intended. His early plays and poetry were not universally accepted or understood. Almost immediately, they encountered vocal opposition in Ireland from the growing nationalist political movement and from the entrenched Catholic establishment. These were powerful social institutions which insisted loudly on their own strongly competing views of the Irish cultural tradition.

Yeats was particularly disturbed by the insensitive imitations of his work by other writers in Ireland who did not share his motivations or understand his comprehensive vision. In his brief poem *A Coat* (1914), he used a memorable image and some harshly rhymed words to communicate his bitterness and disappointment.

I made my song a coat
Covered with embroideries
Out of old mythologies
From heel to throat;
But the fools caught it,
Wore it in the world's eyes
As though they'd wrought it.
Song, let them take it,
For there's more enterprise
In walking naked.

Yeats found he was unable to defend his all-embracing vision of a shared national culture from insensitive imitators and commercial exploiters, and he reacted angrily by turning away from these troubling controversies. He chose instead the personal freedom to explore every realm of the human imagination. He escaped imaginatively from his many tormentors in his native land by throwing off the beautiful garment he had created.

This incomprehension or denial of deeper purposes should bring to mind the extensive commercial activities of foreign and Iranian carpet companies beginning in the 1870s. Mainly in response to increasing European interest, they introduced new methods of carpet production on a large scale. Generally ignoring or intentionally neglecting the possibility of genuine spiritual and religious meanings, the newly established companies followed different standards. They were frequently willing to alter carpet designs substantially in order to satisfy the aesthetic preferences and decorative requirements of international buyers.

The determined opposition to Yeats from religious, political and economic interests in Ireland found an Iranian echo two and three decades later in the very comparable experiences of the writer Sadeq Hedayat. After the official suppression of his literary group in 1936, Hedayat responded to the dangerous situation in a way remarkably similar to Yeats. Unable to communicate his intended meanings directly in the Iran of his day, he turned to the mental refuge of mysticism and to the other cultural resources of the imagination from Europe to India.

For more than a year in 1936 and 1937, he also found a temporary physical refuge by living in Bombay in India. While continuing to write, Hedayat used his time in voluntary exile to expand further the great range of his literary resources. He studied the old pre-Islamic Persian language and some of the ancient texts that had been preserved by the Parsees, the Zoroastrian community in Bombay. Interwoven in complex combinations, these many influences all appeared in his most difficult work, the surreal novel *Buf-e Kur* (*The Blind Owl*) which was first published in India in 1936.

In his wide-ranging explorations of the world's literatures and religions, Yeats seemed to be drawn inexorably to a place and time very distant from modern Ireland. In his most mystical work, *A Vision* (1919), he found an inspired model for the unified culture he was seeking. He discovered this comprehensive vision of human possibility in the cultural life of Byzantium in the early sixth century.

> I think if I could be given a month of Antiquity and leave to spend it where I chose, I would spend it in Byzantium a little before Justinian opened St. Sophia and closed the Academy of Plato. I think I could find in some little wine-shop some philosophical worker in mosaic who could answer all my questions, the supernatural descending nearer to him than to Plotinus even, for the pride of his delicate skill would make what was an instrument of power to princes and clerics, a murderous madness in the mob, show as a lovely flexible presence like that of a perfect human body.
>
> I think that in early Byzantium, maybe never before or since in recorded history, religious, aesthetic and practical life were one, that architect and artificers – though not, it may be, poets, for language had been the instrument of controversy and must have grown abstract – spoke to the multitude and the few alike. The painter, the mosaic worker, the worker in gold and silver, the illuminator of sacred books, were almost impersonal, almost perhaps without the consciousness of individual design, absorbed in their subject matter and that the vision of a whole people. They could copy out of old Gospel books those pictures that seemed as sacred as the text, and yet weave all into a vast design, the work of many that seemed the work of one, that made building, picture, pattern, metal-work of rail and lamp, seem but a single image; and this vision, this proclamation of their invisible master, had the Greek nobility, Satan always the still half-divine Serpent, never the horned scarecrow of the didactic Middle Ages.

This description presents an elaborated vision of Yeats's early ambition to construct a unified literary and visual culture in Ireland.

This poetic evocation of the cultural life of sixth-century Byzantium is surprisingly reminiscent of the many activities in a different place and time that were described so sympathetically by Fred Richards. As it was in 1931, the Isfahan bazaar is a human world much closer to us in time. However, that world and its curiously harmonious way of life do not seem so very far removed from the central aspects of Yeats's vision of an ideal community. The poet envisaged a human community where religious, aesthetic and practical life were totally unified in a common understanding, all woven into a vast design.

The work of many that seemed the work of one that Yeats was able to find in this imagined Byzantium is an echo of some words of the poet Percy Shelley a century earlier. In his eloquent essay *In Defence of Poetry*, Shelley had described the total form of the literary imagination as "that great poem, which all poets, like the cooperating thoughts of one great mind, have built up since the beginning of the world." Losing individual consciousness, the artists of ancient Byzantium and modern Isfahan were absorbed in their subject matter which was their great poem, their vision of a whole people.

This recalls the lifetime ambition of Arthur Upham Pope to discover or impose a unified vision on the entire history of Iranian art. Pope was determined to give to the many contributions to *A Survey of Persian Art* the character of the achievement of a single mind, his rigid model of a unified and coherent national culture. Four decades later, in his article in *A Survey of Persian Handicraft*, Pope returned to this personally controlling metaphor when he studied the prehistoric pots that had been discovered in the region of Susa in the 1960s. Given his strong preconceptions about the unity of the historical development of Iranian art, it was very predictable that he would describe these ancient pots as the products of the whole community or the expression of a common mind.

A related motivation to discover or create a social unity in contemporary Iran may be seen to lie behind Mohammed Ali Jamalzadeh's humane dream of a common language. As expressed in the short story collection *Yeki Bud, Yeki Nabud* and his other writings, Jamalzadeh imagined and helped to create a shared language and literature in which all Iranians could truly communicate. His constant goal was similar to the early ambitions of his contemporary W.B.Yeats for his native Ireland. Jamalzadeh sought the ideal of a unified national culture to which every Iranian could contribute in meaningful ways.

At a different imaginative level, Ananda Kentish Coomaraswamy attempted another difficult unifying task through his prodigious scholarship. His primary aim in his later years was to describe what he sometimes called the common universe of discourse of all religious traditions. Behind all apparent differences of customs and beliefs, he believed in the possibility of a shared symbolic language which would communicate universal human concerns. According to Coomaraswamy, it would be found contained in its many expressions in the religiously inspired art of traditional cultures.

Among all artists and craft workers, Yeats excludes only the poets from his imagined coherent culture. This is an intended reference to the much earlier exclusion of artists and poets by Plato from his ideal republic. It is also an ironic allusion to his own bitter experiences of literary and social controversies in Ireland. In a slightly concealed way, Yeats was objecting again to the crude misinterpretations and the uncomprehending imitations his work had inspired in his native land.

For Plato and even for Yeats despite these many controversies, the city or the national community was the place where the individual realized his authentic self in interaction with others. In *The Enneads*, Plotinus makes the same point: "Humanity gave being human to Socrates: the particular human is so by participation in humanity." In the MacKenna translation, "the individual man exists by participation in the universal." This participation that creates the individual is through the common culture and the shared rituals of the city which enact a subordination to the divine reason that is revealed in cosmic patterns.

Yeats was very familiar with the philosophy of Plotinus, and he was strongly influenced by its transcendent vision of the spiritual life. This influence was initially through his studies of metaphysical philosophy and the poetry and visual art of William Blake. It was reinforced later through the majestic translation of *The Enneads* that was to be the life's work of his friend Stephen MacKenna in Dublin, a meticulous version that required several decades to complete.

The vision of Byzantium that Yeats would return to later in his poetry can be dated very precisely, a little before two significant historical events. The Byzantine emperor Justinian opened St. Sophia in 527, and he closed the ancient Academy of Plato in Athens and Alexandria in 529. As a direct consequence of the second event, there was a substantially increased influence of neo-Platonism and all Greek philosophy on Iranian culture in the following years. Soon after the closing of the Academy of Plato, some of the exiled philosophers found a physical and philosophical refuge in another empire. They were welcomed to Iran by the Sassanian king Khosrow Anushirvan (ruled 531-578) at the beginning of his long reign.

The Tehran carpet illustrated is tentatively dated c.1875, a critical time of rapid social change in Iran. After several years of devastating droughts and famine at the beginning of the decade, there was an increasing openness to new influences and solutions. Nasir al-Din Shah Qajar (Nasreddin Shah) toured Europe in 1873 as an important signal of the strong contemporary desire to encourage substantial reforms and modernization in a traditional society.

The design of the Tehran carpet from this period depicts an idealized crown as its central feature. Universally recognized as the primary symbol of the monarch and the nation, the royal crown may also be seen as a symbolic ideal of the common mind or the human understanding. Our hope for the monarch is that he will help us to resolve the many contradictions of our fallible human nature. Like the mind of every person, the king has been given the difficult task of reconciling the contradictory desires of all members of the national community. At first in his own life and then for his subjects, he must find ways to bring to a unity the competing desires to live in order and in freedom.

The ideal king must act as an embodiment or reflection of the shared values of the nation, and his immortality is a representation of the timelessness of these values. His moral conflicts are not his alone, but are those of each person and all mankind. Properly seen, the royal crown is not a symbol of arbitrary power and unlimited personal pride. It is a common possession not unlike the common language, a reflection of the historical enterprise and achievements of the nation. The jewels of the crown are to be seen as an actual and a symbolic representation of buried treasures, the many precious stones that are also shown at the base of the design of the Tehran carpet.

In a shared endeavor, the nation has brought these concealed treasures from darkness to light. The royal crown displays in visible form the great efforts and endurance of the entire community over many centuries and millennia. As the accepted symbol of the hard-won historical unity of a human community, the jeweled crown may be considered to have both human and divine origins. This may also be suggested in the design by a less conspicuous parallel element, the single vase indicating the hidden source of all. The crown and the vase seen together are another representation of the primary duality of the roles of king and dervish in Iranian culture. In imagination, the jewels of the royal crown are the same as the *ganj* sought by the dervish, the hidden treasure that is to be found in deserts and ruined places.

The image of the tree and serpent in the Tehran carpet may be interpreted as a visualization of the always troubling dichotomy of necessity and freedom. The snake is confined to an earthly existence, while the sheltering tree deeply rooted in the earth points to another realm. The snake is seen climbing the tree in a parody of the spiritual ascent. Unlike the serpent, the symbol of matter, the bird nesting in the tree is a true symbol of the soul's freedom. Disregarding all dangers, the bird attempts to rescue its innocent young fledgling from the snake representing the snares of the material world.

For Iranians, the snakes in the carpet design must recall the two black snakes that grew from the shoulders of the tyrant Zahhak who is the supreme villain of Persian mythology. Each day, these voracious snakes were fed by Zahhak with the brains of two children. This cruel oppression lasted many years until it was eventually ended by a violent rebellion of the whole nation.

The uprising was initiated by the blacksmith Kaveh who had already lost sixteen of his seventeen children to Zahhak and the two snakes. The rebellion is led by the noble Feridoun who, since infancy, had been hidden in the mountains from the cruel tyrant. For some years of his childhood, Feridoun was raised by a dervish who shared some of his secret knowledge with him. There were two prime symbols of the rebellion. One was the leather apron of the blacksmith that became the flag of the rebels, and the second was the iron mace with a cow's head design that Kaveh made as a weapon for Feridoun.

When he began to write the *Shahnameh*, Ferdowsi experienced a personal vision of limitless evil. This was a terrifying vision that came to him when he woke in his garden on a pitch-dark night. In an unforgettable image that recalls the misrule of Zahhak in ancient times, Ferdowsi described the feeling of overwhelming evil as a visible presence appearing to the eye on each side like a black snake with a gaping mouth. This experience and the *Shahnameh* itself, the royal crown, the iron mace of Feridoun used to overcome Zahhak, and Kaveh's leather apron loaded with jewels by Feridoun and later kings: all share a common significance. In their different ways, they symbolize the great central theme of Iranian thought. They represent an escape from darkness and tyranny by the shared efforts and imaginative vision of the whole community.

6.1 Tehran *Crown* *(c.1875, 2.84 x 1.98)*

The royal crown is understood as a symbol of physical protection and the common enterprise of the nation. The dervish crown symbolizes the protection provided by eternal spiritual values.

The design of the Qom prayer carpet may be seen as a creative synthesis of themes from Zoroastrianism and Islam. As a prayer carpet, it is a constant reminder of the religious obligations of every Moslem, especially the obligations to pray five times each day and to make the pilgrimage to Mecca at least once in a lifetime. The central design is a celebration of the renewal of nature at *Nouruz* when all the animals of earth, air and water become magically infused with new life.

The symmetry of this design is another expression of the theme of the earth coming into balance at the spring equinox. This balance between left and right is most profoundly understood as representing a human balance between matter and spirit or between earth and heaven. In the whirling dance of the dervishes in the *sama*, this fundamental unity of creation is symbolized or embodied in a very simple way. As the dancers turn about the *gotb*, their left hands are turned down toward the ground and their right hands are turned upward to the sky. The turning dervish reaches to grasp both earth and heaven.

Hovering just above the niche design in the Qom prayer carpet is a representation of the *Simorgh*. This was the mythological bird that was seen in ancient Iran as the most powerful protecting spirit. At the times of greatest danger to the Iranian nation, the *Simorgh* would descend from its distant mountain home at the boundary of the human world. It would suddenly appear to rescue the king or the great hero Rustam and restore the situation. According to a well-known story in the *Shahnameh*, Rustam's father Zal was raised as a child in the nest of the *Simorgh*. In a quiet way, the Qom designer has made a strong visual statement about the historical unity of Iranian culture by incorporating this Zoroastrian image of divine protection and national identity in an Islamic prayer carpet.

6.2 Qom *Prayer Carpet* *(c.1960, 2.08 x 1.35)*

Prayer carpets imitate the form of the ***mihrab****, the mosque prayer niche indicating the direction of Mecca. All creation is shown in harmonious submission to the divine pattern.*

This creative synthesis of religious and historical images can be found most explicitly in the *zir haq* carpets of the 1930s. It may also be found expressed in more subtle ways in very many carpet designs. The earlier Turshiz (now Kashmar) carpet made c.1900 has an intriguing pictorial design that shows strong influences from Zoroastrianism and Sufism. The central theme of the pattern is the cycle of the four seasons and the normal activities associated with each season.

These ordinary human activities were celebrated by Zardosht (Zoroaster) as defining our common humanity. The mysterious tower in the central medallion is believed to represent the famous astronomical observatory at Nishapur, the great medieval city in Khorasan that was destroyed during the Mongol invasion of Iran in the early thirteenth century.

Like the sixth-century Byzantium imagined by Yeats, the fabled beauty and wealth of Nishapur before the devastating conquest are remembered with longing in Persian literature as symbols of the limits of human knowledge and achievement. At least in memory and imagination, the entire city was viewed as the realization of the divine pattern in an earthly form. In this remembered Nishapur, the religious, aesthetic, and practical dimensions of daily life were seamlessly unified. They all shared in a transcendent common vision of human possibility.

In the Kashmar carpet design, the world turns through the four seasons as the stars and planets turn about the celestial axis represented by the tower in the central medallion. The tower may also be seen as a symbolic representation of the *gotb*, the *shaykh* of the dervish order, in the whirling dance. Like the *gotb* in the *sama*, the observatory tower of Nishapur was a profound cultural image of the subordination of all human activities to the celestial order. Represented in very many different forms, this unifying vision is the core image of Iranian spiritual culture.

The Sufi writer Fariduddin Attar of Nishapur lost his life in the devastating violence of the Mongol invasion. In his many writings, Attar often combined the essential images from Zoroastrianism, Christianity, and Islam in creative ways that served as models for many subsequent writers and for the philosophers of Sufism. He followed the example of another writer from Nishapur. In the eleventh century, Omar Khayyam had used Zoroastrian and Christian images extensively in his poetry.

Attar presents a poetic vision of a whole people in his best-known work, *Mantiq at-tayr (The Conference of the Birds)*. The title is a reference to the passage in the *Quran* where we learn that King Solomon knew the language of the birds. Attar's lengthy work describes a meeting of the birds of all varieties to discuss their great need to find a king to rule them. As the story begins, they have come to realize their need for a wise monarch who will be able to unite them despite their many differences.

The *hudhud* (the crested hoopoe) immediately enchants the other birds with his eloquent description of the *Simorgh*, the fabulous bird whose nest was to be found on *Kaf* mountain at the end of the world. The peacock is told that his exile from paradise will be ended if they reach the home of the *Simorgh*; the humble pigeon will be able to fly to the farthest limits of the sky; the hawk will be released from the dark hood that conceals the two worlds. The *hudhud* establishes his credibility with the other birds by reminding his attentive listeners that Solomon had trusted him as his messenger to the Queen of Sheba. Enchanted by his story of their true king, the birds ask the hoopoe to guide them to the *Simorgh*.

Even before they set out, some of the more fearful birds change their minds and decide not to go. They hesitate when they learn of the perils of the journey and when they remember what must be left behind. The love struck nightingale refuses to be parted from the rose. The cautious peacock says that his only goal is to return to paradise, not to visit the unknown *Simorgh*. The duck will not leave the clean waters in which he lives for the unfamiliar hardships of an arid desert. The hawk cannot bear to leave the comforts of his privileged life at the court. The owl decides to continue his solitary life seeking concealed treasures among deserted ruins.

The birds who do find the courage to embark on the long desert journey must pass through seven barren valleys before they reach their goal. The names of the valleys correspond to the seven stages of a Sufi initiation; quest, love, knowledge, detachment, unity, bewilderment, and spiritual poverty. Some of the birds do not survive to complete their arduous travels. Repeatedly, the hoopoe encourages the others by his wise stories, and he inspires them to continue by his poetic descriptions of the wonders of their destination. After their hardships, thirty birds (*si morgh* in Persian) manage eventually to reach the threshold of the glorious court of the *Simorgh*.

Only after they have reached a state of complete exhaustion and total poverty are they admitted to the presence of the king of the birds. At the great moment when they encounter the *Simorgh*, the thirty birds see in astonishment that they are themselves a second *Simorgh*. Their king explains that he is a mirror in which all who come before him will see themselves reflected. After their spiritual journey, the *si morgh* who have survived all the hazards are rewarded for their constancy by experiencing this transforming revelation.

In their exhausted condition, the thirty birds who have made the journey are able at last to see themselves without any illusions. After their many humbling experiences, the impoverished birds have learned to see what they truly are as individuals and in relation to others. Reinforcing this spiritual message, *The Conference of the Birds* ends with a moving admonition from Attar to his readers. He urges them to act accordingly in their own lives and to gain a true appreciation of themselves now that they have been shown the Way.

6.3 Kashmar *Cycle of the Seasons* *(c.1900, 3.86 x 3.05)*

The four seasons and the observatory tower are reminders of the cosmic pattern. The universe turns endlessly about the fixed pole joining earth and heaven.

6.4 Bakhtiari
Hudhud
(c.1920, 2.00 x 1.48)

The crested hoopoe was Solomon's messenger and the spiritual guide to the ***Simorgh****. Like the* ***hudhud*** *gazing at its own reflection, we will learn to contemplate our double nature.*

The Bakhtiari prayer carpet dated c.1920 includes the *hudhud* in the design, always easily recognizable by the tufts of feathers on its head. In an otherwise very colorful design, the image of the crested hoopoe is woven in undyed grey and white wool. This reinforces the Sufi interpretation of the *hudhud* as a symbol of the dervish in the role of a messenger or spiritual guide. The hoopoe's crest or crown recalls the *taj* of the dervish, and it may also be seen as an imaginative reminder of the royal crown. In their hazardous search for their true king, the other birds choose the hoopoe to rule over them on the journey. Both temporal leader and spiritual guide, the *hudhud* may be seen as another cultural image of the unity of the ideal roles of the king and the dervish.

In this Bakhtiari carpet, the symmetrical paired image has the significance of the hoopoe regarding its own reflection, a clear reference to the culminating moment in Attar's work. This pairing is another representation of the primary theme of Sufism, the recognition of the

6.5 Bakhtiari
Enclosed Garden
(c.1900, 1.93 x 1.30)

The peacock longs to escape from the beautiful garden where it has been confined. Despite the ease of its present life, it looks beyond the boundary and cries to return to its home in paradise.

duality of matter and spirit. The red field may be viewed as a concealed animal skin design that expresses the conception of the Sufi mystic as an embodiment of spiritual wisdom.

The gold vase from which the pattern grows suggests the divine source of all patterns. Like all material forms, the vase is a *zaher* that contains a *baten*, an external form that encloses an inner essence. A gentle wind blowing across the mouth of the vase produces repeatedly the barely audible sound *hu, hu, hu* which we now hear as a *zikr Allah*, a remembrance of the hidden source. The design of this carpet is seen most profoundly as an emanation from that source. Like the Simorgh, it is a mirror that reflects back to us our true nature.

The second Bakhtiari carpet dated a few decades earlier to c.1900 presents an unusual image of a peacock gazing longingly beyond the limits of an enclosed garden into what appears to be an empty desert. In *The Conference of the Birds*, the peacock chose not to make

the difficult journey to the *Simorgh*. The shrill raucous cry of the peacock is conventionally heard in Persian poetry as expressing its sadness in exile from its true home. With constant longing, it looks in the design beyond the walls of its beautiful enclosure. The peacock's only desire is to escape from its confinement and return to its first home in India or in Paradise, the original enclosed garden.

The designer of this intriguing carpet has consciously explored the limits of creative expression of the form. The four abstracted flowers in the corners of the field seem to be designed intentionally to defeat our conventional expectations. They are drawn very haphazardly in the *gol feranghi* or "foreign flower" manner, perhaps to concentrate the mind on the more essential things. The border has a most extraordinary fragmented design, including a mysterious disassembling of an abstract bird that resembles cubist art. Like travelers on a spiritual journey, the viewers of this carpet have the difficult challenge of reassembling these distorted fragments into a coherent pattern.

The very finely knotted Isfahan carpet (c.1965) is best interpreted as a creative portrayal of the spiritual journey. The central medallion in grey wool and the extensive use of undyed wool, not very usual in a fine carpet, are already the first signs of a likely Sufi motivation of this design. We notice that the animals are drawn mostly in undyed wool, a subtle suggestion of the holy dervish who is engaged on the spiritual quest. The dramatically drawn *Simorgh* is another revealing element of the design. Representing the divine presence and grace, the mythical *Simorgh* has caught an innocent rabbit or the dervish that it represents in a moment of forgetfulness. The fabulous bird has carried the rabbit upwards in the final stage of the heavenly ascent.

In the field design of the Isfahan carpet, we encounter the *ahu*, the gazelles or musk deer that are commonly seen as symbols of the spiritual traveler. They are attracted to the hanging lamps suspended from the branches of the cosmic tree. Guided by beauty and the visible light of these lamps, the innocent gazelles are embarked on the soul's journey. They continue the long ascent toward the divine inner light, the restless journey to complete union with the Real.

There is another important detail of the design that we should notice on our own journey to a comprehensive understanding. The *ahu* seem to have been preceded on their path by another spiritual guide, the *hudhud*. Inconspicuously, the crested hoopoe may be seen at the highest point of the field design. After the many difficulties of the soul journey to self-understanding, the *hudhud* is shown completely at rest, peacefully contemplating its reflection.

As a young boy in the early thirteenth century, Jalaluddin Rumi traveled with his father, a renowned religious scholar, from their native city Balkh in present day northern Afghanistan. They were seeking a place of refuge far removed from the impending threat of the Mongol invasion. It was not until ten years after leaving their home that they settled permanently in Konya in Turkey. This cosmopolitan city was then the prosperous and relatively secure capital of the Seljuk kingdom.

6.6 Isfahan *Spiritual Journey* *(c.1965, 2.41 x 1.57)*

The distracted animals moving in every direction are all on the mystical path to understanding. Darkened lamps suggest the pilgrims will be guided by divine light.

The story of Rumi's meeting with Attar in Nishapur on his journey to safety has been told many times. Attar is said to have predicted at this meeting that the young boy would open a door in the heart of love. In Rumi's poetry, there emerges a portrait of an ideal human community engaged in the most ordinary daily activities. To each of these normal activities, he always manages to give an ingenious spiritual interpretation.

In this comprehensive vision of humanity, each member of the community was involved in a single common endeavor, the great task of building the tent of God. In their different ways, the followers of all professions and occupations were engaged together in praising the One.

> There is one praise for the rope-maker, another for the carpenter who makes the tent-poles, another for the maker of the tent-pins, another for the weaver who weaves the cloth for the tent, another for the saints who sit in the tent and contemplate in perfect delight.

For Rumi, the great task of constructing a true home for mankind is not to be imagined as the work of a single mind. It is the freely shared activity of all minds and all bodies.

Nothing in the human and natural worlds seemed to escape Rumi's loving attention. He celebrated the most common everyday experiences which, in his poetic imagination, always took on a profound metaphorical significance. In Rumi's imaginative vision of human possibility, the man of God is a king who may be discovered disguised behind the cloak of a dervish.

Love may appear in Rumi's poetry in the most unexpected ways, perhaps embodied in the person of a cook, a weaver, or a tailor. Another time, love may reveal itself disguised as a police chief who has the ability to open the prison of this world. We learn from Rumi that love may appear in the marketplace, perhaps concealed as a seller of keys that can unlock the heart. One time, the secret of the passionate lovers was learned by all when a jar fell from the roof. At that sudden moment of revelation, everything was changed forever for the lovers. The container *zaher* had fallen into ruins and revealed the essence *baten*.

What is to be done when we learn that a neighbor has fallen ill? Rumi immediately asks a practical question, "What medicine was prescribed?" Some decades earlier, Attar had written in his poetry, "When you have no pain, how could the medicine come?" A century after Rumi, Hafez repeated the same question; "Love's physician has the healing breath of Jesus Himself and is full of compassion; but if He find no pain in you, how will He administer a remedy?"

Perhaps, as the words of these writers suggest, pain and illness are not without their compensations. For Rumi, Attar, and Hafez in their shared vision of a troubled humanity at times of great dislocations and life-threatening dangers, there is one medicine that has the power to cure all illness and suffering. That healing medicine is love of the One.

There have been some attempts in the modern period to make local rituals and celebrations serve other national purposes, not always with the results intended. In October 1977, a major *Festival of Popular Traditions* sponsored by the Pahlavi government was held in Isfahan. A similar event had taken place in Shiraz in 1976. Only one or two generations before, the tribal traditions on display at the new festivals had been seen officially as unfortunate signs of cultural backwardness which were to be ignored or actively suppressed.

6.7 Qashqai
Kourosh Shah and the Lion
(c.1960, 2.13 x 1.51)

Another folk image recalls an ancient ritual performed at the spring equinox. Kourosh Shah or Cyrus the Great slays a lion to renew the empire divinely protected by Ahura Mazda.

In an abrupt reversal of policy by the national government, these neglected traditions were now to be celebrated in large-scale public exhibitions. Usually presented in substantially modified forms, they were to be reclaimed and encouraged as an important part of the Iranian heritage. It should not be surprising that some parts of the programs of the arts festivals in Shiraz and Isfahan proved to be very controversial.

Many objected strongly to the public display of the craft products and social rituals of the different nomadic groups in an insensitive "culture bazaar." The performances of "tribal dancing" by Bakhtiari, Qashqai and other tribal groups produced intense negative reactions from many observers. They criticized the carefully rehearsed performances which were completely divorced from the traditional social contexts and spiritual values that had given them significant personal and cultural meanings.

As another sign of the changing values during this period, an *Institute for Traditional Performance and Ritual* was established in Tehran to conduct academic investigations of disappearing tribal and folk customs. As one of its first public activities, the new research institute sponsored a major academic conference called *The International Symposium on Ta'ziyeh* that was held in 1976 during the Shiraz festival.

The conference participants presented their research on the *ta'ziyeh*, the unique religious theater of Shi'a Islam. This was a centuries-old popular theater comparable in many ways to the Christian passion plays of medieval Europe. The scholarly contributions to the symposium by Iranian and international authorities were later collected in the conference proceedings *Ta'ziyeh: Ritual and Drama in Iran* (1979) edited by P.J.Chelkowski.

In the traditional *ta'ziyeh*, a word which means "mourning" or "consolation," the whole community organized public performances on a very large scale. Most often, the dramatic performances reenacted the violent events of the tragic martyrdom of Imam Hossein at Karbala in 680 on the tenth of Moharram. Chelkowski describes the common vision that temporarily united social opposites and found a full creative expression in these lengthy performances.

> Uniting rural folk art with urban, royal entertainment, it admits no barriers between the archetype and the human, the wealthy and the poor, the sophisticated and the simple, the spectator and the actor. Each participates with and enriches the other.

6.8 Azerbaijan **Ta'ziyeh** *(c.1948, 2.80 x 1.30)*

An emotional folk image from Soviet Azerbaijan recalls the riderless black horse that continued the journey from Karbala to Baghdad. It became the first sign of the mournful fate of Hossein.

Almost all members of the local community were involved in some way in the elaborate preparations for the much anticipated event. They each contributed to the *ta'ziyeh* according to their means and their abilities.

> The men brought their most precious objects – crystal, lamps, mirrors, china, and tapestry – to decorate the walls of the *takiyeh* [theater]. Even the most humble objects were accepted as they were given or lent with religious devotion. ... The women provided refreshments, the children of the aristocracy served water, a symbol of the Kerbela martyrs' thirst, and sweetmeats to all spectators, rich and poor alike.

This common endeavor gave to all present a powerful public demonstration of the humane ideals and social beliefs of Shi'ism. Each year during the sacred month, the *ta'ziyeh* performances helped to create in the participants the strongest feelings of belonging to a human community organized around shared emotions, values and historical experiences.

The American writer John Dos Passos happened to be present in Tehran in 1922 at the time of the annual performance of the mourning ceremonies. In his travel journal *Orient Express* (1927), he recorded his immediate impressions of the impressive ritual with a novelist's practiced eye.

> In Teheran the tenth of Moharram dawns in terror and dismay. All night the streets have been turbulent with torches and chanting and the hollow sound of bare breasts beaten in unison. In the early half light the streets are full of watercarriers offering cups of water to passersby in memory of the terrible thirst they suffered in the tents of Kerbela. Now Hosein is receiving the first charge of the horsemen of Amr, the first flight of arrows.
>
> In a big square in the bazaars the crowd is densest. On a roof chairs have been set for the diplomatic corps, Europeans in frock coats and uniforms, in white flannels and Palm Beach suits as if for a garden party, ladies in pastel-colored dresses, all guarded by a small contingent of Riza Khan's gendarmes.

The foreign audience seemingly dressed for a garden party and the gendarmes of Reza Khan were new and discordant elements. Lacking a common understanding shared with the deeply involved participants, these curious onlookers could not have failed to change almost completely the nature of the mourning observances.

We may hope that these objective witnesses so incongruously present at the *ta'ziyeh* in Tehran were attending the event at least for its great ethnological and aesthetic interest. Their intrusive presence recalls the somewhat similar motivations fifteen years later of the writer Ella Maillart when she was in the tomb chamber of Imam Reza in Meshed. As she admitted with obvious embarrassment in her recollection of the incident, it was her profoundly disturbing presence at the holiest shrine that destroyed the pilgrimage experiences of the two old men.

In *Islamic Art and Spirituality*, Seyyed Hossein Nasr describes the framework of shared belief that is necessary in order to comprehend the significance of this transcendent social ritual. He points out an important distinction between the performance of the *ta'ziyeh* and the more familiar conventions of European theater.

> [The *ta'ziyeh*] can have efficacy and meaning only in the traditional context for which it was meant. The audience is as much a part of the play as the actors, and both participate with all their body and soul in the events of sacred history that are retold on the stage. A skeptical audience, which because of lack of faith cannot participate wholeheartedly in the tragedy of Imam Hossein and his companions, already destroys through its presence the drama's spiritual climate.

The mourning ceremonies required from the spectators very much more than a willing suspension of disbelief. They demanded an emotional engagement and a participating response that fully respected the history and shared values of the community.

The *ta'ziyeh* can never become a tourist event or an aesthetic experience for connoisseurs without destroying entirely its social and religious significance. This profoundly meaningful cultural phenomenon that Chelkowski and Nasr were describing with scholarly interest was not something they could easily observe for themselves. At the time they were writing, the *ta'ziyeh* had become a distant memory. After several years of increasing restrictions, performances of the mourning ceremonies in the cities of Iran were finally banned in 1935 by the reform-minded government of Reza Shah.

In October 1971, Mohammed Reza Shah Pahlavi led the excessive public celebrations of the two-thousand-five-hundredth anniversary of the founding of the Persian Empire by Cyrus the Great. The week of lavish ceremonies and extravagant historical pageants began with a more austere and solemn ceremony. This took place at the ancient tomb of Cyrus in Pasargadae located near the famous ruins of the royal city Persepolis.

As the principal actor in this unprecedented ritual performance, the Shah addressed directly the revered memory of the founder of the Achaemenian dynasty.

> "We cherish thy undying memory, and, at this moment when the new Iran renews its bond with its proud past, we all hail thee as the immortal hero of Iran, as the founder of the oldest empire of the world, as the great emancipator of history, as the noble son of humanity. ... Rest in peace, for we are awake, and we will always stay awake."

Once again, modern Iran was being exhorted to arise from its centuries-long sleep. By remembering its ancient heritage, the nation will reawaken to its true destiny.

At the time of *Nouruz* in 1976, Mohammed Reza Shah repeated this too-common error of misusing history and long-established traditions for current purposes when he decreed a new reform of the official Iranian solar calendar. Henceforward, it would be dated from the year of the coronation of Cyrus. In late 1978, this highly unpopular decree was rescinded during the chaotic last weeks of the Pahlavi period. The original Islamic calendar that had been replaced in 1925 by his father's order was hastily reintroduced.

6.9 Rafsanjan *Tulip Design* *(c.1910, 3.97 x 2.92)*

Tulip flowers in the medallion, corners and border are images of martyrdom and mourning. Flowering briefly after the adversity of winter, blood red tulips recall the defeat of Imam Hossein at Karbala.

اصفهان حبیب

The thirteen days of *Nouruz* or "the day of renewal" are a time when all members of the community join in a genuine celebration whose origins are believed to be even older than the coronation date of Cyrus. In contrast to the officially imposed ceremonies of the brief Pahlavi period, it is a time when individuals freely renew the ordinary conversations with each other that define a true community.

Judging from his lengthy descriptions in *The Glory of the Shi'a World,* it is evident that Percy Sykes entered into the spirit of this popular celebration and he made an effort to understand its cultural importance. He describes the extensive preparations before the annual celebration began. One universal custom was known as "house shaking." Each family made sure that every room was swept carefully and all their carpets were taken out of the house to be beaten thoroughly.

Through the voice of the fictional merchant from Kerman, Major Sykes also describes some more unusual local customs that were still commonly seen during the period when he was in Iran.

> It is considered to be auspicious to keep all doors open; and it is the custom to take a good or bad omen from any conversation that may be overheard, the listeners standing on a key, the symbol of opening, and listening with bated breath. …
>
> Girls, too, who hope for marriage, are taken by a woman *mullah* to a place where four roads meet. There they sit with a lock fastened to their dress and offer sweetmeats to passersby. This is termed "luck opening," as everyone who partakes of the sweetmeats first turns the key in the lock and thereby opens the way to good fortune for the damsel.

Sykes includes many other contemporary *Nouruz* customs that clearly had great personal meaning for the participants.

For this special period of the year, the houses were open to all visitors as a visible sign to everyone that their occupants were open to the shared experiences of the community. In a society whose members valued privacy very highly at other times, all entrance doors were kept open. At least symbolically, all thresholds could be crossed at that special time of the year. In a similar way, no social barriers were recognized between individuals and groups in the preparation and performance of the *ta'ziyeh* during the holy month.

Even family conversations were considered to be public during the *Nouruz* celebrations and might be overheard. This was another indication that the inner and outer experiences of Iranian families were no longer separate. Sykes records that this changed again for a brief time as the precise moment of the spring equinox approached.

> The gate of the house is shut an hour before the equinox, and no one is allowed to enter from outside; but, as soon as the New Year commences, the master of the house goes out into the street with some sweetmeats, … .

On the thirteenth day of the celebration, the final day, the houses of the towns and cities were left empty. If only for a few hours on one day, city dwellers willingly readopted the nomadic way of life. Families traveled a short distance from their homes to spend the day in the countryside in order to observe the renewal of nature and share in its beauty.

6.10 Isfahan *Double Vision* *(c.1970, 1.57 x 1.07)*

Spiritual travelers learn to see with outer and inner vision. In this Habib design, the butterflies are images of human souls escaping their confinements in material form to rise toward eternal light.

This cherished custom was another meaningful unification of the inner and outer lives of Iranian families at this joyful time. Far away from the confining walls of their homes, there was no longer any distinction to be maintained between *anderun* and *birun*. In all their variety, the *Nouruz* customs encouraged and enacted a social healing. They renewed personal and social bonds that had been neglected and they helped in countless ways to strengthen the common enterprise of the human community.

The celebration of *Nouruz* is a theme of carpet designs that is very frequently seen, so commonly seen it is rarely explicitly acknowledged. Any design that displays an abundance of flowers, often with animals shown in pairs, is at least partly a reference to the renewal of all life at the spring equinox. In the many arid regions of Iran, this is the only time of the year when flowers are seen in a wild profusion in the countryside.

At the beginning of spring, trees in abundant blossom are to be seen everywhere. Jalaluddin Rumi caught the mood when he wrote that the whole garden opens with laughter at the time of spring. The great treasure that had been hidden from view during the winter months is now revealed and all of the earth's secrets have become manifest.

The Ravar carpet illustrated has an extremely intricate floral pattern which is an unmistakable reference to this happiest time of the year. It has the very recognizable *hazar gol* design, the "thousand flowers" or *mille-fleurs* pattern, that was made in considerable quantity by the Iran Carpet Company. Since the last decades of the nineteenth century, this French-influenced design has been made in many versions, mainly in Kerman and nearby Ravar. The *mille-fleurs* carpet shown here has approximately ten thousand flowers in its beautiful design. This pattern is an ultimate portrayal of the floral abundance of the Iranian New Year.

In *The Wild Rue,* Bess Allen Donaldson describes some of the numerous folk beliefs associated with this time of year. She records there are different winds in the spring that each have a very dramatic effect. Suddenly, they bring the long-awaited gift of new life to the flowers and the trees. It is only at this joyful time of the year that these beneficial winds occur. Their welcome arrival is a signal to all of the end of the harshness and desolation of winter.

> There is a wind also which opens the buds, and another which impregnates the flowers of the trees. The "wind of the pink rose," which comes when the lovely Muhammadi rose is in bloom, is beneficial.

This special rose of Iranian gardens was the original source of the old perfume called attar of roses. The wind of the pink rose or *gol Muhammadi* carries that intoxicating perfume into every home. It cannot fail to enter all persons who will first make themselves empty in order to receive it.

Donaldson records the widespread folk belief that lovers should strive to imitate the nightingale whenever they are in a garden. It is common knowledge that the love struck bird will never leave a garden where the Muhammadi rose is in bloom. The *hazar gol* designs

6.11 Kerman *Hazar Gol* *(c.1970, 3.92 x 3.01)*

Trees dance and flowers sway in the warm spring winds. Through opened doors and windows, the scent of ***hazar gol*** *or a thousand roses penetrates into every home.*

of Kerman and Ravar are expressions of this obsessive love and they make it completely understandable. They show the overwhelming beauty that is created magically by the warm breath of the spring winds. At this time of year, there is no one to be found who will disagree with the impassioned nightingale. The gardens are most beautiful when the pink Muhammadi rose is in abundant bloom at the time of *Nouruz*.

Flowing from an unknown source, the special winds have some other well-recognized effects. Rumi wrote that the branches of the trees are moved to sway and dance by the spring winds of love. Like the dervishes in the *sama*, the branches are moved to dance about their *gotb*. They turn about the unmoving pillar which is the trunk of the tree. The many roses that are now in full bloom eagerly join the dance. They sway in the spring winds and the warm sun, releasing their intoxicating perfume until they throw off their beautiful garments in ecstasy.

There is another more subtle effect of the winds on every vase, on every container and on every external form that cannot join the dance. If we listen very closely, we will find these unmoving containers are all resonating softly with a low-pitched sound in response to the magical winds. If we listen with our inward hearing, we will hear the constantly repeated sound *hu, hu, hu*. We will discover that all containers and everything in the created world have become reminders of God.

In the same way that they open the flowers and the whole garden, the spring winds open the doors and windows of the houses. They carry the key that had been lost, the key with the power to release the occupants from the dark prison of the winter months. Even more, they unlock the hearts of all who know how to celebrate the precious days of renewal that begin each new year. The spring winds return to us the essential key we have been missing, the key that opens a door in the heart of love.

For those who open all their windows and doors and allow their thresholds to be crossed, the life-giving winds that enter will have a transforming power. They will bring an abrupt end to the social isolation of winter. Like breath itself in every living person, they have the ability to join *zaher* and *baten*. They bring together our perceptions of external form and inner essence. If we respond fully to their healing breath, if we truly open ourselves, the perfumed spring winds will unify our outer and inner experiences.

The conclusion of *The Glory of the Shi'a World* presents another compelling vision of the unity of a community. The book ends with an emotional account of the return of the merchant Nurullah Khan to his home in Kerman. On the day before his expected arrival, his closest friends and relatives had ridden out from the city to meet him. In a symbolically meaningful way, they would share in the last stage of the arduous journey.

The next day, as Khan records, he and the other weary pilgrims returning from the holy shrine in Meshed learned to their great joy that they had not been forgotten in their native city. A few miles outside Kerman, their slow-moving caravan was met by what seemed to be half the population of the city.

> Escorted by relations and friends our joyous party entered the city and passed through the bazaars, where all the shopkeepers rose up in our honour, and so to my house. Now my house is by no means small, but when I represent that there was no room for people to stand even in the courtyard, I have explained the matter.
>
> At last my relations and friends had wished me "May Allah protect thee," and, tired out with the long journey and my reception upon returning home, I retired to rest. But before sleep like that of the Seven Sleepers overtook me, a voice from the Unknown reached my ears, a voice of such mellifluous sweetness that its very tones brought repose to my mind. Thrice it thrilled me with the words, "Thy pilgrimage is accepted," and by the grace of the *Imam*, to him be praise, peace, perfect and infinite, filled my soul.

The religious pilgrimage is finally experienced by Nurullah Khan as a journey to home and origins. Its completion is a return to a participation in the wholeness of family and community that is holy.

Like the *Nouruz* celebrations, the pilgrimage remakes and reunifies the complex patterns of life in humanly meaningful terms. It may be said to recreate the individual and the community. It reconnects them or binds them together, the original meaning of the word religion, in a common understanding which is a subordination to the divine pattern. The whole community in Kerman has crossed the threshold of the pilgrim's home. Through opened gates and doors, they have entered his inner being.

After overcoming the countless difficulties of the physical journey, the spiritual seeker finds that he has traveled a greater distance in the mind. He has traveled from temporal to eternal, from motion to rest. For the pilgrim, all meaning is contained in a few sublime words that come from the Unknown. From a concealed source, he hears three times, "Thy pilgrimage is accepted."

At the end of the pilgrimage, the individual discovers he has returned to his authentic self by his renewed participation in humanity. This imaginative reconnection to others is the unity we can know in our everyday lives, and it is a sign of the deeper unity we should continue to seek. Like the intricate design of a Persian carpet, what had been seen before the pilgrimage as a confusing multiplicity is now revealed in its full splendor as a beautiful pattern.

There is a necessary return to ordinary experience after this revelation, but nothing will ever be seen in the same way as before. The religious pilgrim's perceptions of commonplace things and everyday reality have been changed forever. With this transformation of consciousness, the essential goal of the pilgrimage has been achieved. In all its human variety, a diverse community is now seen as a whole people.

7 After-Image

The technical definition of an after-image is the image of a vivid sensation preserved by the retina or any other sense organ after the external cause has been removed. A very loud sound will be "heard" for some moments after the physical cause of the sound has ended. If we stare constantly at a black object for a minute or two and then close our eyes, we will "see" the same object in white. In a surprising reversal, a colored image will produce an after-image in the complementary colors. Green is replaced by red and red by green. Staring at the sun for a short time may produce a permanent black after-image.

This phenomenon is a type of memory, and it is a model of the internalization and transformation of external experience. The after-image provides another mode of vision beyond ordinary seeing. It is also an experience that may be described as mysterious or mystical. Both words are derived from the Greek word *myein* meaning "to close the eyes." We seek the experience of mystery in order to open our eyes again. Only then does it become possible to see the objects of the perceptual world in their true relations. When light returns after the contraction and darkness of prayer, we feel an undefinable expansion. Standing erect with eyes completely open, we become more fully human.

The Greek word *theorema* had the original meaning of something shown or made obvious by a visual display. A *theoros* was an ambassador sent from one city-state to another to serve as a public witness. His assigned task was to observe the religious rituals and festivals that expressed the traditions and wisdom of the community he visited. A *theoria* was the total way of seeing made possible by the observations of the *theoros*. Ideally, the *theoria* of an individual or a city-state was a comprehensive vision of the divine pattern revealed in a human community.

The modern words theorem and theory still retain some of the resonances of these original meanings. Thomas Taylor was the English translator of Plotinus in the late eighteenth century. He volunteered to give some elementary lessons in geometry to his untutored friend William Blake. They reached only as far as the fifth proposition of the first book of Euclid, the proof of the equality of the base angles of an isosceles triangle. Impatiently, Blake interrupted Taylor's mathematical demonstration to assert his own more intuitive understanding of the nature of a theorem and the requirements for a proof. He said to his instructor, "I see with my eyes that it is so, and do not require any proof to make it clearer."

The Persian carpet functions essentially as a *theorema* in the original sense of the word, a symbolic visual display of the deepest cultural values. If it can be said to serve as a decoration, it does so most profoundly in the sense of *decorum* which is a human balance or equilibrium that implies a rectification of character. An encompassing view reaching toward a *theoria* is necessary in order to find or create this equilibrium. By stepping onto the carpet within the framework of this comprehensive vision, we are making the pilgrimage of one step that takes us out of ourselves.

That one step with the right foot across the border of the carpet takes us in imagination from the ordinary material world through the golden door to the intelligible world of ideal

7.1 Meshed **Theorema** *by Emogli* *(c.1910, 5.70 x 3.70)*

Originally from Tabriz, Emogli was the contemporary Meshed designer most admired by Edwards. This accomplished design is a ***theorema*** *expressing an encompassing vision or* ***theoria****.*

forms. The Persian carpet will always be a physical object, a container or *zaher* vulnerable to all the changes and accidents of the material world. At the same time it serves as a constant reminder of the closeness of a permanent ideal realm, the contained or *baten*. This symbolic role is its primary significance.

Throughout his extensive writings, Sadeq Hedayat reenacted the role of the *theoros* in a modern way. He attempted to communicate his personal vision of a human community as it revealed itself through its ordinary conversations and daily rituals. His self-assigned task was to witness the real conditions in contemporary Iran. With few illusions, he observed the actual life of Iranians and then he used eloquent and sometimes angry words to show them as they truly were.

In his writings, Hedayat often used the verb phrase *tazahor kardan* meaning to make apparent, to show, to demonstrate, or to materialize. Like *theorema,* this concept refers to a visual display or demonstration of previously hidden connections and values, and it expresses the opposite of the Iranian cultural norms of ambiguity and concealment. By his frequent use of *tazahor kardan,* Hedayat communicated his characteristic themes of the recognition of the true relations of things and the intangible being given a visible material form.

His novel *Haji Agha* (1945) is set in contemporary Tehran under American and British military rule. It depicts the manipulations and schemes of an old merchant for whom money and the power it brings him are everything. Distrustful of everyone including the members of his own family, Haji Agha conducts his business in an almost public way from the *eyvan,* the entrance porch, of his home.

In Hedayat's disturbing vision of Iranian society, the cunning trader sits there every day like a spider waiting at the center of his web. All the corrupt and innocent types of wartime Tehran are drawn to visit Haji Agha to do their business with him and to serve his ends. In the novel, this suggestive image becomes an uncompromising demonstration of all the distorted personal and social values of the time. It is a visual showing of the current relations of things that may be interpreted as a harsh parody of the failed ambitions of Reza Shah and his regime.

This modern demonstration suggests an unfavorable comparison to a much earlier time. Each year at the time of Nouruz in ancient Iran, the kings of the world assembled at Persepolis. They traveled great distances to pay their annual tribute to their sovereign and to celebrate the renewal of life at the spring equinox. In the main ceremony, the regional kings passed in a majestic procession before the *eyvan,* the reviewing platform of the Achaemenian rulers. This impressive ritual is famously commemorated in the relief sculptures at Persepolis. It expressed the eternal values and unbreakable unity of the Persian empire. The splendor of the royal procession was a visual display to the whole world of the power and justice of the Achaemenian king of kings.

A less impressive *eyvan* in front of a Tehran home is the setting for Hedayat's bleak vision of a disunited modern Iran. Among all the people passing in procession before the modest throne of Haji Agha, only an impoverished young poet has the courage to stand up to the local tyrant. Despite his poverty, the poet angrily refuses to write a poem on democracy that had been requested by the old merchant to further his latest unworthy scheme. Haji Agha's current plan was to claim authorship of the poem and then to use it to support his most recent ambition to be elected to the national legislature.

7.2 Kashan *Maryam and Isa* *(c.1900, 1.98 x 1.35)*

In the early modern period, many Kashan pictorial rugs displayed the central stories and images of Iranian culture. Mary and the child Jesus are shown before an idealized vision of Jerusalem.

In *Buf-e Kur (The Blind Owl)*, Hedayat explores the troubled consciousness of his central character. For reasons we never learn, he is a recluse who lives an owl-like existence. He rarely leaves the one room he occupies in a derelict area at the edge of an unnamed city. In Iranian popular beliefs, owls choose to live alone in deserts and abandoned places. They hunt at night since they are almost blind in daylight.

Like a dervish endlessly repeating his *zikr Allah* in the *kharabat* or ruined place, this solitary character occupies himself mindlessly by painting the same scene repeatedly on *kalamdan*, wooden pencases. He lives a disembodied existence in which reality continually dissolves and reforms for him in dreamlike ways: "The shadow that I cast upon the wall was much denser and more distinct than my real body. My shadow had become more real than myself."

In an opium-induced reverie, this unnamed painter with almost no remaining connections to the world around him becomes possessed by a comprehensive vision. He experiences a total revelation of his place in the cosmos.

> At this moment my thoughts froze. A unique, singular life was created in me, because my life was bound to all the existences that surrounded me, all the shadows that trembled around me. I felt an inseparable, deep relation with the world, with the movements of all creatures and with nature. All the elements of my self and of nature were related by the invisible streams of some mind-disturbing, agitating current. No thought or image was unnatural to me; I could understand the secrets of ancient paintings, the mysteries of difficult philosophical treatises, and the eternal foolishness of forms and norms, because at this moment I was participating in the revolution of the earth and the planets, in the growth of the plants and in the activities of the animal world. The past and the future, far and near, shared my sentient life and were at one with me.

This is a description of the ultimate participating response to the universe. It comes from a man seemingly cut off from the world, living the confined and isolated life of the prisoner in Plato's cave.

By some effort of the imagination, the solitary pencase painter becomes completely aware of his surroundings. From the extreme narrowness and contraction of his life, he undergoes an unbounded expansion. All limits enclosing him suddenly dissolve, and he realizes that he embodies all of existence. Within himself, he contains the past and the future, the far and the near. In this comprehensive religious vision, he experiences an overwhelming feeling of unity with all creation.

Sadeq Hedayat has been described paradoxically as the least Iranian and the most Iranian of writers. In his search for an authentic national culture, he introduced contemporary European models into what had been a mainly traditional literature. The unprecedented diversity of his interests seemed at first to have no underlying unity. They included everything past and future or far and near. Some of his books disturbed unprepared readers with their strongly critical views and by ranging between unfamiliar extremes of realism and surrealism. The many Iranian cultural references in his works have made them very difficult to translate adequately into other languages.

Hedayat's encouragement of creative innovations in literary forms did have some definite limits in certain areas. Apparently contradicting his willingness to experiment freely with foreign prose forms, his strong preference in Iranian poetry was for the usual themes and the strict metrical conventions of the classical poets. On occasion, he used his notable critical and satirical abilities to reject the fledgling experiments of his time in modernist poetry.

In his own life, Hedayat was following long-established Iranian traditions in another way. To a remarkable extent, he reenacted in a modern form many of the cultural roles of the impoverished *qalandari* dervishes. He became the *rend* who challenges convention in the *kharabat*, the reprobate who prefers to live in ruined places. In the popular imagination, he was similar to the *malamati* who seeks to offend in protest against the hypocrisy of the world. For someone who was unusually sensitive to the power of words from an early age, his name may have suggested to him the course that his life would take. Chosen by his great-grandfather, the family name Hedayat has the meaning of a spiritual guide and is related to Sufism. His given name Sadeq means the truthful one.

Like the fictional character in *Buf-e Kur*, no thought or image was unnatural to him. No aspect of reality could be neglected in his determined quest for a unified understanding. At various times in his life, Hedayat rejected opportunities to live in a more socially and economically stable way. He seemed to be following the central advice of Plotinus to cut away everything. To finance his journey to India in 1936, he sold some of his few possessions including many of his precious books.

Mojtaba Minovi was one of the original four members of the *Rab'a*, the short-lived but very influential group of writers that met informally in the coffeehouses of Tehran in the 1930s. After Hedayat's death by his own hand in Paris in 1951, Minovi recalled their impassioned literary discussions with fond nostalgia.

> Each of us had his own, distinct personality. ... Normally we gathered in teahouses and restaurants and, if drinking is not considered a deviation from righteousness, at times we even consumed liquids harder than water! One could even hear us debate issues critically and with utmost vigor. ... We fought for freedom and we fought with zeal. Hedayat was the hub of our operation. At first we thought that by recognizing Hedayat's value as a literary figure we were encouraging him, but soon it was obvious that he encouraged us. He was the center and we were the satellites revolving around him.

This passage concludes with the essential metaphor of Iranian culture. For Minovi and the others of the *Rab'a*, Sadeq Hedayat came to be seen in the same way as the *gotb* at the *sama*. What had been a disorganized multiplicity of different personalities, partial understandings and conflicting motivations was transformed by his steadfast example into an unbreakable unity.

This final perception of Hedayat's unifying role was a profound reversal of ordinary meanings. From being a seemingly marginal figure in his country, a *rend-i kharabat* who lived in ruins and rejected normal behavior, Hedayat became the leading writer of his time. His defiance of literary and social rules renewed the core human meanings of these rules. For those who knew him well, he became gradually an image or embodiment of the unmoved center about which the world turns.

Minovi's personal observations had some ancient precedents. Ten years after beginning his arduous journey home from Troy, Odysseus was finally allowed by vengeful Poseidon to be cast up on the shores of his native Ithaca. His protector Athena gave him the temporary disguise of an aged man clothed in rags. Completely without resources, he was given shelter and cared for by a humble swineherd. For twenty years, this old servant of Odysseus had remained faithful to the memory of his absent king.

In this simple refuge, Odysseus waited impatiently to recover his strength and he began to plan his drastic revenge against the many suitors of Penelope. When he asked the poor man why he had shown such hospitality to a defenseless stranger, the old swineherd gave a memorable answer. He told Odysseus that all wanderers and beggars come from Zeus. We know that this comparison was not original to the swineherd or to Homer in *The Odyssey*. Long before them, this divine analogy was deeply embedded in language and religion as an essential part of the common understanding.

In the Greek world, the holy men who wandered the earth were called the *planetai* and the same word was used for the five planets, the restless wanderers of the night sky. From Greek mythology, we recall that the celestial planets themselves were descended from Zeus. On their endless journeys, the earthly wanderers imitated the motions of the divine planets. Three millennia later, Mojtaba Minovi and the other writers discovered in Sadeq Hedayat what the faithful old man had recognized immediately in his unknown visitor. He became for them an embodiment in human form of the timeless pattern of the cosmos, the universe turning eternally about the One.

Communication through metaphors and symbols is an essential aspect of any coherent human community, and the ability to interpret and employ a culture's symbolic language is the prime requirement to be considered a member of the community. To know a language, it is not sufficient to know only its vocabulary and grammar. We must be able to use that language to communicate meaningfully and share an understanding. By remembering and reenacting the common understandings, we become a true participant in a community.

In ancient Greece, *symbola* were originally the two broken halves of a clay tablet or of a fragment of pottery. They were used to indicate an agreement or contract between two people. Each person would keep one of the two pieces as a memory device or a token of their agreement. The separated fragments were later brought together when the contract was honored as a visible sign of a wholeness that had been recovered. The word *symbola* evolved to have the meaning of any mutually agreed sign of recognition; for example, the signs and gestures that identified the members of a secret society.

During almost fifty years of continuous involvement in the carpet business, Arthur Cecil Edwards was unable by his own admission to find symbols in Persian carpet designs. Despite this remarkable failure, his many professional activities in England and Iran were highly symbolic in something like the original sense of recovering a wholeness or a unity. And he did use a common metaphor with great personal meaning to describe this recovery when he compared his final journey to a pilgrimage.

Returning to Iran after a long absence, he found an uncertain nation that had been broken apart by economic depression, military occupations, and political instability. With tireless enterprise and ingenuity, the unlikely pilgrim attempted to find practical ways to heal the wounds of the country. His ambitious goal was to revive Iran's principal artistic activity which had been after agriculture its most important source of employment and after oil its most important export product.

During an eventful half century, the forms of Iranian culture took hold of the English businessman as they have with every other conqueror of Iran in history. His neglected first book *A Persian Caravan* indicated he was an acute and sympathetic observer of the human dimensions of Iranian life. Not unlike a dervish, Edwards went everywhere and crossed almost every threshold in his journey throughout Iran in 1948 and 1949. He describes entering even the sacred precinct of Meshed but only by invitation from the religious leaders of the shrine. Taking advantage of his temporary presence in the city, they asked him to examine the many old carpets in the shrine collection.

During his long pilgrimage, Edwards reenacted the recognized cultural role of the dervish in a second fundamental way. We remember, in his own words, that he had recently retired from worldly concerns to pursue a task that had long been in his mind. In words he did not use but very probably would have accepted, this great task of his last years was to devote himself completely to his image of the Beloved. His primary task in traveling and writing was to find ways to reveal the comprehensive or divine pattern as it expressed itself through carpet weaving in the Iranian community of his time.

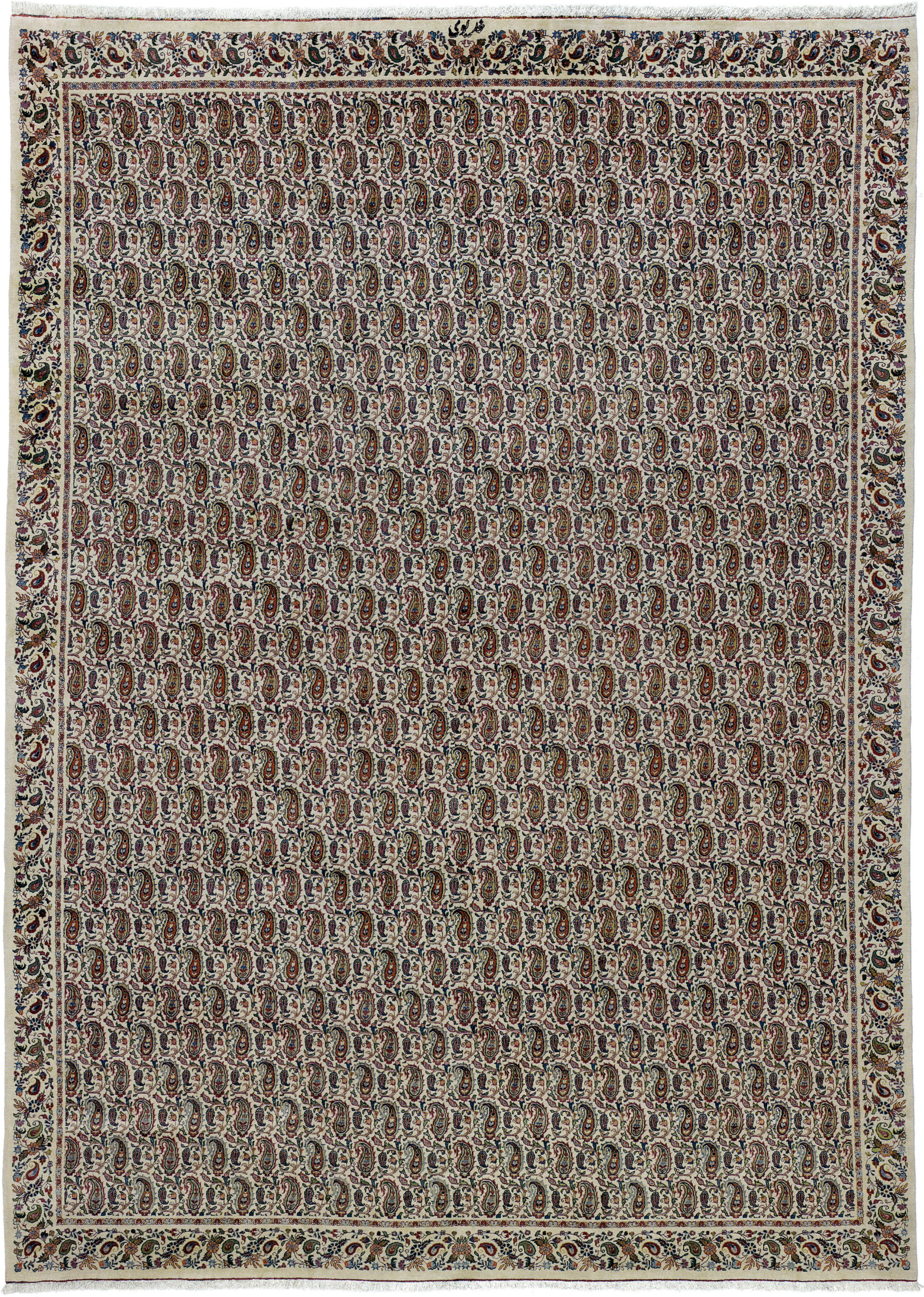

The resulting book *The Persian Carpet* is in some significant ways reminiscent of a common form in medieval Persian poetry. It resembles the long poems describing the poet's arduous desert journey to the king or noble patron with the hope of gaining his favor or alerting him to social problems. The detailed technical knowledge Edwards communicates is impressive, but this is not his only contribution. The many brief anecdotes labeled "conversation pieces" scattered throughout the book strongly suggest the author was seeking another type of communication. The medieval poets and Edwards in his different way were all seeking to recover a wholeness that had been broken.

This is the concealed book Edwards intended to write, a book about *symbola* and conversations, and it is the one he did write. In his studies of the Basseri people of the Khamseh Federation, the Danish ethnologist Fredrik Barth came to understand that they recreated their primary cultural meanings in all the ordinary activities of their annual migration cycle. No less than the Basseri nomads, Edwards was striving in his year-long migration to go far beyond understandable commercial motivations. He was seeking to experience and renew the transcendent personal and social meanings of Persian carpets.

Not always content to be an objective surveyor, he sometimes allowed himself to become a *theoros*. He became a witness of a community's rituals who was himself transformed by his observations and experiences. In his survey, he reached toward the comprehensive vision of a *theoria*. With all his limitations of language and background that made some forms of symbolic communication impossible for him, Edwards did seek to reveal and participate in an idealized vision of the Iranian community.

However, since this is the modern world, his vision of a whole people does not take place at the magnificent court of the *Simorgh* on the distant summit of *Kaf* mountain. His journey of 8,500 miles does not end with the writer seated honorably at the king's table or in attendance at the *dargah* in *Golestan*, the court of the royal palace in Tehran. The author does not report hearing a voice from the Unknown saying three times that his pilgrimage has been accepted.

Instead, Edwards concludes his book in a less imaginative and more contemporary way. He first summarizes briefly what he had seen during his travels. Then, at great length, he describes numerous detailed recommendations for the future development of the carpet industry in every part of Iran. In the spring of 1949, he presented these many sensible recommendations at a national conference in Tehran sponsored by the Ministry of Economy. In that restricted modern sense, perhaps Edwards did find a place at the *dargah* and a seat at the king's table or council of state at the end of his desert journey. We may even choose to believe that his pilgrimage was accepted.

7.3 Meshed ***Boteh*** *Design* *(c.1920, 4.80 x 3.38)*

Edwards looked back with longing to the great period of Meshed design from 1900 to 1930. This repeating pattern by Khadivi contemplates the meanings of ***boteh, kashkul*** *and* ***zikr Allah****.*

Arthur Upham Pope wrote the books he intended to write, and he did it with a single-minded certainty and industry that must inspire admiration. His limitations were partly those of his time when it seemed possible and necessary to create a new modern world. The social goal of many in those years was a scientifically organized way of life, one that would be disentangled from the backwardness and local customs that others might call tradition or the simple rules of human life.

Near the end of his long career, Pope recalled the strong personal emotions he had experienced at the moment of his first arrival in Iran almost fifty years before.

> You all know with what ecstasy the pilgrim greets the first gold glint of the dome of Imam Reza as he comes over the distant hills. It was the same for me as I came up out of hot and dusty Iraq to Qasr-i Shirin. … I would soon see the land of the great artists, the great poets, the many saints and the noble architecture that could not be transmitted by a few poor photographs.

Despite the evident enthusiasm, this is not a promising beginning. The pilgrim's ecstasy at the first sight of the golden dome of the shrine of Imam Reza is more truly a forgetfulness of self in the revelation of a religious experience. It is more an abandonment of personal ambitions than it is their fulfillment.

The experience of ecstasy is not something everyone knows or can know. To achieve true ecstasy requires a retirement from worldly concerns, a mental state that is more self-forgetful and absentminded than it is single-minded. In a very humble way, we may learn this regretful truth from some simple folk beliefs and customs concerning the pilgrimage route to Meshed. They were recorded by Bess Allen Donaldson in our usual source, *The Wild Rue*.

> Under favourable conditions the pilgrim gets his first view of the Shrine of Imam Reza at a point about sixteen miles from Meshed, and there is a saying that if a person cannot see the golden dome from this vantage point, then evidently his spiritual vision has been dimmed by sin. Oftentimes they will pretend to see it when it is actually not visible, so as not to be unfavourably judged by their companions.

This is another reminder that there are two very different kinds of vision. As we should know, even children's stories in Iran begin with this reminder: *Yeki bud, yeki nabud*.

The more familiar way of seeing perceives the ordinary world of appearances and material form. To achieve the other type of sight requires an abandonment of self and this world which is the root meaning of ecstasy. The empirical vision that can be transmitted by means of poor or even good photographs should never be confused with the spiritual vision of the sincere religious pilgrim. That profounder vision must be a revelation uniting human and divine.

When he wrote that great design has the authority of logic, Pope may have revealed an important clue to understanding the self-imposed limitations of his approach. In the Greek and Roman worlds, the ideal education was based on the division of the seven liberal arts into the *trivium and the quadrivium*, a division that survived into medieval Europe. The three subjects of the *trivium* were grammar, rhetoric and logic. These were seen as preparation for the study of the four subjects of the *quadrivium* which were arithmetic, geometry, astronomy and music.

7.4 Kerman *Herati Pattern* *(c.1960, 3.97 x 2.89)*

In the fifteenth century, Timurid Herat was the principal center of Iranian culture. Each element of the Herati design represents a turning about a fixed center, a microcosm of the cosmic pattern.

Fundamentally, Pope remained at the preparatory level of grammar, rhetoric and logic in his studies of Iranian art. His many beautiful words were primarily decoration, lacking a full appreciation of essential spiritual content and social context. This neglect prevented his *Survey of Persian Art* from rising to the level of a *theoria* or comprehensive vision. He was not unlike some pilgrims approaching the shrine of Imam Reza who pretended to see things that remained invisible to them.

For his exhibition of the history of Iranian art in London in 1931, great numbers of art objects were removed for the first time from the places and contexts and from the spiritual culture that had given them transcendent meanings. Beyond the principal goal of demonstrating the historical continuity of Iranian art, his secondary purpose in the exhibition was to display to European and American connoisseurs the evident decorative and aesthetic values of these many objects.

Ananda Kentish Coomaraswamy went beyond Pope's emphasis on the three subjects of the *trivium*, analyzing traditional art instead by means of the *quadrivium*. In the antique world, the well-understood purpose of studies of the four subjects was to educate the mind to perceive images and material forms in terms of the eternal patterns of the cosmos. Criticizing some approaches of his contemporaries to the aesthetics of religious art, Coomaraswamy wrote, "To have lost the art of thinking in images is precisely to have lost the proper linguistic of metaphysics and to have descended to the verbal logic in philosophy."

A favorite example used by Coomaraswamy to illustrate his preferred methods was the analysis of a word. We know we are never satisfied with admiring only the beauty of the sound of a word, but instead we always seek its meanings in the total context of human communication. We attempt to speak that word not in isolation, but with the resonances of all other words and all experiences. By speaking that single word or by contemplating a religious image in this connected way, we are participating in the eternal conversation and the great memory that define humanity.

We have seen that the ideas of Greek metaphysical philosophy have had the profoundest influence on Persian art and carpet design. This came about primarily through the philosophy of Sufism, the royal workshops or *kitabkhana* of the Timurid and Safavid dynasties, and the Sufi guilds of artisans which have been active for centuries throughout Iran. This profound influence of Islamic mysticism on all forms of Iranian art continues until the present day.

In manifold ways which have been so thoroughly assimilated that they would now be difficult or impossible to trace in detail, the philosophy of Plotinus has been a decisive source of ideas and images for Iranian art and culture. To mention one very significant instance, the philosophy of Ibn Sina (Avicenna) in the eleventh century controversially synthesized Aristotelian metaphysics with Quranic creationism. Avicenna's approach followed many of the innovations developed by Plotinus and his immediate successors more than seven centuries before.

Several times in history, the writings of this third century philosopher have played a similarly influential role in European culture. In the fifth century, Augustine adapted the pagan philosophy of Plotinus and the neo-Platonists to serve the needs of Christianity in its early development as a universal religion. The traditions and practices of Christian mysticism derive in large part from Plotinus, and many of these were taken over later by the followers of Islamic mysticism.

One millennium after Augustine, Italian Renaissance artists of the late fifteenth century incorporated the ideas and the related images of the metaphysical philosophy of Plotinus in their paintings. These ideas had been made newly available through the contemporary Latin translations of Marsilio Ficino. The poetry and prose of William Blake and the English Romantic movement were directly affected by the contemporary translation of parts of *The Enneads* by Thomas Taylor. The comprehensive translation by Stephen MacKenna was a strong influence on his friend William Butler Yeats in Ireland and on other twentieth-century writers.

Despite all of these highly significant examples of his influence over many centuries, Plotinus has remained a mainly unacknowledged source. Historically, he has been confused very often with Plato and Aristotle by the poets and philosophers of Sufism. Continuing this long tradition, his works have remained largely unknown by non-specialists. This neglect and even concealment of his crucial influence echo strangely the central concern of his mystical philosophy, the recognition of the hidden source that is the cause of all life.

In all the world's cultures, there is one very remarkable exception to this undeserved neglect. As we might reasonably expect, Plotinus remains a living presence in Iranian popular culture. There are many proverbial sayings and stories frequently heard in ordinary conversations that are attributed to Lohman, the name for Plotinus in the Persian language, or that feature the legendary philosopher in a prominent role. In more concealed ways, we have argued, the profound influence of his metaphysical philosophy on Islamic mysticism may be seen in the traditional designs of Persian carpets.

In *The Enneads*, there are numerous poetic metaphors used by Plotinus to suggest the nature of the hidden source behind all creation. He reminds us that the abundant life spreading through a large tree depends on the invisible roots. The most well-known of these metaphors was the comparison of the divine to a spring that flows eternally, "a spring that has no source outside itself; it gives itself to all the rivers, yet is never exhausted by what they take, but remains always integrally as it was." The works of Plotinus themselves have proved over time to have some very comparable qualities.

Plato had questioned the place of art and artists in his ideal republic. He criticized art as an imitation of an imitation, at least twice removed from the Real. Plotinus saw art very differently, not only as the imitative expression of the artist but primarily as an emanation through the artist from the original source. For Plotinus, great design does not have only the authority of logic. Much more significantly, it has in his philosophy the authority of the divine.

> No doubt the wisdom of the artist may be the guide of the work; it is sufficient explanation of the wisdom exhibited in the arts; but the artist himself goes back, after all, to that wisdom in Nature which is embodied in himself; and this is not a wisdom built up of theorems but one totality, not a wisdom consisting of manifold detail coordinated into a unity but rather a unity working out into detail.

Here again is the central theme of the personal embodiment of divine wisdom that underlies Sufism. The attempt to embody or express the divine pattern in material forms is the primary inspiration for Islamic visual art.

The image or object itself when seen with empirical vision is far less important to Plotinus than the material embodiment of a transcendent source that it represents. He asks his readers, "For who, if he is able to contemplate what is truly real, will go after its image?" From Plotinus, we cannot fail to learn the great lesson that finds a creative expression in the designs of Persian carpets. A material thing becomes beautiful by communicating in the thought that flows from the divine. That is the fundamental reason why we may use the beauty of material objects to contemplate the truly real which is the divine thought.

In his studies of the cosmological significance of the designs of Indian temples, Coomaraswamy repeats this universal theme found in all traditional religious art, the human embodiment of the divine pattern.

> The human frame, the constructed temple, and the universe being analogical equivalents, the parts of the temple correspond to those of the human body no less than those of the universe itself. ... The temple has, for example, windows and doors from which the indweller can go forth, or conversely return to himself; and these correspond in the body to the "doors of the senses."

The well-remembered words of Hallaj in the ninth century, "I am the Real, the Creative Truth," lie at the core of Sufism and its inheritance from Greek philosophy. These heretical words may now be understood as the bold assertion by Hallaj that his human frame was to be seen as an analogical equivalent of the universe.

This transcendent idea of Platonic philosophy, the symbolic analogy of human and divine, has been expressed in religion and philosophy in many different ways. It is the guiding principle for the mystical journey to a unified vision. Plotinus wrote, "The man formed by this mingling with the Supreme must, if he only remember, carry its image impressed upon him." In the language of this mystical philosophy, Mansur al-Hallaj was claiming

7.5 Kerman *Turning Dance* *(c.1910, 3.89 x 2.95)*

In contemplating this hypnotic design by Rashid Farokhi, the 256 ***botehs*** *soon create the illusion of a turning motion. Responsive viewers will find ways to join the whirling dance.*

that he had become an embodiment of the cosmic design. Hallaj believed he had reached the ultimate goal of the spiritual traveler. He carried the image of the Supreme impressed upon him.

Hallaj probably knew he was following some advice given by another mystical philosopher more than six centuries before: "Strive to bring back the god in yourselves to the Divine in the universe." These were reported to be the final words of Plotinus to his followers before his death in 270. His last words reinforce this essential message of the human assimilation of the divine pattern, and they summarize the deepest purpose of the spiritual journey.

In the sixth-century Byzantium imagined by Yeats in his mystical work *A Vision,* he found the single shining image that displayed the cultural unity he had sought in all the world's cultures. Like William Blake a century before him, Yeats described this poetic image of wholeness descended from the supernatural as an embodiment. It was experienced as a lovely flexible presence like that of a perfect human body.

In 1939, in the last few days of his life, Yeats attempted to summarize what he had learned after so many years of earnest searching for social coherence and human meaning. Using words that bring to mind Hallaj and Plotinus, he wrote, "Man can embody truth, but he cannot know it." This recalls the spiritual experience that overwhelms the participants at the moment of revelation in the *sama*. The *gotb* and the whirling dancers of the dervish order become seen in the ritual dance as an embodiment of the eternal pattern that is divine truth.

The ideal unity in this world is described by the Persian carpet at the abstract level of forms and concepts. The carpet is the meeting place of king and dervish. In the mind, it reconciles the duality of reason and imagination. There is another unity created and expressed by the carpet that is equally fundamental. This is a complete union at the ordinary level of physical form, an unbreakable material synthesis that is created by the hands and minds of two women.

The woman in the garden lives in the enclosed world of the home. She weaves the carpet out of the materials raised and gathered by the woman in the waste land, the nomadic woman who lives beyond the margins of the settled community. One woman knows the organized and protected world of a permanent home and a stable community. She follows the inner rhythms and the many rules of a complex human culture. In comparison to her more settled existence, the other woman lives in an endlessly changeable world without visible boundaries.

The nomadic woman is *bi khane,* without a home. The only fixed shelters she knows are the human and the cosmic frames. In her life of wandering, she follows the powerful external rhythms of unbounded nature. As a material object, the Persian carpet transforms and internalizes these external experiences. In the same way, the carpet transforms the inner experiences of the woman in the enclosed garden and gives them an external material form.

These two women may never meet in person or they may have only the briefest of encounters in the bazaar or at the garden gate, but they share intimately a common enterprise. Through their great labors, they unite in the carpet the duality of their different lives. Visibly and tangibly, the carpet expresses in this way a complete physical union of *anderun* and *birun*, of *baten* and *zaher*, and of inner meaning and outer form.

By their combined efforts, the two women create a total union of the realms of necessity and freedom. The Persian carpet is the golden door between these two realms. It is the door in the garden wall, the door that makes possible the union of inner and outer experience. The Persian carpet is the meeting place of the woman in the enclosed garden and the woman in nature. In imagination, it becomes the place where they discover that they share a greater common vision.

In the two small Tabriz textiles illustrated, we may recognize these and many other themes. The textiles might be described uncharitably by connoisseurs as souvenir art until we remind them that all religious art is souvenir art. Nothing in the created world can be rejected in the spiritual pilgrim's quest for total vision. We can neglect nothing in the search for the comprehensive understanding that may come in a moment of unawareness or forgetfulness when we least expect it.

7.6 Tabriz *Woman in a Garden* *(c.1965, 0.61 x 0.50)*

The woman's black hair is a symbol of divine light, the illumination needed to see all things in their true natures. Only in total darkness does the cosmic pattern become most clearly visible.

7.7 Tabriz *Woman in Nature* *(c.1965, 0.63 x 0.56)*

Modest images from daily life may reveal profound spiritual meanings. Is there always a concealed design behind the visible pattern?

In the enclosed garden of one design, the love struck nightingale sings endlessly through the night to the object of his devotion. Doubling this central theme of Sufism, the moth dancing tirelessly about the candle's flame is another familiar image of obsessive love. In ancient Greece, the moth or butterfly was the *psyche*, the same word that was commonly used for the human soul. The moth's difficult metamorphosis and its erratic flight toward the light have one commonly understood symbolic meaning. They have long served as a visual representation of the difficult journey of the soul from its dark imprisonment on earth to its true home in the divine light of heaven.

The moth and candle may also represent a retelling of the famous story of the martyrdom of Mansur al-Hallaj, the story of his joyful annihilation in the flame of love. Always pointing to the One, the candle and Hallaj are consumed by that fire. The moth sees the flame as the divine threshold, the *dār-e Mansur*. To the perceptive mind, the moth's whirling flight about the candle reenacts the turning dance of the dervishes about the *gotb* in the *sama*. In different earthly forms, they recall the more regular motions of the five planets and the stars about the fixed pole joining earth and heaven.

The image of the candle consumed by the heat and light of the flame conveys another transcendent meaning. The candle's flame may act on the receptive mind in the same way as the small fire of the *boteh* thorn bush over which people leap joyfully on *Chahar Shanbeh Suri* before the beginning of *Nouruz*. Both fires may be understood as visualizations of the transformation of matter to spirit. Wordlessly, they show it may be possible to follow the primary command of Plotinus to cut away everything. The two small flames are able to burn away all substance, leaving only essence.

Reflecting the candle's light, the beautiful face of the woman in this design should also be seen in a special way. Like the polished heart of the dervish, her face is a mirror that reflects a greater beauty. Her chain of pearls is a reminder of a chain of inheritance that begins with the hidden source of all creation. Like the jewels of the royal crown, the pearls were lost in darkness until they were discovered and brought to light by the great efforts of the whole community.

The flowering trees shown behind the woman are in full blossom, a universal symbol of spring and the renewal of all life. The fragrant blossoms serve to forcefully remind us of the rhythms of our breathing and they magnify the effect on the mind of the slightest wind. They produce a strong scent everywhere that is another suggestion of the omnipresence of the concealed source.

This woman in the garden at night brings to mind the faithful servant of Ferdowsi who related the story of Bijan and Manijeh in the *Shahnameh*. More than one thousand years ago, as the poet began his life's work, retelling this old story was her answer to Ferdowsi when he awoke suddenly and called out for light in terror of the surrounding darkness. The dark night itself and the flickering candle's feeble light are daily reminders to every person that they should seek another way of seeing.

Like Bijan and Joseph miraculously escaping from their hopeless confinements in dark wells, the many symbols of love and the divine source that are to be found in this modest textile may provide us with a means of escape from all darkness. We remember that the humble moth, the *psyche*, escaped from its narrow confinement in a dark cocoon to rise to the source of light.

The nomadic woman represents a visualization of freedom, but this is not a freedom that comes from making choices, from dominating others, or from controlling the external environment. Like the nomadic Basseri of the Khamseh Federation, she knows the true freedom that comes from living within the framework of an imaginative vision that patterns and gives meaning to all her experiences. Like the wandering dervish whose few possessions may be covered by his small animal skin, she knows the material poverty that makes spiritual wealth and true love possible.

She exercises the ancient right of the poor to glean from the fields after the harvest. This is a right at least as old as that of the poet to sit at the king's table or of the dervish to cross all thresholds. From a time now lost to memory, the nomadic woman has had the unquestioned right to gather and use the plants of the waste land to make dyes and medicines and to feed her sheep. Her sunburned face reflects the full light of the sun as she journeys endlessly in search of what will sustain her family for another day and another year.

In the design of this small textile, there is an awkwardly drawn rainbow barely visible behind the nomadic woman. This image is a vision of the *haft-rang*, the seven colors that color all of creation. These colors of the rainbow are reflected from the seven summits of *Kaf* mountain, the distant home of the *Simorgh* at the boundary of the two worlds. We remember the beautiful dowry carpet the young Qashqai weaver was to lose so regretfully to the two merchants. We may imagine it was woven by Zolaikha with wool she had dyed with her own hands in these seven colors and more.

The sheltering rainbow may be seen in many ways. It is the bow of the legendary hero Rustam protecting ancient Zoroastrian Iran, the sign of God's covenant with Noah and the people of Israel, and the two-edged sword *Zulfiqar* of Ali defending the truth of Islam. All are manifestations of God's grace reaching down to earth. In the villages of Iran, the rainbow is sometimes imagined as the little rug made by Fatima, the beloved daughter of the Prophet Mohammed. In the modern world of science, it is the reflected and refracted light of the sun, the material source of all life on earth. The rainbow is the spectrum of colors that revealed the physical nature of light to Isaac Newton, a phenomenon he studied in solitude in a darkened room.

Most simply, the rainbow is the welcome sign of a recent rain, the after-image of an essential requirement for the continuance of all life. It may signal the joyful return of light and safety after a time of darkness and danger. Perhaps most profoundly, the rainbow serves in this design as a symbol like light itself. It is a reminder of the ability to perceive non-material things. Held by her own compelling vision of the rainbow and all outer experience, the nomadic woman continues on her endless journey. Following her inner vision of human possibility, she turns away from the seven-colored rainbow and the larger world. Like the moth turning toward the light, she turns toward that vision.

7.8 Qashqai
Open Field
(c.1970, 1.78 x 1.08)

Set against the green color identified with the Quran, the open red field suggests the consciousness of the dervish who has become empty in order to receive God.

All paradises are lost paradises. We must turn away from the paradise of the art object and the enclosed world it has created. What do we take away as an after-image? What do we turn toward? In the simplest terms, the experience of a Persian carpet is a sequence of perceptions. At first sensory, these perceptions are then assembled into an overall perception which is no longer sensory.

Initially, the elementary rhythms of the border design are experienced and understood. As in the ritual performance of the *sama*, these regular patterns impose a breath-based rhythm, the symbol of time and the sign of essential life, on our further perceptions. Breathing is now experienced less as a physical sensation than as an unending expansion and contraction, an alternation of inner and outer. This repeated inhalation and exhalation inspires a deeply felt mental experience. There is a constant reversal of meaning which is most profoundly understood as a repeated turning from life to death to life again.

Then the complexity of the central design is scanned, organized and seen as a unity. From the simple rhythm of breath, it is now the more complex rhythms of nature that are the controlling forces, the divine harmonies of the sun, the moon and the stars that drive all earth-based rhythms. Depending on our preparation, a seemingly disordered multiplicity will eventually be revealed as a coherent pattern. There is a spiraling movement in the mind

7.9 Baluchi
Human Essence
(c.1960, 1.20 x 0.79)

The outlined shape in this Afghan prayer rug expresses the essence of human identity. Represented by animal skins, the dervishes embody the eternal pattern which turns about the ***gotb*** *or axis of the universe.*

from rhythm and motion in the external world to pattern and rest in an internal world. To the spiritual traveler, this is experienced as an ascent along the cosmic axis in the direction from human to divine.

In imagination, we move from the multiplicity of the material world to the unity of the intelligible realm. This is a metaphor for the human understanding where the perception and assimilation of elementary patterns give reason to believe that the more complex patterns of perceptual experience may be comprehended in humanly meaningful terms. In this mental journey, we attempt to move from design to designation, from seeing the design to seeing through the design, from information to in-formation. Through the carpet and all the resources of the common culture, we may hope that what we have learned from aesthetics and objective science will become embedded in ethics and subjective conscience.

On our journey to a shared understanding, we reenact the controlling experience of Greek philosophy and its most compelling image. Ariadne's clue of thread again leads Theseus out of the labyrinth of chaotic sense impressions into the intelligible world. The Persian carpet trains the senses and the mind to construct a single unified vision. It does this by uniting the dualities of experience and imagination, of matter and spirit, of motion and rest. Following Plotinus, Hallaj, Yeats and Hedayat in learning to embody the wisdom

اصفهان = داوری

in nature, we first achieve an understanding of the carpet as a material embodiment itself of the cosmic design. The Persian carpet is seen as a *theorema,* a visual display of the timeless pattern known as spiritual wisdom.

We do not forget that the carpet must always be a perishable display. Like all material containers, its substance will become essence. There is an unexpected reversal in our perceptions at the moment when carpet patterns seem to escape from their confinement in material forms. Opening ourselves completely to their subversive influence, they may enter the imagination and begin to pattern all of our experiences. Recalling Nizami's view of his poetry, the design of the carpet now teaches us the nature of our own design.

Through the carpet, we recognize again that our fragile substance will become essence. These reversals of understanding and our evolving responses are finally experienced as a subordination or a personal submission to the divine pattern. Through contemplating the carpet design and all designs, inner and outer experience become inseparably unified in a common vision. That submission to the timeless unchanging design behind all visible patterns is the core meaning of Islam and all religions.

These ideals are to be found in a most beautiful synthesis in the small Isfahan carpet (c.1970) signed by the master designer Davari. The border of this carpet forcefully imposes the rhythm of breath on the viewer, an endlessly repeated expansion and contraction. We may then notice a possibly significant detail. The major design element of the border is repeated precisely twelve times. The brilliant white field of the carpet is seen as a symbolic representation of the woolen cloak or the animal skin of the dervish. The intricate medallion represents the heart or the inner essence of the holy wanderer.

Brought to a polished perfection, the heart has become a mirror that flawlessly reflects the Divine. The central medallion in this compelling design expresses this primary meaning of Sufism, the internalization or embodiment of the divine pattern, in another subtle way. The medallion may be seen as an elaborated vision of the familiar double square which is the most elementary sign of the duality of existence brought to a unity. The double square appears about to double again in a dynamic process that will end only when we reach the circle, the universal symbol of the One.

In the field design of the Isfahan carpet, the sixteen soul birds are flying restlessly in all directions. Seeking to escape forever from the snares and changeable forms of this world, they are attracted to the twelve shining images brilliantly colored in a lustrous gold. These golden images of spiritual freedom are believed to be stylized representations of the head of the *tabar*. They represent the essence of the two-edged axe of the wandering dervish, the weapon that cuts through all dualities and points toward the Real.

Borrowing the words of Plotinus, we know the design is beautiful because it communicates in the thought that flows from the Divine. The carpet design represents in material form the transcendent ideal of a submission to the religious wisdom of the twelve Imams who are believed in Shi'a Islam to be the true inheritors of the final revelation of Allah. This ideal is the perfected divine wisdom that the enlightened dervish on the mystical journey has learned to embody.

7.10 Isfahan *Twelve Images* *(c.1970, 1.80 x 1.09)*

Conveying motion and rest, this Davari pattern communicates the timeless peace of the wanderer who has completed the long journey. He has become an embodiment of the divine.

غالبا این قدرم عقل کفایت باشد
من و انکار شراب این چه حکایت باشد

The small Turkoman textile from Afghanistan depicts the simplest of scenes and yet it may be seen to contain many of the most important themes of Sufism in a profoundly meaningful way. Two musk deer, a mother and her child, have been grazing peacefully in the full light of the sun. They are in an open space surrounded by the dark forest. Sheltered between two trees in flower in spring or heavy with fruit in autumn, the scene presents a portrait of unconditional and unbounded love. In the abstracted design, the mother seems to be alert. Perhaps she has become aware of another presence.

The simple scene recalls a poetic image that occurs frequently in the literature and visual art inspired by Sufism. By a mysterious alchemy, the gentle musk deer are able to transform ordinary grass, the humblest plant growing nearest the earth, into the most precious scent. Like the divine essence, that scent pervades all creation. In a very subtle way, the modest image before us suggests we may perform almost the same miracle as the musk deer. We may discover for ourselves the magic alchemy capable of transforming the most ordinary experiences into sustaining rituals that embody and renew the deepest human meanings.

آهو

For the mystic traveler who was seeking self-annihilation and union with God, the shy musk deer were rarely or never seen. However, they left behind them a trail of scent indicating the correct path to follow through the wilderness to reach the One. In the Persian language, the musk deer or gazelle is the *ahu*. Beyond its primary meaning, this word has acquired a more profound cultural significance in Islamic mysticism. It is often intended in Sufi poetry to be heard as a concealed reminder of *ya hu*, the most common *zikr Allah* or remembrance of God.

7.11 Tabriz *Divine Union* *(c.1970, 1.53 x 0.95)*

At the center of a turning vortex of mystical meanings, an ideal image of male and female displays the union of all dualities in the comprehensive vision.

7.12 Turkoman ***Ahu*** *(c.1960, 0.79 x 0.69)*

Musk deer are rarely seen but their enticing scent lingers for a time like an after-image. The traveler may use this reminder of another unseen presence to find the narrow path to the One.

Very inconspicuously, this single word *ahu* has been woven into the design of the Afghan textile. Is it significant that *ahu* has been woven or written vertically, in the direction that points between heaven and earth? We begin to suspect that the weaver has presented us with an intended challenge to our understanding. Through the hidden clues provided by one short word and a seemingly uncomplicated image, the quiet musk deer may serve us once more as a guide on the mystical journey. Following the trail of this spiritual guide, we will continue to move from concealment to revelation.

If we look very closely, we may find in the shapes alone of the three letters of the single word *ahu* the most intense concentration of the meanings of the way of life of the dervish. The letter a (*"aleph"*) is drawn as a representation of the tabar, the two-edged axe that points toward the One. The letter *u* (*"vav"*) is written in the shape of the *kashkul*, the begging bowl used to receive alms. Through their material forms, these two letters have themselves become spiritual symbols. They visibly indicate, *tazahor kardan*, that the dervish strives to unite in his person the active and passive as he seeks total union with the One.

The *a* and *u*, representing male and female, outward and inward, and all dualities, are joined in the word *ahu* by the third letter *h* (*"heh"*). We recall that repeatedly saying the letter *h* acted as a common *zikr Allah* in Islamic mysticism. Spoken with the outward breath, saying the letter produces the emptiness required to receive God. Even more than a spoken remembrance of God, the final letter of *Allah* is most profoundly seen as a symbol of the divine essence.

On the mystical journey, the dervish seeks without rest to escape from all the transitory illusions of this world. In a moment of unawareness, he will find himself helplessly caught between the two arms of the letter *h*. In the word *ahu*, it may be the divine essence itself that has been caught between the *tabar* and the *kashkul*, the primary symbols of the dervish and his way of life.

Protected by the simple *haft-hasht* border, the red field of this modest textile may be seen as a representation of the animal skin, the *pustin*. Moving from outer to inner experience, the dervish on the soul journey has taken into his inner being the spiritual meanings of this scene and of all scenes. Forgetting himself completely, the holy wanderer has become an embodiment of the wisdom in nature. He has become a personification of the divine essence.

The Shaykh Safi design of the majestic Ardebil carpet in London carries the same meanings that may be found concentrated in the three letters of the word *ahu*. They both express the union of all dualities in the divine essence. By the most fragile human and material means, the Ardebil carpet and the small Turkoman textile attempt the same transcendent task. Like the dervish and every pilgrim on the spiritual journey, like the shapes of the letters of the word *ahu*, they strive to give the intangible a material form. They all seek to display the essence of the world.

7.13 Meshed *Shaykh Safi Design by Saber* *(c.1920, 6.38 x 4.70)*

Continuing a chain of creativity, the master weaver Saber trained with Emogli. The dominant purple-red color identified with Meshed weaving is a reminder of the martyrdom of Imam Reza.

The place where the gentle musk deer are quietly grazing is a vision of the first temple. The clearing in the forest is the original sacred space. In imagination, the carpet may be a similar refuge, a place of light and imagined safety surrounded by darkness and danger. The fullest judgment of a Persian carpet or any art work will take us beyond the welcome shelter of this temporary refuge. It will result in a lasting reconnection to humanity which is the truest meaning of any religious experience.

The ideal judgment begins in a contemplation which requires from the viewer a creative response. This personal response may take many forms but it is always an identification, an assimilation of a pattern, followed by an understanding which is a subordination to a comprehensive vision. This will then lead to a renewed participation in the common language. We will return to a full participation in the conversation and the shared rituals that express the wisdom of the human community and bind it together.

In the conversation we are about to rejoin, we must re-pair everything that has been broken or held apart. We will be seeking to discover the comprehensive unity that lies concealed behind all dualities and multiplicities. What is required from the viewer of the carpet design before this return is a transformation of consciousness, a rectification of character which is a reconstruction in the mind of that original temple. The contemplation inspired by the Persian carpet will take us far beyond the threshold of entrancing forms. It will take us past the *eyvan* of material appearances into the interior of that temple.

The ideal judgment of a work of art, the ideal creative response, will be a conversion. This is first a decision to turn away temporarily from material form to live in the mind in an ideal imagined world. Then it is a return to an ordinary world that has been transformed. This personal conversion is an experience we will share with others in the unending conversation that defines the human community. That true conversation is a turning together like the constant turning in the whirling dance, like the turning of the *planetai,* an endless turning that is properly understood as a turning to face God.

The border of the carpet attracts our attention again, briefly delaying our return to the community. The border does permit a steady contemplation of the main design, but it does this in an active way. It is not simply a passive frame isolating the central pattern. The principal colors of the border and field are usually complementary colors, very often red and blue symbolizing earth and sky, human and divine, and all dualities.

Acting similarly to the subtle effects of the reciprocating designs of the minor borders, these complementary colors prepare the mind for a constant alternation of meaning. They act on the barely conscious mind to produce a continual oscillation between the realms of matter and spirit, of earth and heaven, of content and form, of substance and essence, of ethics and aesthetics, of seen and unseen.

The major repeating elements of the principal border may often be interpreted to have another archetypal significance. This is beyond the role they share with the minor guard borders in imposing the rhythm of breathing on our subsequent perceptions. They may represent a memory, an after-image, of the bases of the columns supporting the constructed temples that were built in imitation of these forest clearings. The wood and stone columns of these ancient temples were themselves a symbolic representation of the trees that formed the original boundaries of the first sacred spaces.

The border design of the carpet remembers this ancient origin. Like the bounding chain that declares an area is *bast* or enclosed, these repeating elements of the border are a signal to the traveler through life of the refuge of a divine sanctuary. Like the enclosing columns of the first temples, like the bounding trees of the forest clearings, the major elements of the border act to create in the receptive mind a protected space. The border of the carpet encloses and designates a sacred space.

We must turn away at last from the Persian carpet, from all humanly created images and words, and from all ideal forms and conceptual thinking. Crossing the border, we seek to escape from what has become in its turn a place of contraction and confinement. We do this by returning to another book created from the surrounding forest, the unbounded book of nature that is the familiar image of reality. This is a return to present time and lived experience, to material form and ordinary perception.

Where do we begin our exile from the ideal world we have dreamed together? After our journey, will we find that the ordinary world has been transformed? If we go to the nearest playground for small children, an open clearing in the modern forest, or if we visit it in memory or imagination, we will find that we see everything in a new way. We will not be allowed to enter this enclosed and protected garden. We may only watch from a distance or pass silently by.

There are perhaps thirty or forty children in the garden, but they are moving too rapidly to be counted. We see the sandbox, the wading pool, the fountain and the goldfish pond, some tall shade trees, the swings, the ladder and slide, the seesaw, and the roundabout. All of these are present, if only in the imagination. It is early afternoon and the bright sun is moving to its highest point in the sky.

Everywhere we look we notice there are abundant flowers in at least the seven colors of the rainbow. A few pet animals and the many birds sheltering in the trees have awoken from their midday torpor, and they are now responding noisily to the loud rhythms of the children's play. This is a moment when the all-embracing vision may descend. For those who are prepared to receive it, the vision will appear before them as a lovely flexible presence like that of a perfect human body.

The two children on the seesaw are oscillating repeatedly between the realms of earth and heaven. They are learning to feel and embody the total metaphors of balance and justice. Several small children are nervously climbing the seven-stepped ladder and slide for their first time. In every part of their bodies, they are experiencing the unfamiliar fears and dangers of the spiritual journey. And then they discover the surprise and delight of the return in an instant to a transformed world.

One brave child in the playground tries to reach the center of the rapidly turning roundabout. As he turns unsteadily around that unmoving center, it becomes for him the fixed pole about which the entire universe turns. On the swings, a courageous young girl travels so high she almost leaves the earth. Reaching far beyond herself, she tries in vain to touch the golden door of heaven. She does swing high enough to begin to see the pattern of her world.

Some laughing children are exploring the two worlds by playing hide and seek. A few children are busy making imaginary things from the wet red clay they have found near the base of the ever-flowing fountain. Some other children begin singing a familiar song, "Pass me the blue, oh the blue, pretty blue; pass me the blue, oh, the blue." While they sing, their hands reach above them as if they could grasp a portion of the sky and bring it down to earth. What their folded hands enclose today is only emptiness, but that does not seem to lessen their joy. The singing children chant faster and faster until they lose the rhythm and their song breaks down in torrents of laughter.

One solitary child stands by herself among the trees at the boundary, uncertainly remaining half in shade and half in sun. Tired from her running, she stays quietly apart, content for the moment to observe the others and to wonder at the beauty of the garden. Losing all awareness of herself, she moves unknowingly to the tallest tree on the garden's border to sleep and dream for a time in its welcoming shade. As the sun descends slowly from the cloudless sky, another observant child looks up and is the first among them to see it falling. A short time before, he was one of the children singing. He points to the distant sun and he begins to cry, suddenly fearful that this perfect day will end.

If we let them finish their play, these children will weave the fabric of creation out of their experiences. Here is the single shining image, the vast design, the vision of all that reflects what we truly are. When night does come and motion becomes rest, the rhythmic whirling dance of the children's play will be seen in the planets and the stars. This enclosed garden is the original sacred space, the first meeting place of human and divine, and the carpet is its after-image. *This is where we begin.*

7.14 Tabriz *Garden Design* *(c.1960, 5.93 x 3.93)*

An anonymous designer, unnamed weavers and many others contributed to this carpet. A multiplicity of materials and motivations has become a unified image of the soul's tranquility in a whole understanding.

Bibliography

Ackroyd, Peter. *Blake*. London: Sinclair-Stevenson, 1995.

Attar, Farid-Ud-Din. *The Conference of the Birds*. London: Penguin, 1984.

Bakhtiar, Laleh. *Sufi: Expressions of the Mystic Quest*. London: Thames and Hudson, 1976.

Baldick, Julian. *Mystical Islam: An Introduction to Sufism*. New York: New York University Press, 1989.

Barth, Fredrik. *Nomads of South Persia: The Basseri Tribe of the Khamseh Confederacy*. Boston: Little, Brown, 1961.

Bashiri, Iraj. *The Fiction of Sadeq Hedayat*. Lexington, Ky: Mazda, 1984.

Beeman, William O. *Language, Status and Power in Iran*. Bloomington: Indiana University Press, 1986.

Bell, Clive. *Art*. London: Chatto and Windus, 1914.

Bell, Gertrude. *Persian Pictures*. London: Ernest Benn, 1928.

Benjamin, S.G.W. *Persia and the Persians*. Boston: Ticknor and Co., 1887.

Berenson, Bernard. *Aesthetics and History*. New York: Pantheon, 1948.

Browne, Edward G.

A Year Amongst the Persians. Cambridge: Cambridge University Press, 1927.

Poems from the Persian. London: Ernest Benn, 1927.

Byron, Robert. *The Road to Oxiana*. London: John Lehmann, 1950.

Chelkowski, P.J. *Ta'ziyeh: Ritual and Drama in Iran*. New York: New York University Press, 1979.

Coomaraswamy, Ananda K. *Selected Papers 1, 2, 3* (ed. Roger Lipsey) Princeton: Princeton University Press, 1977.

Dhamija, Jasleen. *Living Tradition of Iran's Crafts*. New Delhi: Vikas Publishing House, 1979.

Donaldson, Bess Allen. *The Wild Rue*. London: Luzac and Co., 1938.

Dos Passos, John. *Orient Express*. New York: Harper and Brothers, 1927.

Dwight, H.G. *Persian Miniatures*. New York: Doubleday, Page and Co., 1917.

Edwards, Arthur Cecil.

A Persian Caravan. New York: Harper and Brothers, 1928.

The Persian Carpet: A Survey of the Carpet-Weaving Industry of Persia. London: Duckworth, 1953.

Esfandiary, F.M. *Identity Card*. New York: Grove Press, 1966.

Filmer, Henry. *The Pageant of Persia*. Indianapolis: Bobbs-Merrill, 1936.

Fry, Roger. *Vision and Design*. London: Chatto and Windus, 1920.

Forbes-Leith, F.A.C. *Checkmate: Fighting Tradition in Central Persia*. New York: Robert M. McBride, 1927.

Gerson, Lloyd P. *Plotinus*. London: Routledge, 1994.

Ghazzali, Abu Hamid al-. *The Niche for Lights*, in *Four Sufi Classics*. London: The Sufi Trust, Octagon Press, 1980.

Gluck, Jay and Sumi Gluck. *A Survey of Persian Handicraft*. Tehran: A Survey of Persian Art, 1977.

Harnack, Curtis. *Persian Lions, Persian Lambs*. New York: Holt, Rinehart and Winston, 1967.

Hedayat, Sadeq.

The Blind Owl (trans. D.P.Costello). London: John Calder, 1957.

Haji Agha (trans. G.M.Wickens). Austin: University of Texas, 1979.

The Pearl Cannon (ed. Iraj Bashiri). Lexington, Ky: Mazda, 1986.

Hill, Donald L. (ed.) *The Renaissance: Studies in Art and Poetry* by Walter Pater (1893 text). Berkeley: University of California Press, 1980.

Jamalzadeh, Mohammad Ali. *Once Upon a Time (Yeki Bud, Yeki Nabud).* New York: Bibliotecha Persica, 1985.

Kashani, Jamal. *Iran's Men of Destiny.* New York: Vantage Press, 1985.

Katouzian, Homa. *Sadeq Hedayat: The Life and Literature of an Iranian Writer.* London: I.B.Tauris, 1991.

Lentz, Thomas and Glenn Lowry. *Timur and the Princely Vision.* Washington: Smithsonian Institution Press, 1989.

Maillart, Ella K. *The Cruel Way.* London: William Heinemann, 1947.

Meisami, Julie Scott. *Medieval Persian Court Poetry.* Princeton: Princeton University Press, 1987.

Merritt-Hawkes, O.A. *Persia: Romance and Reality.* London: Ivor Nicholson and Watson, 1935.

Morrison, George (ed.) *History of Persian Literature.* Leiden: E.J.Brill, 1981.

Mumford, John Kimberly. *Oriental Rugs.* New York: Charles Scribners' Sons, 1901.

Nasr, Seyyed Hossein. *Islamic Art and Spirituality.* Delhi: Oxford University Press, 1990.

Payne, Robert. *Journey to Persia.* London: William Heinemann, 1951.

Plotinus. *The Enneads (trans. Stephen MacKenna).* London: Faber and Faber, 1956.

Pope, Arthur Upham.

An Introduction to Persian Art since the Seventh Century A.D. London: Peter Davies, 1930.

Persian Architecture: The Triumph of Form and Color. New York: George Braziller, 1965.

and Phyllis Ackerman (eds.)

A Survey of Persian Art from Prehistoric Times to the Present. Tehran: Soroush Press, 1977.

Raine, Kathleen. *Yeats the Initiate.* London: Allen and Unwin, 1986.

Rice, Cyprian. *The Persian Sufis.* London: George Allen and Unwin, 1964.

Rist, J.M. *Plotinus: The Road to Reality.* Cambridge: Cambridge University Press, 1967.

Richards, Fred. *A Persian Journey.* London: Jonathan Cape, 1931.

Schimmel, Annemarie.

Mystical Dimensions of Islam. Chapel Hill: University of North Carolina Press, 1975.

The Triumphal Sun: A Study of the Works of Jalaloddin Rumi. London: East-West Publications, 1980.

I am Wind, You are Fire: The Life and Work of Rumi. Boston: Shambhala, 1992.

Shahrokh, Meskoob. *Iranian Nationality and the Persian Language.* Washington: Mage Publishers, 1992.

Sykes, Percy M.

Ten Thousand Miles in Persia. London: John Murray, 1902.

The Glory of the Shi'a World: The Tale of a Pilgrimage. London: Macmillan, 1910.

Vaziri, Mostafa. *Iran as Imagined Nation: The Construction of National Identity.* New York: Paragon House, 1993.

Wiesinger, Rita J. *Light Me a Candle.* Bombay: Shakuntala Publishing, 1973.

Yeats, W.B.

The Collected Plays of W.B. Yeats. London: Macmillan, 1934.

A Vision. New York: Macmillan, 1956.

References

0. Preface

iv Browne 3
Bell 102-3

1. Yeki Bud, Yeki Nabud

2 Filmer 364-7
3 Merritt-Hawkes 106, 87, 204
4 Byron 82, 208
14 Nizami in Meisami 243
17 Jamalzadeh in Morrison 199
18 Shahrokh 41
19 Payne 64-5
Merritt-Hawkes 251
20 Hedayat in Katouzian 52, 212-3, 225, 222
21 Esfandiary 57-9, 61, 69, 72
22 Browne 279, 289, 117
23 Browne 282
24 Dwight 177, 180-1,
25 Dwight 186, 183

2. The Persian Carpet

29 Dwight 196-7
30 Dwight 205, 217
31 Edwards (1953) v, 287, 311
32 Benjamin 82, 423
34 Benjamin 315
35 Sykes 21,199
36 Richards 238
The Antiquarian, Feb.1931, 30
37 Pope in Gluck 15
Pope (1930) 2, ix, 130, 120
38 Pope (1977) xv
Pope (1977) xvii, 1
39 Edwards (1953) 13, 17
41 Edwards (1953) 17, 51
43 Mumford 56
45 Dwight 179-80
47 Edwards (1953) 18
48 Mumford 85
Berenson 103
Pater in Hill 106,104
49 Bell 25
Fry 29
50 Coomaraswamy 1 167,175,174
51 Coomaraswamy 1 xxxiv, 195
Dwight 74
52 Forbes-Leith 115
53 Edwards (1953) 96-7, vi
55 Edwards (1953) 160
57 Edwards (1953) 368, (1928) 43
Browne 282

3. The Wild Rue

59 Hedayat in Katouzian 85; in Bashiri 143
Yeats in Raine 53
61 Yeats in Raine 54
Donaldson vi-vii
62 Donaldson 21
64 Donaldson 21, 59
65 Merritt-Hawkes 59, 195
Sa'adi 301
66 Sykes iii-iv
67 Wiesinger 87
Edwards (1953) 97
69 Blake in Ackroyd 209
Wiesinger xii, 103-4
70 Beck 65, 124,
71 Beck 155, 188
73 Dhamija 2

74 Dhamija in Gluck 277
77 Barth 147, 153
78 Edwards (1953) 36
80 Harnack 86-88
82 Gluck 8
Pope in Gluck 13
83 Edwards (1953) 90

4. The King's Threshold

87 Merritt-Hawkes 172-3
88 Merritt-Hawkes 257-8
89 Merritt-Hawkes 258
Bell 94
90 Browne 486, 161
Donaldson 194
91 Browne 57
93 Sykes 142
94 Merritt-Hawkes 235, 237
99 Edwards (1953) 287
103 Edwards (1953) 306
Donaldson 116
107 Merritt-Hawkes 80
110 Schimmel (1975) 270

5. The Golden Door

123 Plotinus 434, 56-8
125 Schimmel (1992) 203
127 Ghazzali 128
132 Nasr 70-1
Sykes 253-4
136 Plotinus 150
139 Maillart 106
141 Maillart 108
142 Maillart 109
Edwards (1953) 161
Payne 8

6. The Vision of a Whole People

145 Donaldson vii-viii
146 Richards 49
147 Richards 49
149 Yeats (1956) 279
150 Plotinus in Gerson 90
162 Schimmel (1992) 363
164 Chelkowski 1
165 Chelkowski 7-8
Dos Passos 94
167 Nasr 79
Kashani 154
169 Sykes 143, 145
170 Donaldson 100,166
173 Sykes 277

7. After-Image

175 Blake in Ackroyd 89
178 Hedayat (1957) 26; in Bashiri 116
179 Minovi in Bashiri 4
185 Pope in Gluck 14
Donaldson 64
186 Coomaraswamy 1 (1977) 296
187 Plotinus 249
189 Plotinus 426
Plotinus in Gerson 217
Coomaraswamy 1 (1977) 5
Plotinus 624
190 Plotinus xii
Yeats in Raine xvi

Index

Published in Canada by TABAR
www.tabar.ca

ISBN 978-0-9784187-0-0

Design by RMS Design
Photography by Paul McCarthy
Set in Palatino LT Std: Light, Italic and Medium Italic
Printed and bound in Canada by Transcontinental Printing
Printed on acid-free paper